Algebra 1
Geometry
Algebra 2

SO-BBW-460

Explorations and Projects Book

The Explorations and Projects Book contains a variety of Explorations and Projects correlated to McDougal Littell's Algebra 1, Geometry, Algebra 2 series. The Explorations are designed to be used with specific lessons while the Projects are designed to be used with specific chapters. Support materials for the teacher include notes on the Explorations and Projects, scoring rubrics for the Projects, and answers to all Exploration exercises and questions.

McDougal Littell
A HOUGHTON MIFFLIN COMPANY
Evanston, Illinois   •   Boston   •   Dallas

Photography Credits

38 *left* John Elk III/Stock Boston
38, 39 © Cathy Melloan
39 Phillip Bailey/Corbis Stock Market
85 John V.A.F. Neal/Photo Researchers, Inc
156 Lewis Portnoy/Pictor
All other photography: RMIP/Richard Haynes

Copyright © 2003 by McDougal Littell Inc. All rights reserved.

Permission is hereby granted to teachers to reprint or photocopy in classroom quantities the pages or sheets in this work that carry a McDougal Littell copyright notice. These pages are designed to be reproduced by teachers for use in their classes with accompanying McDougal Littell material, provided each copy made shows the copyright notice. Such copies may not be sold and further distribution is expressly prohibited. Except as authorized above, prior written permission must be obtained from McDougal Littell Inc. to reproduce or transmit this work or portions thereof in any other form or by any other electronic or mechanical means, including any information storage or retrieval system, unless expressly permitted by federal copyright laws. Address inquiries to Manager, Rights and Permissions, McDougal Littell Inc., P.O. Box 1667, Evanston, IL 60204.

ISBN: 0-618-25523-1

123456789 - DAM - 06 05 04 03 02

CONTENTS

Correlation Chart of Explorations and Projects to McDougal Littell *Algebra 1*

Chapter 1: Connections to Algebra	
1.2 Exponents and Powers	• Algebra 1 Exploration 1
1.3 Order of Operations	• Algebra 1 Exploration 2
1.4 Equations and Inequalities	• Algebra 1 Exploration 3
1.5 A Problem Solving Plan Using Models	• Algebra 1 Exploration 4
Chapter 2: Properties of Real Numbers	• Algebra 1 Portfolio Project for Chapter 2
2.8 Probability and Odds	• Algebra 1 Exploration 5
Chapter 3: Solving Linear Equations	
3.3 Solving Multi-Step Equations	• Algebra 1 Exploration 6
Chapter 4: Graphing Linear Equations and Functions	• Algebra 1 Portfolio Project for Chapter 4
4.2 Graphing Linear Equations	• Algebra 1 Exploration 7
4.5 Direct Variation	• Algebra 1 Exploration 8
4.6 Quick Graphs Using Slope-Intercept Form	• Algebra 1 Exploration 9
Chapter 5: Writing Linear Equations	• Algebra 1 Portfolio Project for Chapter 5
5.4 Fitting a Line to Data	• Algebra 1 Exploration 10
Chapter 6: Solving and Graphing Linear Inequalities	• Algebra 1 Portfolio Project 1 for Chapter 6 • Algebra 1 Portfolio Project 2 for Chapter 6
6.5 Graphing Linear Inequalities in Two Variables	• Algebra 1 Exploration 11
6.6 Stem-and-Leaf Plots and Mean, Median, and Mode	• Algebra 1 Exploration 12

Explorations and Projects Book, Copyright © McDougal Littell Inc.

Correlation Chart of Explorations and Projects to McDougal Littell *Algebra 1*

Chapter 7: Systems of Linear Equations and Inequalities	
7.1 Solving Linear Systems by Graphing	• Algebra 1 Exploration 13
7.3 Solving Linear Systems by Linear Combinations	• Algebra 1 Exploration 14
Chapter 8: Exponents and Exponential Functions	• Algebra 1 Portfolio Project for Chapter 8
8.3 Division Properties of Exponents	• Algebra 1 Exploration 15
Chapter 9: Quadratic Equations and Functions	• Algebra 1 Portfolio Project for Chapter 9
9.2 Simplifying Radicals	• Algebra 1 Exploration 16
9.3 Graphing Quadratic Functions	• Algebra 1 Exploration 17 • Algebra 1 Exploration 18
Chapter 10: Polynomials and Factoring	• Algebra 1 Portfolio Project for Chapter 10
10.2 Multiplying Polynomials	• Algebra 1 Exploration 19 • Algebra 1 Exploration 20
10.4 Solving Polynomial Equations in Factored Form	• Algebra 1 Exploration 21
Chapter 11: Rational Equations and Functions	• Algebra 1 Portfolio Project 1 for Chapter 11 • Algebra 1 Portfolio Project 2 for Chapter 11
11.1 Ratio and Proportion	• Algebra 1 Exploration 22
11.3 Direct and Inverse Variation	• Algebra 1 Exploration 23
11.6 Adding and Subtracting Rational Expressions	• Algebra 1 Exploration 24
Chapter 12: Radicals and Connections to Geometry	• Algebra 1 Portfolio Project for Chapter 12
12.7 Trigonometric Ratios	• Algebra 1 Exploration 25

Correlation Chart of Explorations and Projects to McDougal Littell *Geometry*

Chapter 1: Basics of Geometry	
1.1 Patterns and Inductive Reasoning	• Geometry Exploration 1
1.2 Points, Lines, and Planes	• Geometry Exploration 2 • Geometry Exploration 3
Chapter 2: Reasoning and Proof	
2.1 Conditional Statements	• Geometry Exploration 4
Chapter 3: Perpendicular and Parallel Lines	
3.4 Proving Lines are Parallel	• Geometry Exploration 5
3.7 Perpendicular Lines in the Coordinate Plane	• Geometry Exploration 6
Chapter 4: Congruent Triangles	
4.1 Triangles and Angles	• Geometry Exploration 7 • Geometry Exploration 8
4.2 Congruence and Triangles	• Geometry Exploration 9
Chapter 5: Properties of Triangles	
5.2 Bisectors of a Triangle	• Geometry Exploration 10
5.5 Inequalities in One Triangle	• Geometry Exploration 11
Chapter 6: Quadrilaterals	• Geometry Portfolio Project for Chapter 6
6.2 Properties of Parallelograms	• Geometry Exploration 12
6.3 Proving Quadrilaterals are Parallelograms	• Geometry Exploration 13
6.4 Rhombuses, Rectangles, and Squares	• Geometry Exploration 14
6.7 Areas of Triangles and Quadrilaterals	• Geometry Exploration 15

Explorations and Projects Book, Copyright © McDougal Littell Inc.

Correlation Chart of Explorations and Projects to McDougal Littell *Geometry*

Chapter 7: Transformations	• **Geometry Portfolio Project for Chapter 7**
7.4 Translations and Vectors	• Geometry Exploration 16
Chapter 8: Similarity	• **Geometry Portfolio Project for Chapter 8**
Chapter 9: Right Triangles and Trigonometry	• **Geometry Portfolio Project for Chapter 9**
9.2 The Pythagorean Theorem	• Geometry Exploration 17
9.3 The Converse of the Pythagorean Theorem	• Geometry Exploration 18
9.5 Trigonometric Ratios	• Geometry Exploration 19
Chapter 10: Circles	
Chapter 11: Area of Polygons and Circles	
11.6 Geometric Probability	• Geometry Exploration 20
Chapter 12: Surface Area and Volume	• **Geometry Portfolio Project 1 for Chapter 12** • **Geometry Portfolio Project 2 for Chapter 12** • **Geometry Portfolio Project 3 for Chapter 12**
12.4 Volume of Prisms and Cylinders	• Geometry Exploration 21
12.6 Surface Area and Volume of Spheres	• Geometry Exploration 22

Correlation Chart of Explorations and Projects to McDougal Littell *Algebra 2*

Chapter 1: Equations and Inequalities	
1.3 Solving Linear Equations	• Algebra 2 Exploration 1
Chapter 2: Linear Equations and Functions	• Algebra 2 Portfolio Project for Chapter 2
2.2 Slope and Rate of Change	• Algebra 2 Exploration 2
2.3 Quick Graphs of Linear Equations	• Algebra 2 Exploration 3
2.5 Correlation and Best-Fitting Lines	• Algebra 2 Exploration 4
2.6 Linear Inequalities in Two Variables	• Algebra 2 Exploration 5
Chapter 3: Systems of Linear Equations and Inequalities	
3.1 Solving Linear Systems by Graphing	• Algebra 2 Exploration 6
Chapter 4: Matrices and Determinants	• Algebra 2 Portfolio Project for Chapter 4
4.1 Matrix Operations	• Algebra 2 Exploration 7
4.2 Multiplying Matrices	• Algebra 2 Exploration 8 • Algebra 2 Exploration 9
Chapter 5: Quadratic Functions	• Algebra 2 Portfolio Project for Chapter 5
5.1 Graphing Quadratic Functions	• Algebra 2 Exploration 10 • Algebra 2 Exploration 11
5.2 Solving Quadratic Equations by Factoring	• Algebra 2 Exploration 12
5.6 The Quadratic Formula and the Discriminant	• Algebra 1 Exploration 13
Chapter 6: Polynomials and Polynomial Functions	
6.7 Using the Fundamental Theorem of Algebra	• Algebra 2 Exploration 14
6.8 Analyzing Graphs of Polynomial Functions	• Algebra 2 Exploration 15

Explorations and Projects Book, Copyright © McDougal Littell Inc.

Correlation Chart of Explorations and Projects to McDougal Littell *Algebra 2*

Chapter 7: Powers, Roots, and Radicals	• Algebra 2 Portfolio Project for Chapter 7
7.4 Inverse Functions	• Algebra 2 Exploration 16 • Algebra 2 Exploration 17
7.7 Statistics and Statistical Graphs	• Algebra 2 Exploration 18 • Algebra 2 Exploration 19
Chapter 8: Exponential and Logarithmic Functions	• Algebra 2 Portfolio Project 1 for Chapter 8 • Algebra 2 Portfolio Project 2 for Chapter 8 • Algebra 2 Portfolio Project 3 for Chapter 8
8.2 Exponential Decay	• Algebra 2 Exploration 20 • Algebra 2 Exploration 21
8.3 The Number *e*	• Algebra 2 Exploration 22
8.4 Logarithmic Functions	• Algebra 2 Exploration 23
8.5 Properties of Logarithms	• Algebra 2 Exploration 24
Chapter 9: Rational Equations and Functions	• Algebra 2 Portfolio Project for Chapter 9
9.2 Graphing Simple Rational Functions	• Algebra 2 Exploration 25
9.3 Graphing General Rational Functions	• Algebra 2 Exploration 26
Chapter 10: Quadratic Relations and Conic Sections	• Algebra 2 Portfolio Project for Chapter 10
10.1 The Distance and Midpoint Formulas	• Algebra 2 Exploration 27
10.2 Parabolas	• Algebra 2 Exploration 28
10.4 Ellipses	• Algebra 2 Exploration 29

Correlation Chart of Explorations and Projects to McDougal Littell *Algebra 2*

Chapter 11: Sequences and Series	• Algebra 2 Portfolio Project for Chapter 11
11.3 Geometric Sequences and Series	• Algebra 2 Exploration 30
11.5 Recursive Rules for Sequences	• Algebra 2 Exploration 31
Chapter 12: Probability and Statistics	• Algebra 2 Portfolio Project 1 for Chapter 12 • Algebra 2 Portfolio Project 2 for Chapter 12 • Algebra 2 Portfolio Project 3 for Chapter 12
12.1 The Fundamental Counting Principle and Permutations	• Algebra 2 Exploration 32
12.2 Combinations and the Binomial Theorem	• Algebra 2 Exploration 33 • Algebra 2 Exploration 34
12.3 An Introduction to Probability	• Algebra 2 Exploration 35
12.5 Probability of Independent and Dependent Events	• Algebra 2 Exploration 36
12.6 Binomial Distributions	• Algebra 2 Exploration 37
Chapter 13: Trigonometric Ratios and Functions	• Algebra 2 Portfolio Project for Chapter 13
13.1 Right Triangle Trigonometry	• Algebra 2 Exploration 38 • Algebra 2 Exploration 39
13.2 General Angles and Radian Measure	• Algebra 2 Exploration 40
13.5 The Law of Sines	• Algebra 2 Exploration 41
13.7 Parametric Equations and Projectile Motion	• Algebra 2 Exploration 42
Chapter 14: Trigonometric Graphs, Identities, and Equations	• Algebra 2 Portfolio Project for Chapter 14
14.1 Graphing Sine, Cosine, and Tangent Functions	• Algebra 2 Exploration 43

Explorations and Projects Book, Copyright © McDougal Littell Inc.

Algebra 1
Explorations

According to an ancient folktale from India, a man named Sissa Ben Dahir invented the game of chess. The king of India liked the game so much that he wanted to reward Sissa with 64 gold pieces, one for each square on a chessboard. Instead, Sissa asked for grains of wheat arranged on the chessboard in the pattern shown below.

EXPLORATION
COOPERATIVE LEARNING

Exploring Exponents

Work with a partner.
You will need:
• a chessboard
• a handful of rice

SET UP Use rice to model Sissa Ben Dahir's pattern. Place the grains of rice on a chessboard as shown. Each square should contain twice as many grains as the square before it. Continue this pattern until you run out of rice. Then answer the questions below.

Questions

1. Copy and complete the table. Express each number in the second column as a product of 2's.

2. How many factors of 2 would be in the product for the number of grains on the 30th square? on the 64th square? on the nth square? How do you know?

3. A 50 lb bag of wheat contains about 2,500,000 grains. Use a calculator to estimate the number of 50 lb bags of wheat that must be placed on the 30th square to satisfy Sissa Ben Dahir's request. Why do you think he asked for wheat instead of gold?

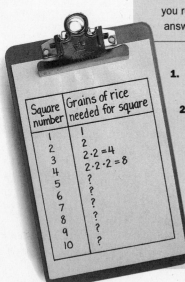

Square number	Grains of rice needed for square
1	1
2	2
3	2·2 = 4
4	2·2·2 = 8
5	?
6	?
7	?
8	?
9	?
10	?

While studying for their math exam, Robin and Jeff had a pizza delivered. The pizza cost $12.50, and they gave the driver a $2.00 tip. To figure out how much each of them should pay, they both used the keystrokes 12.5 [+] 2 [÷] 2 [=] on their calculators. Why did they get two different answers, as shown below?

EXPLORATION
COOPERATIVE LEARNING

Calculator Order of Operations

Work with a partner.
You will need:
• a calculator

1 Reread the paragraph above about Robin and Jeff. Whose answer makes more sense? Why?

2 Try using Robin's and Jeff's keystrokes on your calculator. Did your calculator add first, or did it divide first? How can you tell?

3 Which operation did Robin's calculator do first? Jeff's? How do you know?

4 Press the following keys on your calculator:

24 [÷] 7 [−] 3 [=]

Which operation did the calculator do first?

Now try: 24 [÷] [( ] 7 [−] 3 [ )] [=]

Which operation did the calculator do first this time?

5 Explain how Jeff can use parentheses keys to figure out how much to contribute for pizza. Test your answer on your calculator.

EXPLORATION
COOPERATIVE LEARNING

Patterns and Variable Expressions

Work with a partner.
You will need:
• about 30 toothpicks

SET UP Make as many triangles in a row as you can. Copy and extend the table. Then answer the questions below.

Number of triangles	Number of toothpicks
1	3
2	5
3	7
4	?
5	?
?	?

1
triangle

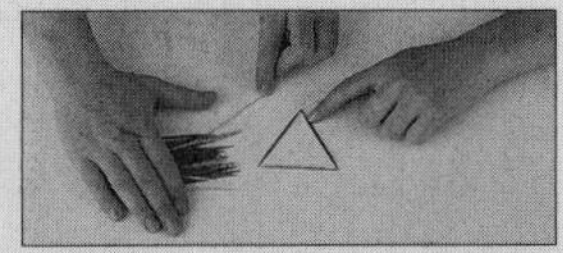

2
triangles

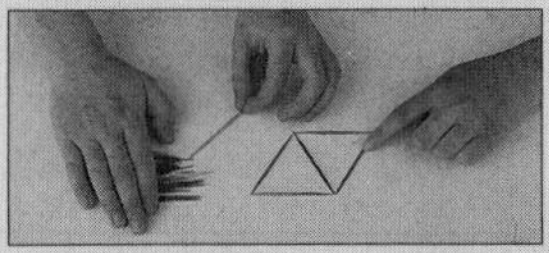

3
triangles

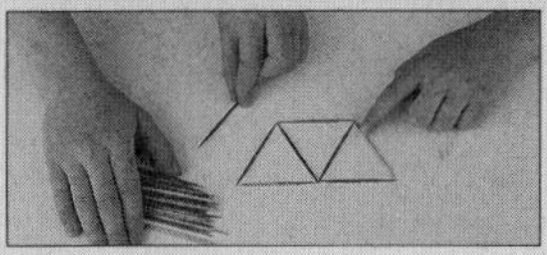

Questions

1. Describe any number patterns you see. What is the relationship between the number of triangles and the number of toothpicks?

2. How many toothpicks do you need to make 10 triangles? 100 triangles? 1,000,000 triangles? How did you get your answers?

3. How many toothpicks do you need to make *n* triangles? Write your answer as a variable expression. Compare your answer to the answers of other groups in the class.

Explorations and Projects Book, Copyright © McDougal Littell Inc.

EXPLORATION
COOPERATIVE LEARNING

Writing an Algorithm
Work in a group of 3–5 students.

1 Work together to write an algorithm that explains how to sit down in a chair. Make each step as clear and precise as possible.

2 Have one of the members of your group follow your algorithm exactly. Did each step work the way you planned?

3 If necessary, revise your algorithm. Have someone in your group test your new algorithm.

4 Compare your algorithm with those of other groups. Are there different steps you could use, or are all of the algorithms basically the same?

EXPLORATION
COOPERATIVE LEARNING

Rolling a Die

Work with a partner.
You will need:

• one die

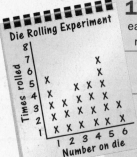

1 How many times do you think each number will occur in 24 rolls? Explain your reasoning.

2 Roll the die 24 times. Record your data on a graph as shown. Were your predictions close to your results?

3 How does your graph compare to the graphs of the other groups in your class?

4 Find the ratio of the number of times each number occurs to the total number of rolls. For example, if 2 occurs 3 times in 24 rolls:

$$\frac{\text{Number of 2's rolled}}{\text{Total number of rolls}} = \frac{3}{24} = \frac{1}{8}$$

5 What do you think the ratios found in Step 4 will be if you combine the results from all the groups in your class? Explain.

6 Combine your results with the rest of the class. Create a class graph and calculate the ratios in Step 4 for each number. Are these numbers close to your prediction in Step 5?

Explorations and Projects Book, Copyright © McDougal Littell Inc.

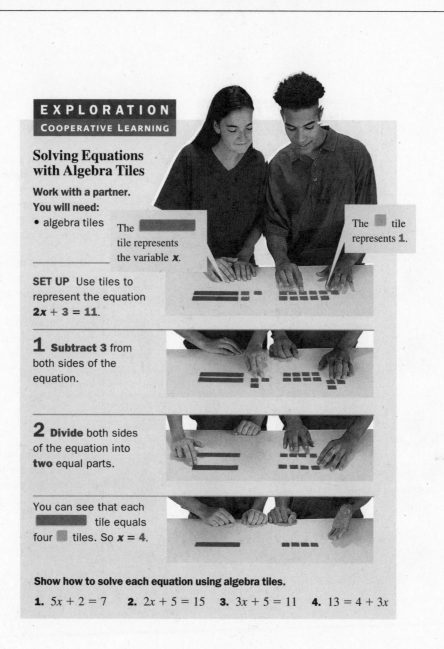

EXPLORATION
COOPERATIVE LEARNING

Solving Equations with Algebra Tiles

Work with a partner.
You will need:
• algebra tiles

The ▬▬▬ tile represents the variable **x**.

The ▪ tile represents **1**.

SET UP Use tiles to represent the equation **2x + 3 = 11**.

1 Subtract **3** from both sides of the equation.

2 Divide both sides of the equation into **two** equal parts.

You can see that each ▬▬▬ tile equals four ▪ tiles. So **x = 4**.

Show how to solve each equation using algebra tiles.

1. $5x + 2 = 7$ **2.** $2x + 5 = 15$ **3.** $3x + 5 = 11$ **4.** $13 = 4 + 3x$

EXPLORATION
COOPERATIVE LEARNING

Graphing Equations

Work with your class.

1 Turn your class into a coordinate grid, as shown. What are your coordinates?

2 Stand up if your coordinates make the equation $y = x - 1$ true. What do you notice about the people standing up?

3 Sit down again. Your teacher will give you other equations. For each equation given, stand up if your coordinates make the equation true. In each case, describe what you observe.

This student is standing because her coordinates, (1, 0), make the equation true.

$$y = x - 1$$
$$0 = 1 - 1$$

Explorations and Projects Book, Copyright © McDougal Littell Inc.

The artist Leonardo da Vinci (1452–1519) studied human proportions in order to make more accurate drawings. He observed that the kneeling height of a person is $\frac{3}{4}$ of the person's standing height. In the Exploration, you will test Leonardo da Vinci's observation.

EXPLORATION
COOPERATIVE LEARNING

Patterns and Direct Variation

Work in a group of at least 6 students.
You will need:
- a meterstick
- graph paper or a graphing calculator

1 Measure and record the kneeling and standing heights of each person in your group.

2 For each person, find the ratio of kneeling height to standing height. Compare your group's results with results from other groups.

Name	Standing height (cm)	Kneeling height (cm)	Kneeling height / Standing height
Tim	156	119	0.76
?	?	?	?

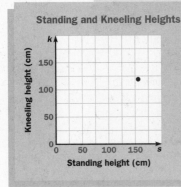

Standing and Kneeling Heights

◀3 Make a graph of your data. Plot a point for each student. Do not connect the points. This **scatter plot** shows the relationship between the two sets of data.

4 Based on Leonardo da Vinci's observation, write an equation for kneeling height as a function of standing height. Graph the equation on your scatter plot.

5 Describe any patterns you see. Do you agree with Leonardo da Vinci's observation? Explain.

EXPLORATION
COOPERATIVE LEARNING

Exploring Linear Equations and Graphs

Work with a partner.
You will need:
- a graphing calculator
- graph paper

GETTING STARTED Set the viewing window on your calculator. The *standard viewing window* uses values from −10 to 10 on both the *x*-axis and the *y*-axis.

1 Graph each equation. For each equation give the slope of the line and write the coordinates of the point where the graph crosses the *y*-axis.

a. $y = 2x$ **b.** $y = 2x + 3$ **c.** $y = 2x - 3$

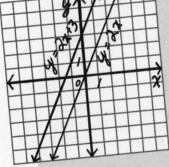

2 Sketch the graphs of the three equations. Describe any patterns you see.

3 Predict what the graph of $y = 2x + 6$ will look like. Predict the slope. Where will the graph cross the *y*-axis? Explain your prediction. Then check it.

4 One way to write linear equations is in the form $y = mx + b$. Based on your observations, what information do the numbers *m* and *b* give you about a graph? Use graphs to support your answer.

Explorations and Projects Book, Copyright © McDougal Littell Inc.

EXPLORATION
COOPERATIVE LEARNING

Creating a Linear Model

Work in a group of 3–4 students:

You will need:
- a paper cup
- a paper clip
- 30 marbles
- 25 pieces of uncooked spaghetti
- 2 chairs of the same height

SET UP Arrange the chairs, spaghetti, and cup as shown.

1 Place marbles in the cup, one at a time, until the spaghetti breaks. Copy and complete the table.

2 Make a scatter plot of the data. Draw a line of fit. Find an equation for your line of fit.

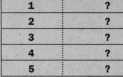

Number of pieces of spaghetti	Number of marbles needed to break spaghetti
1	?
2	?
3	?
4	?
5	?

3 Use your equation to predict how many marbles are needed to break six pieces of spaghetti. Check your prediction using spaghetti.

4 Do you think that moving the chairs farther apart or closer together would affect your results? If so, how? Describe and carry out an experiment to test your theory.

E X P L O R A T I O N
COOPERATIVE LEARNING

Graphing $x - y \geq 1$

Work with a partner.
You will need:
- a ruler
- colored pencils

1 Make a large coordinate grid like the one in the picture. Both axes should extend from −4 to 4. Draw the grid lines.

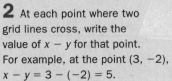

2 At each point where two grid lines cross, write the value of $x - y$ for that point. For example, at the point (3, −2), $x - y = 3 - (-2) = 5$.

3 With a colored pencil, circle each point that represents a solution of the inequality $x - y \geq 1$. What do you notice?

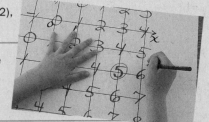

4 Find the point (2.5, 0.5) on your grid. Do you think this is a solution of the inequality? Do you think (2.5, 1.5) is a solution of the inequality? Check your answers.

5 Shade your grid to show all of the solutions of the inequality $x - y \geq 1$. How is the border between the shaded and the unshaded regions related to the inequality $x - y \geq 1$? Explain.

 Explorations and Projects Book, Copyright © McDougal Littell Inc.

EXPLORATION
COOPERATIVE LEARNING

Comparing Game Scores

Work in a group of four.
You will need:
- a bowl
- a narrow cup or glass
- about two cups of dried beans

1 Place the cup upright inside the bowl on the floor.

2 Take turns trying to drop beans into the cup. Stand up straight and hold your arm straight out. You each get one minute. Count the number of beans that land:

- inside the cup (10 points)
- inside the bowl but outside the cup (5 points)
- outside the bowl (0 points)

Record your results in a table.

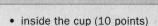

Name	Number in cup	×	10 points	Number in bowl	×	5 points	Number outside bowl	×	0 points
Lisa	18		180	6		30	3		0
?	?		?	?		?	?		?

3 Compute the total number of points for each person in your group. Can you tell who had the best aim by comparing total numbers of points? Explain.

4 Compute the average number of points per drop for each person in your group. Can you use this information to decide who had the best aim? Explain.

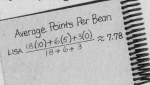

Average Points Per Bean

LISA $\dfrac{18(10)+6(5)+3(0)}{18+6+3} \approx 7.78$

EXPLORATION
COOPERATIVE LEARNING

Comparing Tables and Graphs

**Work in 2 teams of
2 students each.**
You will need:

- a graphing calculator or
  graph paper

Discounts!

CDs $11⁰⁰

Why Pay More !?!

*Join our
CD Club
and get*
8 FREE CDs
*(You must buy at
least 6 more CDs
for $15 each.)*

One team should do Steps 1–4 below.
The other team should do Steps 5–8
on the next page. The teams should
work together on Step 9.

The CD club minimum
is 8 + 6, or 14.

1 Copy and complete the table.

Number of CDs	Cost at store ($)	CD club cost ($)
14	?	?
15	?	?
16	?	?

2 For the values in the table, which way of buying CDs is less expensive? Will this always be the case? Explain.

3 Expand your table. Include rows for 20, 30, 40, and 50 CDs.

4 When will the total cost through the CD club equal the total cost at the discount store? How can you tell? When would you choose the CD club? the discount store? Why?

Exploration continued on next page.

Exploration *continued*

5 Write an equation for the cost *y* of buying *x* CDs from the discount store.

6 Repeat Step 5 for the CD club.

7 Graph the two equations in the same coordinate plane. Set a good viewing window, like the one shown below.

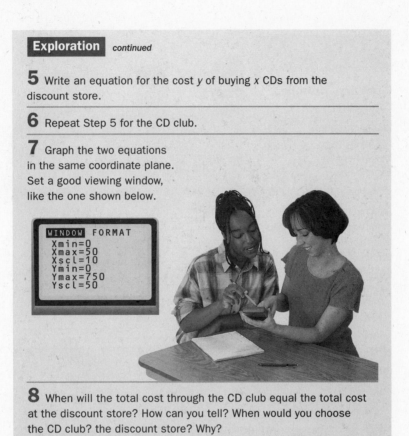

```
WINDOW FORMAT
 Xmin=0
 Xmax=50
 Xscl=10
 Ymin=0
 Ymax=750
 Yscl=50
```

8 When will the total cost through the CD club equal the total cost at the discount store? How can you tell? When would you choose the CD club? the discount store? Why?

9 Discuss your answers to Steps 4 and 8 with the other team. Compare the table method to the graphing method. List some advantages and disadvantages of each method.

EXPLORATION
COOPERATIVE LEARNING

Graphing Multiple Equations

Work in a group of 3 students.

You will need:
• graph paper

1 Choose one of the equations below and graph it. Each of you should choose a different equation.

   a. $2x + 2y = 5$

   b. $4x + 4y = 10$

   c. $6x + 6y = 15$

2 Compare your graphs. What do you notice?

3 Compare the three equations. How are they related?

4 Choose one of the systems of equations below and solve it by graphing. Each of you should choose a different system.

   a. $2x + 2y = 5$
      $5x - 6y = 7$

   b. $4x + 4y = 10$
      $5x - 6y = 7$

   c. $6x + 6y = 15$
      $5x - 6y = 7$

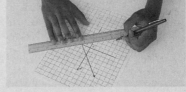

5 Compare your solutions. What do you notice? Explain your results.

6 Which of the systems in step 4 is easiest to solve algebraically? Why?

Explorations and Projects Book, Copyright © McDougal Littell Inc.

Algebra 1 Exploration 15

EXPLORATION
COOPERATIVE LEARNING

Multiplying and Dividing Powers of 10

Work with a partner.
You will need:
- a calculator

Product of powers	Expanded product	Product as a single power
$10^2 \cdot 10^1$	$(10 \cdot 10)(10)$	10^3
$10^4 \cdot 10^2$	?	?
$10^7 \cdot 10^1$	?	?
$10^5 \cdot 10^6$	?	?
$10^0 \cdot 10^3$	?	?

Quotient of powers	Expanded quotient	Quotient as a single power
$\frac{10^3}{10^2}$	$\frac{10 \cdot 10 \cdot 10}{10 \cdot 10}$	10^1
$\frac{10^6}{10^4}$	?	?
$\frac{10^{12}}{10^3}$	?	?
$\frac{10^1}{10^3}$	?	?
$\frac{10^0}{10^2}$	?	?

Copy and complete the tables. Then answer the questions below.

Questions

1. Use any patterns you see in the tables to complete these rules for working with powers of 10:

a. $10^m \cdot 10^n = 10^?$ **b.** $\frac{10^m}{10^n} = 10^?$

2. Use the rules you wrote in Question 1 to simplify each expression. Use a calculator to check your answers.

a. $10^4 \cdot 10^7$ **b.** $10^{10} \cdot 10^3$ **c.** $\frac{10^9}{10^2}$ **d.** $\frac{10^8}{10^{14}}$

Copyright © McDougal Littell Inc.

Comparing Radicals

Work with a partner.
You will need:
- graph paper

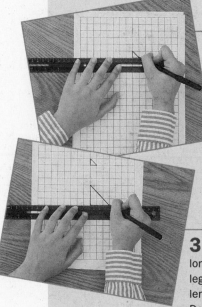

1 Draw a right triangle with legs 1 unit long, as shown. Use the Pythagorean theorem to show that the hypotenuse is $\sqrt{2}$ units long.

2 Draw a right triangle with legs 2 units long. Show that the hypotenuse is $\sqrt{8}$ units long. Divide the triangle into smaller triangles like the one in Step 1 to show that the hypotenuse is also $2\sqrt{2}$ units long.

3 Draw a right triangle with legs 3 units long, one with legs 4 units long, and one with legs 5 units long. For each triangle, write the length of the hypotenuse two different ways. Describe any patterns you see.

4 The number 8 can also be written as the product 4 · 2. You can write $\sqrt{8}$ as $\sqrt{4 \cdot 2}$. How does writing $\sqrt{8}$ this way help explain what you saw in Step 2? How does it help to explain what you saw in Step 3?

EXPLORATION
COOPERATIVE LEARNING

Exploring Nonlinear Graphs

Work in a group of 2–4 students.
You will need:
- graph paper
- a graphing calculator

You want to design a rectangular pen for a dog, using 30 ft of fencing. You decide that the length of each side must be an integer.

Perimeter = 30 ft
Area = 14 ft^2

1 Draw all the pens you can build. Then copy and complete the table. Add rows until you have listed all possibilities.

Length of Side 1 (ft)	Length of Side 2 (ft)	Perimeter (ft)	Area (ft²)
1	14	30	14
14	1		

2 Which dimensions give the dog the most area? Which dimensions give the dog the longest run? Discuss which dimensions you would recommend. Explain your decision.

3 Make a scatter plot of the data. Put the length of Side 1 on the horizontal axis and the area of the pen on the vertical axis. Describe the shape of the graph.

4 Let x = the length of Side 1 of the pen. Write an expression in terms of x for the length of Side 2. Then write and graph an equation for the area of the pen as a function of the length of Side 1. Use a graphing calculator.

5 Discuss with your group how the graphs in Steps 3 and 4 compare.

E X P L O R A T I O N
COOPERATIVE LEARNING

Analyzing the Shape of a Parabola

Work with a partner.
You will need:
• a graphing calculator
• graph paper

1 One person should graph the equations below. Set a good viewing window, such as $-9 \le x \le 9$ and $-2 \le y \le 10$. What do you notice about the shapes of the parabolas?

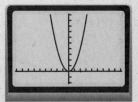

a. $y = x^2$ **b.** $y = 2x^2$ **c.** $y = 3x^2$

2 On graph paper, the other person should sketch what he or she thinks the graph of $y = 4x^2$ will look like in relation to the graphs in Step 1. Use a graphing calculator to check the prediction.

3 Switch roles and repeat Step 1 using the equations below.

a. $y = x^2$ **b.** $y = \frac{1}{2}x^2$ **c.** $y = \frac{1}{3}x^2$

4 On graph paper, sketch what you think the graph of $y = \frac{1}{4}x^2$ will look like in relation to the graphs in Step 3. Use a graphing calculator to check your prediction.

5 Work together to generalize what happens to the graph of the equation $y = ax^2$ as the value of a increases from 0 to 1 and beyond.

6 Work together to generalize what happens to the graph of the equation $y = ax^2$ as the value of a decreases from 0 to -1 and beyond. Try some examples. Be sure to set a good viewing window.

EXPLORATION
COOPERATIVE LEARNING

Finding Products with Algebra Tiles

Work with a partner.
You will need:
- algebra tiles
- ruler
- paper

SET UP Use tiles to find the product $2x(x + 3)$.

1 Draw two perpendicular lines on your paper.

2 Using tiles, mark off the dimensions $2x$ and $(x + 3)$.

3 Create and completely fill in a rectangle using x^2-tiles, x-tiles, and 1-tiles.

4 Count the tiles to see that $2x(x + 3) = 2x^2 + 6x$.

Use algebra tiles to find each product. Make a drawing of each tile model and show its dimensions.

1. $3x(x + 2)$ **2.** $(x + 2)(x + 3)$ **3.** $(2x + 1)(2x + 3)$

4. Choose your own product to model. Make a drawing of your tile model and show its dimensions.

EXPLORATION
COOPERATIVE LEARNING

Modeling Dimensions with Polynomials

Work in a group of 4 students.
You will need:
- rectangular pieces of paper that are not square
- a ruler

Each of you should build a box and write
expressions for its dimensions
as outlined in Steps 1–8.

1 Fold a rectangular piece of paper into 16 equal parts as shown.
Always fold toward the front of the piece of paper.

Fold in half...	then in quarters...	then turn and repeat.

Exploration continued on next page.

Explorations and Projects Book, Copyright © McDougal Littell Inc.

Exploration *continued*

2 Hold your paper with the longer side facing you and fold the outer flaps back in as shown.

3 Fold in the four corners so the edges line up with the horizontal fold lines as shown.

4 Fold back two vertical strips in the middle, one to the left and the other to the right, to "lock" the corners.

5 Lift up gently as shown to form your box.

6 Unfold your box as shown. Measure the length and the width of the original piece of paper. Also measure the width of the vertical strips that you folded back.

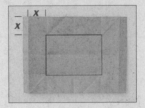

7 What do *x* and the region outlined in red represent in terms of the box?

8 Use your measurements from Step 6 to write expressions for the length, width, and height of the box in terms of *x*.

9 Compare expressions with those of the members of your group. How are the expressions alike? How are they different?

EXPLORATION
COOPERATIVE LEARNING

Factors, Intercepts, and Solutions

Work with a partner.
You will need:
- graphing calculators

1 One of you should graph equations 1–4 while the other graphs equations A–D. Match the equations that have the same graph.

STANDARD FORM	FACTORED FORM
1. $y = x^2 + 2x - 3$	**A.** $y = x(x - 4)$
2. $y = x^3 - 12x^2 + 44x - 48$	**B.** $y = (x + 3)(x - 1)$
3. $y = x^2 - 4x$	**C.** $y = x(x + 3)(x + 1)$
4. $y = x^3 + 4x^2 + 3x$	**D.** $y = (x - 2)(x - 4)(x - 6)$

2 Find the x-intercepts of each graph in Step 1. Then look at the factored form of the equation for each graph. How are the x-intercepts and the factored form related?

3 Suppose you want to solve the polynomial equation $x^2 - 6x = 0$. How can the graph of $y = x^2 - 6x$ help you solve the equation? How can the factored form $x(x - 6) = 0$ help you solve the equation?

Explorations and Projects Book, Copyright © McDougal Littell Inc.

E X P L O R A T I O N
COOPERATIVE LEARNING

The Capture-Recapture Method

Work with a partner.
You will need:
• a large coffee can
• a bag of dried beans
• a marker

Follow Steps 1–4. Then answer the questions below.

1 Pour the bag of beans into the can.

2 Take out a handful of beans, mark them, and record how many you marked.

3 Put the marked beans back into the can. Mix the beans thoroughly.

4 Take out another handful, or *sample*, of beans. Record the number of marked beans and the total number of beans in your sample.

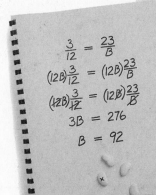

$$\frac{3}{12} = \frac{23}{B}$$

$$(12B)\frac{3}{12} = (12B)\frac{23}{B}$$

$$(\cancel{12}B)\frac{3}{\cancel{12}} = (12\cancel{B})\frac{23}{\cancel{B}}$$

$$3B = 276$$

$$B = 92$$

Questions

1. Let B = the unknown number of beans in the can. What is the fraction of beans that are marked? (Your answer will involve B.)

2. What fraction of beans in your sample were marked? How do you think this fraction relates to the fraction from Question 1?

3. Ayita marked 23 beans. Then she took a sample of 12 beans and found 3 marked. Use Ayita's method and the fractions you found in Questions 1 and 2 to estimate the number of beans in your coffee can.

EXPLORATION
COOPERATIVE LEARNING

Exploring Rectangles with Equal Areas

Work with a partner.
You will need:

- 36 algebra unit tiles
- graph paper

1 Arrange the 36 tiles to form a rectangle. What are the length and the width of the rectangle?

2 Use the algebra tiles to form as many rectangles as you can with area 36. Copy and extend the table to record the length *l* and the width *w* of each rectangle.

ℓ	w
12	3
3	12
2	?
?	?

3 Graph the data pairs (*l*, *w*) from your table in a coordinate plane.

4 **a.** Could a rectangle with area 36 be 4.5 units wide? If so, what would the length be?
b. Draw a smooth curve passing through the points you graphed. Explain why it makes sense to connect the points.

5 Can a rectangle be 0 units long? What happens as the length of the rectangle gets very small? Adjust your graph if necessary.

6 Write an equation relating *l* and *w*. Describe how the length of a rectangle affects its width if the area is constant.

Explorations and Projects Book, Copyright © McDougal Littell Inc.

EXPLORATION
COOPERATIVE LEARNING

Subtracting Rational Expressions

Work with a partner.
You will need:
- a ruler
- graph paper

1 Look at the diagram. Explain how it shows that $\frac{1}{2} - \frac{1}{3} = \frac{1}{6}$.

2 Draw a diagram to show that $\frac{1}{3} - \frac{1}{4} = \frac{1}{12}$.

Questions

1. Look for a pattern in the equations from Steps 1 and 2. Use this pattern to complete the following equations.

    a. $\frac{1}{4} - \frac{1}{5} = \underline{\ ?\ }$ **b.** $\frac{1}{5} - \frac{1}{6} = \underline{\ ?\ }$ **c.** $\frac{1}{6} - \frac{1}{7} = \underline{\ ?\ }$

2. Now use the pattern you found to complete this equation.
    $\frac{1}{x} - \frac{1}{x+1} = \underline{\ ?\ }$

EXPLORATION
COOPERATIVE LEARNING

Constructing Similar Triangles

Work with a partner.
You will need:
- a rectangular sheet of paper
- scissors
- a protractor
- a ruler

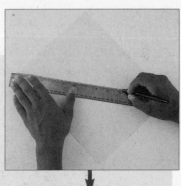

SET UP Cut along the diagonal of a piece of paper to make two triangles. Label the corners of one triangle *A*, *B*, and *C* as shown. Fold the unlabeled triangle to make a line parallel to the shortest side. Cut along this line and label the corners of the smaller triangle *D*, *E*, and *F* as shown. Then answer the questions below.

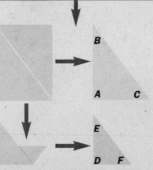

Questions

1. Copy and complete the tables. Give lengths to the nearest millimeter.

2. What do you notice about the angles of △*ABC* and △*DEF*?

△*ABC*			△*DEF*	
Measure of ∠*A*	?		Measure of ∠*D*	?
Measure of ∠*B*	?		Measure of ∠*E*	?
Measure of ∠*C*	?		Measure of ∠*F*	?
Length of $\overline{AB}$	?		Length of $\overline{DE}$	?
Length of $\overline{BC}$	?		Length of $\overline{EF}$	?
Length of $\overline{AC}$	?		Length of $\overline{DF}$	?

3. Find each ratio. What do you notice? (*AB* stands for the length of $\overline{AB}$.)

   a. $\dfrac{AB}{DE}$ b. $\dfrac{BC}{EF}$ c. $\dfrac{AC}{DF}$

4. The triangles you made are called *similar* triangles. What do you think it means for two triangles to be similar?

Explorations and Projects Book, Copyright © McDougal Littell Inc.

Algebra 1
Projects

Analyzing Change

Would your school feel more crowded if enrollment increased by 50 students? It depends on the size of your school. If your school has 1000 students, enrollment would increase by 5%. If your school has 100 students, enrollment would increase by 50%. Knowing a percent change often gives you more information than a numerical change.

PROJECT GOAL Your goal is to investigate the percent change in something that interests you.

Collecting Data

Work with a partner. Decide on a topic for your investigation. You can collect data yourself, or you can find statistics in a newspaper, a magazine, or an almanac. Your data should include at least four numerical values that change from one time to another.

Some possibilities are:

- the populations of your state and four nearby states in two different years

- the number of cars passing through a green light in the morning and afternoon at various intersections

Use a table or spreadsheet to record and analyze your data. For example, suppose you want to explore a surge in the popularity of in-line skating.

1. **USE A SPREADSHEET** to record the number of in-line skaters in four regions of the United States for two different years.

2. **USE A FORMULA** to calculate the percent change from 1992 to 1993 in the Northeast.

$$\text{Percent change} = \frac{\text{New value} - \text{Old value}}{\text{Old value}} \cdot 100$$

Edit   Format

Normal

In-Line Skating

D2		=((C2–B2)/B2)*100		
	A	**B**	**C**	**D**
1		1992	1993	Percent change
2	Northeast	1,720,000	2,889,000	67.97
3	North central	2,646,000	3,963,000	49.77
4	South	2,306,000	2,899,000	25.72
5	West	2,692,000	2,808,000	4.31
6				
7				
8				

3. **FILL DOWN** to find the percent change in the other three regions of the country.

Explorations and Projects Book, Copyright © McDougal Littell Inc.

Making a Graph

Present your results visually. Your display should make it clear which quantities increased and which decreased. You can choose any of these types of displays, or you may have an idea of your own.

- a bar graph
- a colored map
- a histogram

Presenting Your Analysis

Write a report, make a poster, prepare a video, or give a presentation explaining your results.

Remember to:

- Include your original data. Explain how you measured and recorded the data.

- Describe how you did your calculations. (If you used a spreadsheet, include a copy and explain how you used it.)

- Explain your visual display.

- Explain the difference between a positive percent change and a negative percent change.

- Try to draw conclusions from the percent change or from the original data.

- Discuss reasons why these changes may have occurred.

Self-Assessment

What have you and your partner learned about percent change? Describe what you think went well in your project. Describe what you think did not work as smoothly as you would have liked. If you could do the project again, what would you do differently? Why?

PORTFOLIO PROJECT

Functions of Time

Many of the changes you see are examples of functions. A graph of a function can help you see a pattern in the change.

PROJECT GOAL Collect and graph data about something that changes over time. You will look for patterns in your graph.

Collecting Data

Work with a partner. Choose an event that occurs in the world around you. Whatever you choose should be easy to measure and should change noticeably within minutes, hours, or days.

Some possibilities:

- the height of a pedal on a moving bicycle

- the temperature at each hour of the day

- the number of cars in a fast food restaurant's parking lot at different times of the day

- the number of people going into a mall on different days or at different hours

Investigate and record what you observe. For example, suppose you decide to investigate how the height of a bicycle pedal changes over time.

1. MEASURE the height of the pedal in different positions.

2. RECORD when the pedal is in each position. Making a video can help you see a change that happens quickly.

3. ORGANIZE your data in a table or spreadsheet.

Explorations and Projects Book, Copyright © McDougal Littell Inc.

Making a Graph

Use your data to make a graph of the function. Do you see a pattern? What do you think happens between the points that you plot? Does it make sense to connect the points?

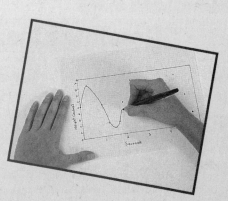

Presenting Your Ideas

Write a report, make a poster, or give an oral presentation explaining your graph. Describe what you observed and discuss any patterns you see. Describe the domain and the range of your function.

You may also want to look through books, magazines, and other sources at the library. Can you find data about functions like the one you investigated? How do the data compare with yours?

Before giving your presentation, you may want to show your classmates your graph without the title or the labels to see if they can guess what you observed.

Self-Assessment

Describe what you and your partner learned about collecting and graphing data. For example, how did you decide what to investigate? How did you decide on values to use for the axes of your graph? Did you discuss ideas together? Did you divide up some of the work? What might you do differently next time?

PORTFOLIO PROJECT

Creating Linear Puzzles

Computer graphics programs use equations to determine each shape in a picture. Displaying a line on a computer starts with finding an equation of the line and specifying its endpoints. You can use this idea to create a puzzle with linear equations.

PROJECT GOAL | Design and create a book of linear puzzles for other students in your class to solve.

Designing the Puzzles

Work in groups of five or six to create a book of linear puzzles. Here are some hints for designing your puzzles:

1. **CHOOSE A SHAPE OR LETTER** for your puzzle that you can draw using straight lines. **DRAW** your design on a coordinate plane. Make sure that the endpoints of the line segments are on grid intersections. Keep your design secret from the other members of your group.

Choose a shape that has line segments with at least four different slopes.

Solution

2. **FIND** an equation in slope-intercept form of each line in your design. Write an equation for each line segment on a separate sheet of paper.

3. **PROVIDE INFORMATION** about the endpoints of each line segment. Write inequalities that describe the smallest and largest x- or y-values for each line. Add this information to your set of equations. This list is your puzzle. Your drawing is the solution.

Puzzle

Equation	Endpoints	
$y = \frac{3}{2}x + \frac{1}{2}$	$x \geq 1$	$x \leq 5$
$y = -2x + 18$	$x \geq 5$	$x \leq 8$
$y = -\frac{1}{2}x + \frac{5}{2}$	$x \geq 1$	$x \leq 5$
$y = \frac{2}{3}x - \frac{10}{3}$	$x \geq 5$	$x \leq 8$
$x = 5$	$y \geq 0$	$y \leq 8$

Explorations and Projects Book, Copyright © McDougal Littell Inc.

Checking Your Work

• Exchange puzzles within your group and solve them by graphing the lines described by the equations and inequalities.

• Check to see if your drawing matches the solution.

• Write an evaluation of the puzzle you solve. Give suggestions for improvements if you have any.

Assembling Your Puzzle Book

Collect a copy of the puzzle and solution made by each member of your group. Use these puzzles to make a book with instructions for solving and creating puzzles.

Remember to include:

• names of puzzle designers

• instructions for solving

• an answer key

You may want to extend your report to explore some of the ideas below:

• Images on a computer monitor are made up of tiny dots called pixels. Each pixel has a coordinate based on its distance from one corner of the monitor. How do computer programmers use pixel coordinates to generate images on a computer screen?

• Chess players move pieces according to a specific set of rules. Find out what these rules are. Then write a set of equations to describe the paths of different pieces as they are moved from one end of the chess board to the other.

Self-Assessment

In your report, describe which puzzles were the most challenging to solve. Why were they challenging? How could you have made your puzzle more challenging? What general advice would you give someone who is trying to create a puzzle?

PORTFOLIO PROJECT

Making a Profit

Have you ever wondered how prices are determined? People who make a product must determine how much money to charge so that they make a *profit*. Profit is the money remaining after expenses are subtracted from income.

PROJECT GOAL Determine the expenses of making cookies and decide on a selling price so that you earn a profit.

Financial Plans

Work with a partner. Choose a cookie recipe you want to make.

1. CALCULATE EXPENSES

• **INGREDIENTS**
Calculate or estimate how much the ingredients in one batch of cookies cost. For example:

Cost of 1 cup of sugar =

$$\frac{\text{Cost of a bag}}{\text{Cups per bag}} = \frac{\$1.89}{10} \approx \$.19$$

• **TIME**
Calculate the cost of your time to make one batch.

$$\frac{\text{Labor}}{\text{costs}} = \frac{\text{Hours}}{\text{worked}} \times \frac{\text{Hourly}}{\text{pay}}$$

• **FIXED EXPENSES**
Assume that you must pay $25 for a permit to sell cookies.

2. CALCULATE INCOME Research a reasonable price to charge for selling your cookies individually. How much income can you make per batch?

Explorations and Projects Book, Copyright © McDougal Littell Inc.

Analyzing Your Data

Use a table and a graph to model expenses and income as functions of the number of batches sold. What is the point at which you make a profit? Write and solve an inequality to show another method of finding the point at which you make a profit.

Making a Report

Write a report about your cookie-making venture. Describe the decisions that you made concerning ingredients, labor costs, and pricing. Include your table, your graph, and a discussion of income and expenses.

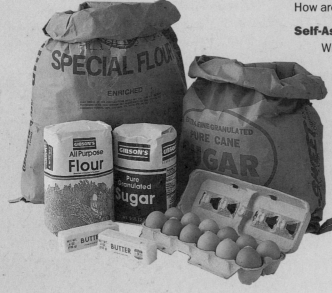

You may want to extend your report by examining some of the ideas below:

• Survey friends and neighbors to find the price they would be willing to pay for a cookie. Display that data and any conclusions you can make from the data.

• How do cookie manufacturers' prices differ from your price? Why do you think this is so? How are their expenses different from yours?

Self-Assessment

Write a paragraph explaining your decisions. Which method, making a table, making a graph, or writing an inequality, works best for you?

Describe how you did research. For example, how did you find out what the minimum wage is or what local businesses pay workers for similar work?

What was the most difficult aspect of the project? the easiest? Why?

PORTFOLIO PROJECT

Designing a Stairway

Have you ever found it difficult to climb a narrow or steep stairway? Stairs may appear to be all the same, but slight changes in the riser/tread ratio can greatly affect the safety and the cost of stairs.

Iowa City

PROJECT GOAL Compare the dimensions of stairways in your community with some accepted rules for stairs, so that you can better design your own stairway.

Designing a Stairway

Work with a partner.

1. COLLECT riser and **tread** data for at least five different stairways. Take notes about how easy or hard it is to climb each stairway.

Number	Location	Tread Length (in)	Riser Length (in)
1	Near Gym	10	7

2. DECIDE on an ideal riser/tread ratio. Explain your decision.

Chicago

3. DESIGN your own stairway. Suppose the total distance from one floor to the next is 105 in. Determine lengths for the risers for a 9 in. tread and an 11 in. tread. Then make a scale drawing of your stairway.

riser   tread

Analyzing Stairway Standards

Codes have been written to increase stair safety. Codes often concern the riser/tread ratio, lighting around stairs, and handrail height. Here are two generally accepted rules for stairway construction:

RULE 1: The sum of one riser and one tread should be from 17 in. to 18 in.

RULE 2: The sum of two risers and one tread should be from 24 in. to 25 in.

New Mexico

1. Make a graph showing all the riser/tread data that meet the conditions of these rules. (*Hint:* You will graph four inequalities.)

2. On the same coordinate grid, graph the data you collected about stairs as ordered pairs. Also graph the ordered pair for the stairway you designed.

3. Describe any patterns you see. Did all the stairways follow the generally accepted rules? Did any not follow the rules?

Presenting Your Results

Give a report that includes your graph, your table, and your scale drawing. Write a paragraph comparing your local stairways' dimensions with the accepted rules for stairs. Give your recommendations for riser/tread ratios.

You may want to extend your report by examining some of the ideas below:

• Learn more about constructing stairs, including how a carpenter's square is used.

• Collect photographs of stairways from other periods of time and from other countries.

• Find the slope for each stairway on your list. Then find the range of slopes for the stairways.

• Interview architects and/or carpenters in your area. Ask what they would consider the best riser/tread ratio for stairs.

Questions

1. What was the most interesting stairway you've designed?

2. What's the difference between designing a stairway for a home and for an office building?

3. What different types of stairways have you designed?

Self-Assessment

What method(s) did you use to create your graph? How did you and your partner decide on an ideal riser/tread ratio? Overall, was there enough variety in the stairs you studied to give you a sense of how the riser/tread ratio affects stairway use? What was the most difficult aspect of the project? the easiest? Why?

PORTFOLIO PROJECT

Models for Spirals

Many patterns found in nature can be modeled by mathematical equations. One pattern that often appears in flowers, spider webs, and sea shells is the spiral. In this project, you will use exponential equations to create a spiral.

PROJECT GOAL Find an exponential formula that models a spiral. Then create your own spiral.

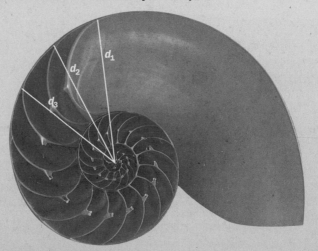

Measuring the Nautilus Shell

Work with a partner. Find a photograph of a nautilus shell, or use the one shown here. Measure the distance in millimeters from the center of the spiral to the outside corner of the first chamber. Label this distance d_1 as shown. Measure the corresponding distances for the next seven chambers. Label these distances d_2, d_3, and so on.

Calculating the Ratios

As you move inward along the spiral, the distances you measure become shorter. They are decreasing exponentially. Organize the distances you measured in a table or spreadsheet. Find the ratio of the distance for each chamber to the distance for the previous chamber.

	A	B	C
	Spiral Project		
	A	**B**	**C**
1	n	dn	dn+1/dn
2	1	10	0.95
3	2	9.5	
4	3	8.6	
5	4	7.7	
6	5	7.2	

Explorations and Projects Book, Copyright © McDougal Littell Inc.

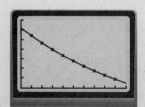

Modeling the Spiral with an Equation

Let r = the mean of the ratios you found. Substitute your values for d_1 and r into the formula below to create an equation for d_n, the distance for the nth chamber.

$$d_n = d_1 \cdot r^n$$

Calculate values for d_n by substituting values of n into your equation. How close do the calculated values come to the distances you measured? Make a scatter plot of your data and graph your equation in the same coordinate plane. Describe your results.

Creating Your Own Spiral

1. CHOOSE values for r and d_1. Make sure your r-value is between 0 and 1.

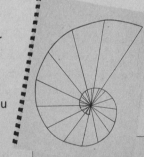

2. DRAW a line segment of length d_1.

3. MULTIPLY the length of the line segment you drew by r. Draw a line segment of this new length at a 25° angle to the previous line.

4. REPEAT Step 3 until the lengths become very close to zero.

5. CONNECT the endpoints of the line segments with a smooth curve.

Find an equation to model your partner's spiral. How does the spiral change when you increase the value of r? when you increase the value of d_1? Write a paragraph answering these questions. Include sketches of your work.

Self-Assessment
Tell what you liked and didn't like about this project. How did you and your partner divide up the work in the project? Describe any difficulties you had and discuss how you solved problems. What would you do differently if you were to do the project over again? List some ways you could extend your study of spirals.

PORTFOLIO PROJECT

Investigating Gravity

Downhill skiers take advantage of steep slopes to ski faster. Gravity enables them to accelerate as they go down the slope. Objects are pulled toward the ground because of gravity. The bigger the object, the greater its pull on other objects. Since Earth is the biggest thing around, it pulls objects (like skiers) toward it.

PROJECT GOAL Explore how gravity affects the time it takes a ball to roll down a ramp.

Collecting Data

Work with a partner to recreate an experiment first performed by Galileo Galilei over four hundred years ago. Measure the time it takes a solid heavy ball or marble to roll down a ramp for at least ten different distances. Here are some key steps you should follow:

1. MAKE a ramp by taping two meter sticks together side by side in a "V" shape.

2. PLACE one end of the ramp on a stack of books so that the other end forms a 10° angle with the floor. Check the angle with a protractor.

3. USE a stopwatch to measure the time it takes a ball to reach the end of the ramp. Record the time and the distance for ten starting points.

Based on your observations, how long do you think it would take the ball to roll 55 cm? How far would the ball roll in 0.75 s?

Explorations and Projects Book, Copyright © McDougal Littell Inc.

Comparing Graphs

Galileo showed that a ball rolling down an inclined plane accelerates at a constant rate. The equation below shows the relationship between the amount of time t in seconds that a solid ball rolls and the distance d it travels along a ramp inclined at a 10° angle:

$$d = 0.61t^2$$

• Calculate how long it would take a ball to roll 55 cm. Compare this value to the value you estimated using your scatter plot. What might explain any differences?

• Sketch a graph of the equation $d = 0.61t^2$ in the same coordinate plane as your scatter plot. How do the graph and the scatter plot compare?

Writing a Report

Write a report about your experiment. Include a brief description of your procedure. Describe the relationship between the distance a ball travels and the time it takes to travel that far.

4. MAKE **a scatter plot of the data. Put time in seconds on the horizontal axis and distance in meters on the vertical axis.**

You may want to extend your report to explore some of the ideas below:

• What effect does doubling the time a ball rolls have on the distance it travels?

• Will the results of the experiment change if you change the angle of the ramp? If so, how?

• Will the results of the experiment change if you use a lighter or a heavier solid ball? Why or why not?

Self-Assessment

Identify the mathematical skills you used to analyze the relationship you explored in this experiment. What are some possible sources of error in the way you collected your data? Describe how you and your partner worked together or could work together in the future to minimize errors.

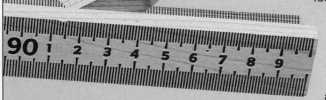

PORTFOLIO PROJECT

Volume and Weight

Dolls and action figures are scale models of human beings, but not all such models are shaped like real people. You can learn something about the accuracy of a doll's proportions by measuring its volume.

PROJECT GOAL   **Find out how much a doll or an action figure would weigh if it were a real person.**

Taking Measurements

Work with a partner to measure the volume of a model (either a doll or an action figure) by measuring the amount of water it displaces. You may want to do the experiment several times to be sure you are getting reliable results.

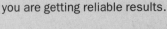

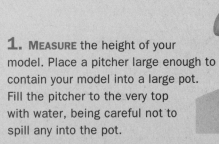

1. MEASURE the height of your model. Place a pitcher large enough to contain your model into a large pot. Fill the pitcher to the very top with water, being careful not to spill any into the pot.

2. TAPE over any places where water might leak in if your model is hollow. Then completely submerge your model in the water without letting your fingers go beneath the surface.

3. REMOVE your model and pitcher from the pot. Then use measuring cups and spoons to measure the volume of the water that was displaced, or spilled over, into the pot. This is the volume of your model.

4. CONVERT the volume of your model to liters using the conversion chart at the left.

U.S. Customary Units	Metric Units
1 cup	0.24 liters
1 tablespoon	0.015 liters
1 teaspoon	0.005 liters

Explorations and Projects Book, Copyright © McDougal Littell Inc.

Calculating Weight

The polynomial equation below shows the relationship between the volume of a real person V_p and the volume of a scale model V_m, in liters.

$$V_p = V_m s^3$$

The variable s is a scale factor.

$$s = \frac{\text{Person's height (in.)}}{\text{Model's height (in.)}}$$

Suppose the doll or action figure that you measured were a real person.

- About how tall do you think the person would be? What is the scale factor s for your model?

- What would be the person's volume?

- How much would the person weigh? Use the formula below to help you find out. The average weight density for males is 2.34 pounds per liter. The average weight density for females is 2.31 pounds per liter.

$$\text{Weight} = \text{Volume} \times \text{Weight density}$$

Writing a Report

Summarize your experiment. Be sure to include:

- a brief description of the procedure you used

- the data you collected

- your calculations

- a discussion of some possible sources of error

Analyze your results. Is the weight you calculated realistic? Why or why not? If not, what could the designers of the model do to make the model more realistic? Explain your answer in terms of the volume relationship at the top of this page.

Self-Assessment

Conclude your report with a discussion of what went well for you during this experiment. Also discuss the aspect of the experiment that you and your partner found the most challenging and how you dealt with it. Describe what you have learned about the relationship between the volume of a scale model and the weight of the object it represents.

PORTFOLIO PROJECT

Using a Cartogram

Most maps of the United States show the size, shape, and location of each state. Some other maps are drawn so that each state's size is distorted to reflect a particular group of data, such as population. This type of map is called a cartogram.

For example, although Colorado is only a little larger than Wyoming, in 1990 it had approximately seven times as many people. The cartogram shows how these states look when their sizes are distorted to represent population instead of area.

PROJECT GOAL Make a cartogram of a selected group of states. Then make a poster of your cartogram.

Gathering Data

Work in a group of 2–3 students. First choose a set of statistical data to illustrate with your cartogram. Some possible topics are:

- number of physicians
- amount of land suitable for farming
- amount of a natural resource produced each year, such as oil or coal

Select three to five neighboring states to show on your cartogram, and find the relevant data for each. Organize the information in a table. For example, this table shows the population densities of Nebraska, Iowa, and Illinois.

State	Population density, 1993
Nebraska	20.9
Iowa	50.4
Illinois	210.4

Constructing Your Cartogram

Use a computer drawing program or graph paper to form the shapes of the states in your cartogram with squares.

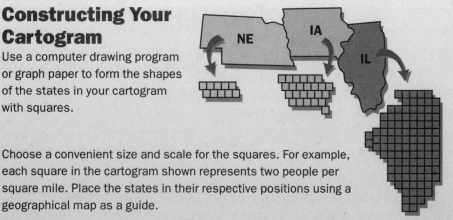

Choose a convenient size and scale for the squares. For example, each square in the cartogram shown represents two people per square mile. Place the states in their respective positions using a geographical map as a guide.

Making a Poster

Display your cartogram on a poster. Label each state and describe the scale you used. Include a labeled geographical map of the states and a table of the data.

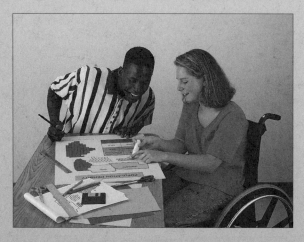

You and your classmates can extend your study of cartograms by exploring some of the ideas below:

• Create a class cartogram of the entire United States.

• Make three or four cartograms that illustrate different data for the same group of states.

• Start a scrapbook of cartograms that you find in newspapers, magazines, or reference books.

Self-Assessment

Write a paragraph explaining your project. Describe how you chose the scale and how you created each state. Why is it important to use the same sized squares for all the states? How does it help to have a geographical map next to your cartogram? Describe any difficulties you had. What would you do differently if you were to do the project over again?

PORTFOLIO PROJECT

Balancing Weights

Have you ever ridden a seesaw or teeter-totter? Often you must adjust your position on the board to balance with the person on the other end.

PROJECT GOAL Explore the relationship between weights and their distances from the center of a balance.

Making a balance

Work with a partner to make a balance, as shown.

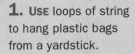

1. USE loops of string to hang plastic bags from a yardstick.

2. HANG the balance using string and a binder clip attached to the middle of the yardstick.

3. PUT different numbers of marbles in the bags.

4. SLIDE the bags until they balance.

Exploring Inverse Variation

1. Let b = the distance from bag B to the center of the balance. Record the distance b to the nearest $\frac{1}{4}$ in., and record the number of marbles in bag B.

2. Use tape to hold bag A in place. Put a different number of marbles in bag B and move it until both bags are balanced again. Record the distance b and the number of marbles in bag B. Repeat this step at least six more times.

3. Make a scatter plot of your data. Write an equation for the distance b as a function of the number of marbles in bag B.

Explorations and Projects Book, Copyright © McDougal Littell Inc.

Exploring Rational Expressions

4. Add bag *C* to the balance as shown at the right.

5. Adjust the three bags until they balance. Record the number of marbles in each bag and measure the distances *a*, *b*, and *c*. Repeat Step 4 at least 7 times, putting different numbers of marbles in the bags for each trial.

6. For each trial, make the calculations shown at the right. What do you notice?

7. Suppose the bags are balanced and contain different numbers of marbles. If you add *x* marbles to each bag, how far must you move bag *A* so they balance again? Write and simplify a variable expression.

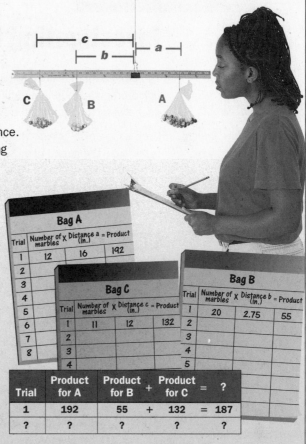

Bag A

Trial	Number of marbles	×	Distance a (in.)	=	Product
1	12		16		192
2					
3					
4					
5					
6					
7					
8					

Bag C

Trial	Number of marbles	×	Distance c (in.)	=	Product
1	11		12		132
2					
3					
4					

Bag B

Trial	Number of marbles	×	Distance b (in.)	=	Product
1	20		2.75		55
2					
3					
4					
5					

Trial	Product for A		Product for B	+	Product for C	=	?
1	192		55	+	132	=	187
?	?		?		?		?

Summarizing Your Results

Write a report about your experiments. Include your data, calculations, and results.

Remember to:

- Explain how the number of marbles in bag *B* affects the distance at which it balances.

- Explain how you constructed the variable expression in Step 7, and show how you simplified it.

You may want to extend your report to include some of the ideas below:

- Find the weight of an object by balancing it with available objects of known weight.

- Ask your science teacher to show you a beam scale. Explain how it works.

Self-Assessment

In your report, describe what you learned while completing this project. You may want to mention things you learned about balances as well as things you learned about how you approach problems and how you work with others.

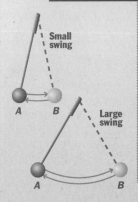

Small swing

A   B   Large swing

A   B

Investigating Pendulum Length

The pendulum of a clock swings back and forth, causing the clock to tick off the seconds. A pendulum clock runs down over time. With each swing, the pendulum travels a slightly smaller distance.

Even as the clock starts to run down, it can still keep good time. This is because the **period** of a pendulum, or the amount of time it takes the pendulum to swing from point **A** to point **B** and back to point **A**, is the same for large swings and small swings.

PROJECT GOAL   Investigate how the length of a pendulum affects the period.

Conducting an Experiment

Work with a partner to design and carry out an experiment in which you measure the period of a pendulum for at least 10 different lengths of string. Here are some hints for organizing your work:

1. MAKE your pendulum by taping several coins to a piece of string. Use a pencil to hold the pendulum away from the table.

2. DETERMINE how many seconds it takes your pendulum to make 10 full swings. Divide by 10 to find the period.

3. ORGANIZE your data in a table. Then make a scatter plot. Put string length on the horizontal axis and period on the vertical axis.

Use a range of string lengths between 10 cm and 30 cm.

Based on your observations, find a string length that produces a period of one second. Can you keep time with this pendulum?

Explorations and Projects Book, Copyright © McDougal Littell Inc.

Using a Formula

The Italian scientist Galileo Galilei (1564 – 1642) showed that the period of a pendulum is proportional to the square root of the length of the pendulum. You can use a formula to describe how the period *P* of a pendulum is related to its length *L*.

$$P = 0.2\sqrt{L}$$ *P* is in seconds and *L* is in centimeters.

• Calculate *P* for the *L*-values you used in your experiment. (Make sure you express the *L*-values in centimeters.) Compare your calculated *P*-values to your measured values. What could cause differences?

• Graph the equation $P = 0.2\sqrt{L}$ on a graphing calculator. How does the graph compare with your scatter plot?

• Use the formula to find *L* when the period is one second. Compare this *L*-value to the length you found from experimenting.

Writing A Report

Write a report about your experiment. Describe your procedure and tell what conclusions you made about the relationship between the length of a pendulum and its period. Include pictures, graphs, and tables to support your ideas.

You may want to extend your report to explore some of the ideas below:

• The first pendulum clock was invented in 1657. How does a pendulum clock work?

• Pendulum clocks have a weight that can be raised and lowered. Why would this come in handy?

• How does the weight of a pendulum affect the period? Design and carry out an experiment to find out.

Self-Assessment

In your report, be sure to describe any difficulties you had. Tell what went well in your experiment and why. Is there anything that you would like to remember for a future experiment, such as a useful way to organize data, or a way to use your data to set up a good viewing window on a graphing calculator?

Geometry Explorations

EXPLORATION
COOPERATIVE LEARNING

Analyzing Patterns

Work with another student.

1 Draw a segment.

2 Add 2 shorter segments.

3 At each new point, draw 2 segments.

4 At each new point, draw two segments half as long as the segments from Step 3. Copy the table, including several more steps. Complete the row for Step 4.

5 Continue the pattern as long as you can. Fill in the table after each step.

6 What patterns do you notice in the figure you drew? Circle three parts of your diagram that look like each other but are different sizes.

7 What patterns do you notice in your table?

8 Predict the total number of segments for the tenth step. Explain.

Step	Number of new segments	Total number of segments
1	1	1
2	2	3
3	4	7
4	?	?

Explorations and Projects Book, Copyright © McDougal Littell Inc.

EXPLORATION
COOPERATIVE LEARNING

Representing Points, Lines, and Planes

**Work with another student.
You will need:**
- three foam trays or
  pieces of stiff paper
- tape
- scissors
- several pieces
  of uncooked spaghetti

**Make a model like the one shown.
The pieces of spaghetti represent
lines and the trays represent planes.**

Tape three trays
together. Poke one
hole in each tray.
Label the holes as
points *A*, *B*, and *C*.

1 On the tray that contains point *A*, draw a line through *A*. Label the
line ℓ. Put a piece of spaghetti through the holes at *A* and *B*. Do line ℓ
and the spaghetti have any points in common other than point *A*?

2 Draw a line on the same tray as line ℓ so that the two lines don't share
any points, even though they continue forever. Label the new line *m*.

3 Add a line to your model that is not on the same tray as line ℓ and
does not share any points with ℓ.

4 Is it possible for two different trays to contain the same line? If so,
add such a line to your model and label it *s*.

5 Is it possible for a line and a plane to have exactly one point in
common? exactly two points in common? no points in common? Give an
example of each possibility, drawing lines on your model as necessary.

EXPLORATION
COOPERATIVE LEARNING

**Investigating Planes and
Their Intersections**

Work with another student.
You will need:
- three index cards
- scissors
- two toothpicks

1 Cut and label the cards as shown.

2 Hold cards *A* and *B* so that they model parallel planes. Can you position plane *C* so it is parallel to both *A* and *B*? Can plane *C* intersect one plane but not the other? Can *C* intersect both planes? If so, how are the lines of intersection related?

3 Use cards *A* and *B* to model intersecting planes. Can plane *C* intersect one plane but not the other? Can *C* intersect both planes?

4 Can three planes form exactly one line of intersection? two lines? three lines? Explain.

5 Draw a pair of intersecting lines on one card. Place one end of a toothpick on the point of intersection and position the toothpick so it is perpendicular to both of the lines. A line that is perpendicular to both lines is perpendicular to the plane of the card.

6 Hold two toothpicks to model two different lines that are each perpendicular to the same card. Describe the relationship between the lines.

EXPLORATION
COOPERATIVE LEARNING

Tracing Networks

Work with another student.

1 Copy each network.

vertex

edge

 A   B   C D   E

2 Try to trace each network without lifting your pencil or retracing an edge. Which networks are traceable?

A vertex is **odd** if an odd number of edges meet at the vertex.

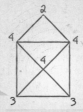

A vertex is **even** if an even number of edges meet at the vertex.

3 For each network, count how many edges meet at each vertex.

4 Copy and complete the table, including a row for each figure. (*Note:* Vertices is the plural of vertex.) Describe any patterns that you notice.

5 Sketch a network with four odd and zero even vertices. Is it traceable?

6 Make a conjecture about how you can tell if a network is traceable.

Network	Number of odd vertices	Traceable?
House	2	Yes
A	?	?
B	?	?
C	?	?

Geometry Exploration 5

EXPLORATION
COOPERATIVE LEARNING

Drafting Parallel Lines

Work with another student.
You will need:

- a straightedge or ruler
- an index card
- scissors

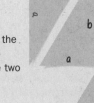

1 Using a straightedge, draw one diagonal of the index card. Cut along the diagonal to form two right triangles, one for each student. Label the two triangles differently, as shown.

2 Each of you should use a straightedge to draw a line *k*. Place your triangle on your paper so leg a lies along *k*. Trace the hypotenuse to draw $\overline{PQ}$. Label ∠1, the acute angle formed by *k* and $\overline{PQ}$.

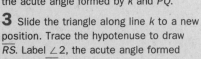

3 Slide the triangle along line *k* to a new position. Trace the hypotenuse to draw $\overline{RS}$. Label ∠2, the acute angle formed by *k* and $\overline{RS}$.

4 Use *k* as a transversal. What is the name for the pair of angles you labeled?

5 How do lines $\overleftrightarrow{PQ}$ and $\overleftrightarrow{RS}$ appear to be related? Compare your results with your partner's results. Make a conjecture based on your results.

Explorations and Projects Book, Copyright © McDougal Littell Inc.

EXPLORATION
COOPERATIVE LEARNING

Comparing Slopes of Lines

Work with another student.
You will need:

• geometry software or graph paper

• a straightedge

1 Lines *j* and *k* are parallel. Find the slope of each line.

2 Graph a different pair of parallel lines. If you are graphing by hand, use the sides of your straightedge to draw the lines. Find the slopes of your lines.

3 Make a conjecture about the slopes of parallel lines.

4 Lines *ℓ* and *m* are perpendicular. Find the slope of each line.

5 Graph a different pair of perpendicular lines. If you are graphing by hand, use a corner of a piece of paper to help you. Find the slopes of the lines.

6 Make a conjecture about the slopes of perpendicular lines.

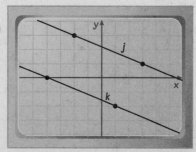

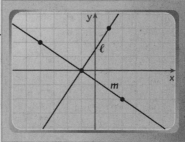

EXPLORATION
COOPERATIVE LEARNING

Sorting Triangles

Work in a group of four students. You will need:
- a set of triangles like the ones at the right

1 One student should write down a "secret rule" that a second student will use to sort the triangles.

2 The second student, the sorter, should choose triangles that fit the rule as the other students watch. At any time, another student can stop the sorter and guess the rule.

One rule might be "triangles with an obtuse angle."

Another possible rule is "triangles with three congruent sides."

3 Repeat Steps 1 and 2 until five rules have been used. Make sure each student has a chance to write a rule, sort the triangles, and guess a rule.

4 Make a list of the rules your group used. What other rules can you think of? What rules did the other groups in your class use?

Explorations and Projects Book, Copyright © McDougal Littell Inc.

EXPLORATION
COOPERATIVE LEARNING

Measuring Exterior Angles

Work with another student.
You will need:
- geometry software
- a ruler and protractor

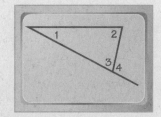

1 Draw a triangle with one side extended, as in the diagram. Find the measures of ∠1, ∠2, ∠3, and ∠4.

2 Round the angle measures to the nearest degree. Record the measures in a table.

m∠1	*m∠2*	*m∠3*	*m∠4*	*m∠1 + m∠2*
26°	78°	76°	104°	104°
?	?	?	?	?
?	?	?	?	?

3 Move one vertex, or draw new triangles, to form at least five different triangles. Record the angle measures for each triangle in your table.

4 Make a conjecture about the measures of the interior and exterior angles of any triangle. Compare your conjecture with other groups.

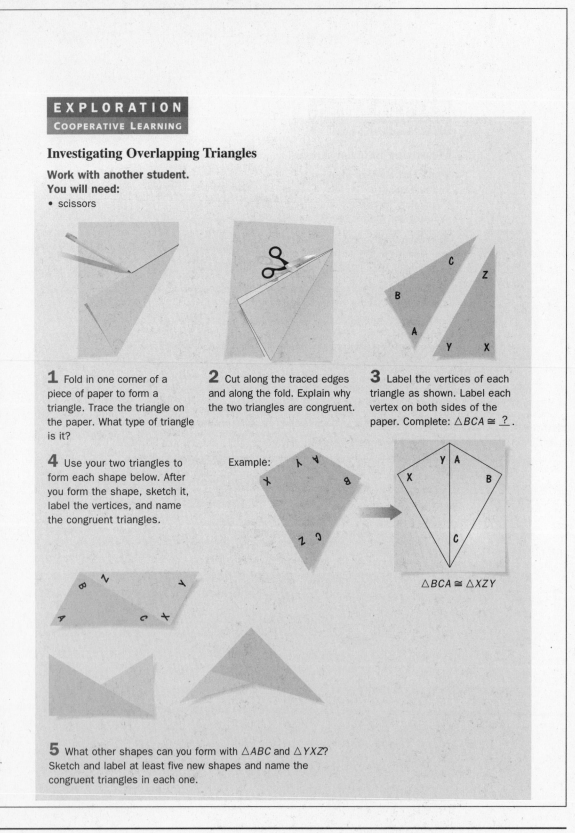

EXPLORATION
COOPERATIVE LEARNING

Investigating Overlapping Triangles

Work with another student.
You will need:
• scissors

1 Fold in one corner of a piece of paper to form a triangle. Trace the triangle on the paper. What type of triangle is it?

2 Cut along the traced edges and along the fold. Explain why the two triangles are congruent.

3 Label the vertices of each triangle as shown. Label each vertex on both sides of the paper. Complete: △BCA ≅ __?__ .

4 Use your two triangles to form each shape below. After you form the shape, sketch it, label the vertices, and name the congruent triangles.

Example:

△BCA ≅ △XZY

5 What other shapes can you form with △ABC and △YXZ? Sketch and label at least five new shapes and name the congruent triangles in each one.

EXPLORATION
COOPERATIVE LEARNING

Circumscribing a Triangle

Work with another student.
You will need:
- patty paper
- compass
- straightedge

1 Draw any △DEF on a piece of patty paper.

2 Carefully fold the paper to form the perpendicular bisector of each side of the triangle.

3 The three perpendicular bisectors should meet at a point. Label this point C.

4 Draw a circle with C as the center and CD as the radius. Describe your results. How do you know that all three vertices are the same distance from C?

5 Compare your results from Step 4 with the results from other groups. Make a conjecture.

6 Check whether your conjecture in Step 5 is true for other triangles. Be sure to try right, obtuse, and acute triangles.

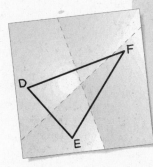

EXPLORATION
COOPERATIVE LEARNING

Comparing Sides of Triangles

Work with another student.
You will need:
• geometry software

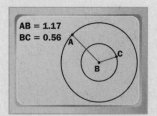

AB = 1.17
BC = 0.56

1 Construct two circles with the same center. Label the center *B*. Construct and label point *A* on the larger circle and point *C* on the smaller circle.

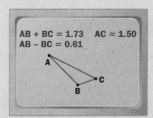

AB + BC = 1.73   AC = 1.50
AB − BC = 0.61

2 Construct and measure $\overline{AB}$ and $\overline{BC}$. Hide the circles so only $\angle ABC$ is showing.

3 Calculate $AB + BC$ and $AB - BC$.

4 Using a different type or color of line, construct $\overline{AC}$. Measure AC.

5 Compare AC with $AB + BC$ as you move points *A* and *C* to different positions on the circles. Compare AC with $AB - BC$. What do you notice?

6 When AC is at its largest value, do $\overline{AB}$, $\overline{BC}$, and $\overline{AC}$ form a triangle? Explain why or why not. Do the segments form a triangle when AC is at its smallest value?

7 If segments $\overline{AB}$, $\overline{BC}$, and $\overline{AC}$ form a triangle, write two inequalities to describe AC in terms of AB and BC.

Geometry Exploration 12

EXPLORATION
COOPERATIVE LEARNING

Analyzing Parallelograms

Work in a group of four students.
You will need:

- lined notebook paper
- a ruler
- patty paper or tracing paper
- a protractor

1 Place a piece of patty paper on the notebook paper. Trace two lines as shown.

2 Turn the patty paper so that the lines on the notebook paper intersect the lines you drew in Step 1. Trace two more lines to form a quadrilateral. This figure is called a *parallelogram*.

3 Measure each side of the parallelogram. What do you notice?

4 Measure each angle. How do the measures of opposite angles compare?

5 Draw a diagonal of the parallelogram and find its midpoint. Draw the other diagonal. What do you notice?

6 Repeat Steps 1–5 at least two more times. Use different side lengths and angle measures for each parallelogram.

7 Make three conjectures about the parts of a parallelogram.

Geometry Exploration 13

EXPLORATION
COOPERATIVE LEARNING

Placing a Parallelogram on a Coordinate Plane

Work in a group of four students.

You will need: graph paper, scissors, straightedge

1 On graph paper, each student should draw a quadrilateral with vertices $E(0, 0)$, $F(6, 8)$, $G(11, 8)$, and $H(5, 0)$. Cut out your quadrilateral and label the vertices on both sides. Color it if you wish.

2 On a separate piece of graph paper, draw coordinate axes. Place the cut-out polygon on the coordinate plane so that all four vertices have integer coordinates. Each student should use a different placement.

3 Trace your cut-out polygon onto your graph paper. Label the vertices E, F, G, and H and write their coordinates.

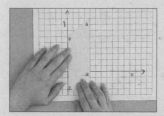 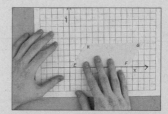

4 Use the Slope Formula to show that $EFGH$ is a parallelogram.

5 Use the Midpoint Formula to show that the midpoint of $\overline{EG}$ is the same as the midpoint of $\overline{FH}$. Which theorem from Section 2.5 does this illustrate?

6 Compare your answers with those of others in your group. How are your answers different? How are they the same?

7 Does the position of a parallelogram on a coordinate plane affect whether or not the diagonals bisect each other? Explain.

Explorations and Projects Book, Copyright © McDougal Littell Inc.

Geometry Exploration 14

EXPLORATION
COOPERATIVE LEARNING

Investigating Diagonals

Work with another student.
You will need:
- four drinking straws
- string
- a protractor

1 Thread the string once through each straw and a second time through the first straw. You should have a movable rhombus.

2 Hold the rhombus steady and use the ends of the string to form its diagonals.

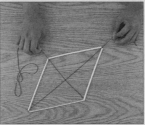

3 Measure the angles that the diagonals form. What do you notice?

4 Measure the adjacent angles at each vertex. How are the measures related?

5 Repeat Steps 2–4 twice more. Adjust the rhombus so that the straws meet at different angles each time.

6 Make two conjectures about the diagonals of a rhombus.

Geometry Exploration 15

EXPLORATION
COOPERATIVE LEARNING

Discovering Area Formulas

Work in a group of three students.
You will need:
- a rectangular sheet of paper
- scissors

1 Cut the paper into two noncongruent rectangles. Label the sides as shown.

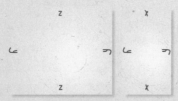

2 Cut along one diagonal of one rectangle to make two congruent right triangles, as shown.

3 How do the base and height (the lengths of the legs) of one triangle compare to the base and height of the rectangle it was cut from? How does the area of one triangle compare with the area of that rectangle? Describe the area of one triangle in terms of its base and height.

4 Use all three pieces to make a rectangle.

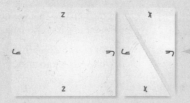

The rectangle's **base** is $x + z$ and its **height** is y. So the area is $A = (x + z)y$.

5 Use all three pieces to make a nonrectangular parallelogram whose *height*, the distance between two of its parallel sides, is y. Write an expression for the base. Does the parallelogram have the same area as the rectangle you made in Step 4? Describe the area of the parallelogram in terms of its base and height.

6 Use all three pieces to make a trapezoid whose height is y. Write an expression for each base and the sum of the bases. Does the trapezoid have the same area as the rectangle you made in Step 4? Describe the area of the trapezoid in terms of its height and the sum of its bases.

Explorations and Projects Book, Copyright © McDougal Littell Inc.

EXPLORATION
COOPERATIVE LEARNING

Comparing Translated Polygons

Work in a group of four students.
You will need:
- geometry software or patty paper
- a ruler

1 Draw points *P* and *Q* on a horizontal line and draw vertical lines through them. Label the lines *m* and *n*. Draw △*ABC* to the left of line *m*.

2 Reflect △*ABC* over line *m* and label the image △*A′B′C′*. Reflect △*A′B′C′* over line *n* and label the image △*A″B″C″*.

> The image of *A′* is *A″*, which is read "*A* double prime."

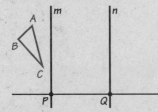 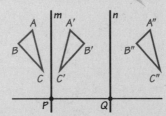

3 What are the orientations of △*ABC* and △*A″B″C″*?

4 Measure *AA″*, *BB″*, *CC″*, and *PQ*. What do you notice?

5 Change the distance between lines *m* and *n* and see what happens to the distances *AA″*, *BB″*, and *CC″*. What do you notice?

EXPLORATION
COOPERATIVE LEARNING

Proving the Pythagorean Theorem

Work in a group of three students.
You will need:
- paper • scissors • ruler

1 Cut out four identical right triangles. In a right triangle, each of the two shorter sides is called a **leg**. The side opposite the right angle is called the **hypotenuse**.

2 Arrange your triangles in a square. Measure each length and find the area of the square. Find the sum of the areas of the right triangles. The area of a triangle is $\frac{1}{2} \times$ height $\times$ base.

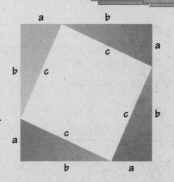

3 Subtract the areas in Step 2 to show that the area of the central square equals the square of the length of the hypotenuse of the right triangles.

$$\begin{array}{ccc} \textbf{Area of the} & = & \textbf{Area of the} & - & \textbf{Area of the} \\ \textbf{central square} & & \textbf{large square} & & \textbf{4 right triangles} \end{array}$$

4 Compare your results with those of other groups.

5 Use *a*, *b*, and *c* for the lengths of the sides of the triangles, as shown. Use algebra to show that in any right triangle, the sum of the squares of the lengths of the legs equal the square of the length of the hypotenuse.

Explorations and Projects Book, Copyright © McDougal Littell Inc.

Geometry Exploration 18

EXPLORATION
COOPERATIVE LEARNING

Analyzing Triangles

Work with another student.
You will need:
- graph paper
- scissors

1 Cut ten squares out of graph paper. Use several different side lengths.

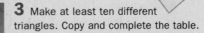

2 Choose three squares. If you can, make a triangle with the three squares. Let c be the length of the longest side of the triangle. Let a and b be the lengths of the two shorter sides.

3 Make at least ten different triangles. Copy and complete the table.

4 What conjectures can you make about the relationship between the squares of the side lengths and the type of triangle?

5 Use your conjectures to predict whether a triangle with the given side lengths is *right*, *obtuse*, or *acute*.

    a. 11, 11, 15
    b. 11, 13, 18
    c. 5, 11, 12

Lengths of sides	$a^2 + b^2$	c^2	Type of triangle
3, 4, 5	25	25	right
4, 4, 5	32	25	acute
?	?	?	?

EXPLORATION
COOPERATIVE LEARNING

Analyzing Ratios in Triangles

Work with another student.
You will need:
- geometry software or a ruler and protractor

1 For each angle measure in the table below, complete these steps:

- One student should draw right △ABC so that ∠A has the given measure.

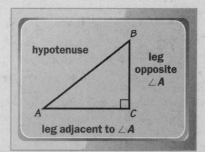

$m\angle A$	$\dfrac{\text{opposite}}{\text{hypotenuse}}$	$\dfrac{\text{adjacent}}{\text{hypotenuse}}$
20°	?	?
40°	?	?
60°	?	?
80°	?	?

- The other student should measure the side lengths of △ABC, calculate the ratios $\dfrac{\text{opposite}}{\text{hypotenuse}}$ and $\dfrac{\text{adjacent}}{\text{hypotenuse}}$, and record these values in the table. Round each value to the nearest hundredth.

2 As $m\angle A$ increases, what happens to each ratio?

3 What value do you think each ratio approaches as $m\angle A$ approaches 0°? as $m\angle A$ approaches 90°? Explain your answers.

4 For what value of $m\angle A$ do you think the two ratios will be equal? Draw a right triangle with this angle measure and find out if you are correct.

Explorations and Projects Book, Copyright © McDougal Littell Inc.

EXPLORATION
COOPERATIVE LEARNING

Investigating Probability Based on Area

Work in a group of three students.
You will need:
- paper
- dried beans

1 Make a target by drawing several shapes that you can find the area of on a rectangular sheet of paper. Shade in your shapes.

2 Place your target on the floor near a wall. Toss a bean against the wall so that it will land on your target. Record whether the bean lands on a shaded part of the paper. If the bean misses the paper, or lands on a border, do not count that toss.

3 Repeat Step 2 until the bean has landed on the target 50 times. Find the percent of the tosses in which the bean landed on the shaded part of the paper.

4 Find the percent of the area of the paper that is shaded.

5 Compare your results in Steps 3 and 4. What do you think is the probability that if a bean lands on the target, it lands in the shaded area? Compare your results and predictions with those of other groups.

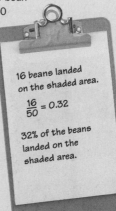

16 beans landed on the shaded area.

$$\frac{16}{50} = 0.32$$

32% of the beans landed on the shaded area.

Geometry Exploration 21

Comparing Volumes

Work with another student.
You will need:

• rectangular pieces of paper
  that are the same size
• tape
• popcorn or dried beans

1 Tape the two
long sides of one
piece of paper
together to form
a tube.

2 Tape together the two short
sides of another piece of paper,
identical to the one used in Step 1,
to form a shorter, wider tube.

3 Stand the long tube on its end and fill it
with popcorn or beans.

4 Place the wide tube around the thin tube,
as shown. Slowly raise the thin tube so that
the contents fill the wide tube. Which tube
holds more? How can you tell?

5 Repeat Steps 1–4 using paper of different
dimensions. Do you get the same result?

6 Do you think the *radius* of a tube or the
height of a tube has more effect on the amount
it holds? Explain your reasoning.

Explorations and Projects Book, Copyright © McDougal Littell Inc.

EXPLORATION
COOPERATIVE LEARNING

Triangles on a Sphere

Work in a group of two or three students.
You will need:
- a basketball, globe, or other sphere-shaped object
- five long strips of paper
- tape
- a protractor

1 Tape one end of a strip of paper to the sphere. Run your finger along the strip to fit it to the sphere. Tape the strip at the other end.

2 Repeat Step 1 for two more strips to form a triangle on the sphere. Label the vertices of the triangle A, B, and C.

3 To measure $\angle B$, hold one of the remaining strips of paper along $\overline{AB}$ and the other along $\overline{BC}$. Tape the two strips together at B. Lay these strips on a flat surface and measure the angle. Repeat to measure $\angle A$ and $\angle C$.

4 What is the sum of the measures of the angles of $\triangle ABC$?

5 Form at least three other triangles of different sizes on the sphere. Find the sum of the measures of the interior angles for each triangle. What do you notice?

Geometry
Projects

PORTFOLIO PROJECT

Classifying Information

How does a music store owner decide how to display instruments? Instruments could be grouped by the type of music performed on them or they could be grouped into types of instrument. The owner might use a classification system. We use systems like this to classify just about everything to help keep track of what we have or know.

PROJECT GOAL Make and use a classification system for something of interest to you.

Using a Classification System

1. Classify a guitar as a *stringed*, *wind*, *percussion*, or *keyboard* instrument by using the diagram below.

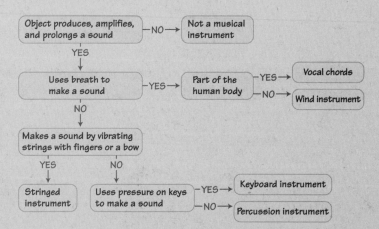

2. Choose some other instruments to classify using the diagram above. Does the diagram classify all of the instruments the way you expect them to be classified? How could you deal with instruments that fit into more than one category?

3. Discuss other ways the diagram could be arranged. Would it make sense to have more than two options in some places? What changes would you make to help classify instruments correctly?

Where Does it Belong?

Develop a system for classifying a group of objects that you collect. If you do not have a collection, choose something that you are interested in, such as types of music or Internet sites.

Draw a diagram for your classification system. Show how to classify at least five different items in the group using your system. If you need to, adjust your classification system.

Presenting Your Project

Make a display of your classification system and how it works. Explain what group of items your system classifies.

Look at some of the other displays. Analyze how well you think one other classification system works. Give a copy of your analysis to the group that created that system.

You may want to extend your project and explore one of the ideas below:

- Interview someone who works in marketing. Describe how they classify customers for various markets.

- Expand the musical instrument diagram. Add branches after the existing instrument categories.

- Research how astronomers classify stars. What type of criteria do they use to categorize a star?

Self-Assessment

What are some important points to remember when developing a classification system? What items are the most difficult to classify? Why?

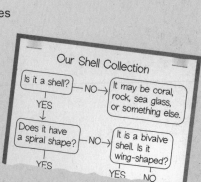

Our Shell Collection

Is it a shell? —NO→ It may be coral, rock, sea glass, or something else.

YES ↓

Does it have a spiral shape? —NO→ It is a bivalve shell. Is it wing-shaped?

YES

YES   NO

Spiral Shells

Coral Rock

Hinged Shells

PORTFOLIO PROJECT

Investigating Symmetry

From hummingbirds to hubcaps, from leaves to ladders, symmetry can be found all around you. Countless natural and artificial objects have symmetry.

PROJECT GOAL Identify objects that have symmetry and analyze transformations that preserve their shapes and sizes.

Reflection, Translation, and Rotation

1. Find five or more objects that exhibit symmetry. At least one of them should be something that is found in nature, and at least one should be artificial. Make sure you have examples of each type of symmetry (reflection, translation, and rotation).

2. Identify a way to transform each object so that the image coincides with the object. Measure the transformation as described below. Then sketch the object. Label the angles and distances you measured.

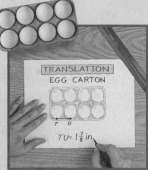

ROTATION Choose a point *R* on the object and locate point *S*, the image of *R* after a rotation. Find the point *O* around which the object is rotated and measure ∠*ROS*, the angle of rotation.

TRANSLATION Choose a point *T* on the object and locate point *U*, the image of *T* after a translation. Measure *TU*.

REFLECTION Choose a point *A* on the object and locate point *B*, the image of *A* after a reflection. Measure *AB* and find the midpoint *M* of $\overline{AB}$. Include the line (or plane) of symmetry in your sketch.

Explorations and Projects Book, Copyright © McDougal Littell Inc.

Presenting Your Results

Make a poster, write a report, or give
a verbal presentation of your results.
Include sketches of each object
that you used. Label each sketch
with the type of symmetry the object
has. On your sketches, label the
points that you used and the angles
and distances that you measured.

You may also want to consider the
following ideas:

- Do any of the objects have more
  than one type of symmetry? Tell how
  many types of symmetry each has
  and explain how you know.

- Choose one of the objects that has
  rotational symmetry. Are there other
  angles that can be used to rotate the object so that the
  image coincides with the object? Explain your answer.

- Do any of the objects that you measured have features
  that make them not truly symmetrical? Explain.

Extending Your Project

You can extend your project by examining some of the
ideas below:

- Describe how symmetry is used by a group that you
  know, such as a marching band or gymnastics team.
  Use sketches or photographs to help you explain
  what types of symmetry are used.

- Ask a graphic designer, scientist, architect, or other
  professional how symmetry is used in his or her field.

Self-Assessment
Describe how you took the measurements of your objects. Were any of
the objects particularly difficult to measure? Why? How did measuring
and sketching the objects improve your understanding of symmetry?

PORTFOLIO PROJECT

Scaling the Planets

Could you make a scale model of the solar
system the size of a football field so that the
scale of the diameter of each planet and the sun is the same as the
scale of the distance between each planet and the sun? If the sun
was the size of a beach ball, how far away would Earth be?

PROJECT GOAL   Create a model of our solar system.

Organizing the Data

1. Find the diameter of the sun and each of the nine planets in our
solar system. You can find this information in an encyclopedia or
almanac. Be sure to record the source of your data.

2. Organize your data in a spreadsheet or table. Label everything
clearly. Include units of measure. Include columns for the dimensions
of the scale model and the actual dimensions of the solar system.

	A	B	C	D	E
1		Diameter at Equator (km)	Mean distance from sun (million km)	Scale diameter (cm)	Scale distance (cm)
2	Sun	1400000	0		
3	Mercury	4870	57.9		
4	Venus				
5	Earth				

3. Choose a convenient size for Earth's scale diameter. Use this
size to calculate the scale for the model. Your scale must use the
same units for Earth's actual diameter and its scale diameter.

21	If the diameter of Earth =	3 cm	This is another
22	then the scale factor is	2.35E−09	expression for
23	and the scale is 1:	425000000	$2.35 \cdot 10^{-9}$.

Explorations and Projects Book, Copyright © McDougal Littell Inc.

Making the Model

1. Use the scale you found to calculate the size of the sun and each planet in a model. If the sizes of the models will be unreasonable, choose a new scale for the diameters.

2. Choose a scale to show the distances of the planets from the sun. Can you use the same scale that you chose for the diameters?

3. Create scale models of the sun and each planet in the solar system. Your models may be two- or three-dimensional. Place these models at their scale distance from the sun.

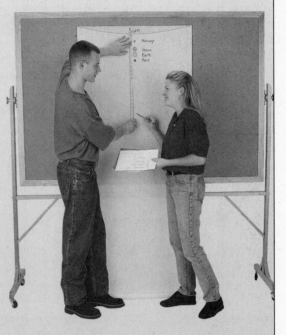

Presenting Your Results

Present your model and data to the class. In your report, you should include:

- the source of your data

- your spreadsheet with an explanation of each formula you used

- a discussion of why you chose the scale(s) that you used for your model

You may want to extend your report by investigating some of these topics:

- Find information about the planets and photos of them to include in your report. Use the Internet, magazines, or other sources. Be sure to include the source(s) you use.

- Find the scale distance between our sun and another star. Include it in your model, if possible.

- Discuss the size of the scale model of the solar system if the diameter of each planet and the distance between each planet and the sun are at the same scale.

Self-Assessment
Explain how you chose the scale you used for your model. How did making this model change your understanding of the size of the solar system?

PORTFOLIO PROJECT

Applying Solar Geometry

The sun can help to heat your home during the winter. The roof of a *passive solar* home allows sunlight to shine in during the winter, when the sun is low in the sky. These roofs also help keep homes cool during the summer when the sun is higher.

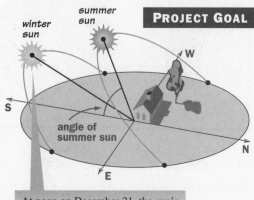

winter sun
summer sun
W
S
angle of summer sun
N
E

At noon on December 21, the sun's angle is 90° − **latitude** − 23.5°.

PROJECT GOAL

Use the angle of the sun to plan the roof overhang for a passive solar home.

Analyzing Angles

The house in the diagrams shown is in Chicago, Illinois, at a **latitude of 42°** north . To find the angle of the sun at noon on the longest day of the year, June 21, use this expression:

$$90° - 42° + 23.5°$$

After June 21, the days shorten until the sun reaches its lowest point in the sky on December 21. You can use the angle of the sun to find the best angle for a roof.

The angle of the roof blocks the sun's rays during the summer.

The angle of the roof allows the sun's rays in during the winter.

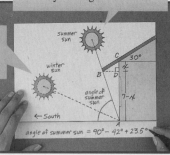

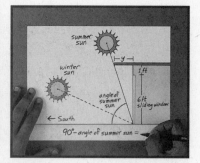

1. Find the amount of overhang, *BC*, of a roof of slope 30° in the Chicago home shown. Explain your method. (*Hint:* Find *BC* in terms of *x* and solve for *x*.)

2. Examine the diagram of a solar home with a flat roof, as shown above. Find the amount of overhang, *y*, that blocks the summer sun.

You can get ideas for your design by looking at homes in your neighborhood.

Designing Your Roof

3. Look up the latitude of your town. Calculate the angle of the sun at noon on the longest and shortest days of the year.

4. Use the angle that you found in Step 3 to design your sloping solar roof. Use trigonometry to find the amount of overhang needed in the summer. Include the dimensions of windows or doors affected by the overhang.

Presenting Your Results

Use diagrams, photographs, or models to illustrate your results. Describe your design and be sure to include these points:

- Describe how a passive solar roof performs different functions at different times of the year.

- Explain the differences between overhangs of flat and sloping roofs. Which type do you prefer, and why?

- How do weather conditions, location, and the direction the house faces affect its solar efficiency?

Extending Your Project

Here are some ideas for extending your project:

- Is there only one correct angle for the roof of a passive solar house? Explain why or why not.

- Why is 23.5° used to calculate the sun's angle? (*Hint:* Find the definition of *ecliptic.*)

- Are there other ways to heat a house using solar energy?

- If possible, talk to an architect to see if your plan is realistic.

Find pictures or make sketches of different roof designs.

Self-Assessment

Did your design for a solar home turn out the way you expected? How did you use trigonometry in your design? Would you consider using some type of passive solar heating if you were building a house? Why or why not?

PORTFOLIO PROJECT

Building the Platonic Solids

A *regular solid* is made of only one type of regular polygon. Over 2000 years ago, the Greek mathematician Euclid proved that only five regular solids, called the *Platonic solids*, are possible. The subject of this activity is the last proposition in Euclid's book, *The Elements*.

PROJECT GOAL Work with a partner to discover the regular solids and investigate how to make nets for them.

Discovering the Five Solids

1. Draw a regular triangle, a square, a regular pentagon, and a regular hexagon using what you know about the angle measures of regular polygons. Cut out six copies of each. Cut out additional copies as needed.

2. Tape three triangles together so that they share a common vertex, as shown below. Can they fold up to form a closed three-dimensional vertex? If so, use another piece of tape to hold the sides together. If not, explain why they don't make a closed vertex.

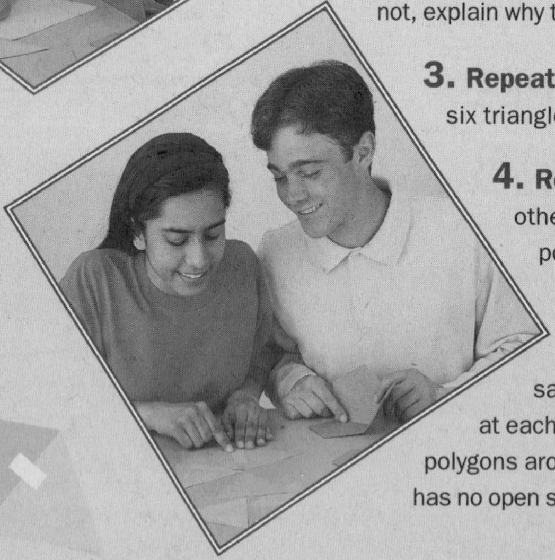

3. Repeat Step 2 for four, five, and six triangles.

4. Repeat Steps 2 and 3 for the other polygons. You will find five possible vertices.

5. Finish constructing the five solids so that the same number of polygons meet at each vertex. Continue adding polygons around each vertex until the solid has no open spaces.

Explorations and Projects Book, Copyright © McDougal Littell Inc.

Use the information at the right to identify each of your solids. Tell what kind of polygons were used for the faces of each solid, and how many polygons meet at each vertex.

tetrahedron ■ **4 faces**

hexahedron (cube) ■ **6 faces**

octahedron ■ **8 faces**

dodecahedron ■ **12 faces**

icosahedron ■ **20 faces**

Making Nets for the Solids

Cut or remove some of the tape from the icosahedron. Leave enough edges attached to keep it in one piece, but separate enough edges so that the pieces lie flat. Sketch the resulting figure. Use your sketch to make an accurate net for the solid from heavy paper. Do the same for the dodecahedron.

Try to make nets for the other solids without taking them apart. Use these nets to make solids out of heavy cardboard.

Extending Your Project

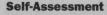

Continue your investigation of Platonic solids by exploring one of the following topics.

• Find all the different possible nets for the tetrahedron. Find at least three nets for each of the other solids. What makes one net easier to assemble than another?

• Count the number of vertices, faces, and edges of each solid. Use a table to record your data. What patterns do you see? Two pairs of Platonic solids are related by their vertices, faces, and edges. Find these pairs and describe the relationships.

Self-Assessment

Describe the work you and your partner did for this project. What did you learn during your investigation? What advice would you give to someone who plans to do this project in the future?

Designing a Cottage

An architect who designs a building must work within certain constraints, such as the area the building will cover. Within these restrictions, there is a lot of room for creativity.

PROJECT GOAL Design a floor plan for a one-story cottage, using specified guidelines.

Understanding the Specifications

You and two other students will design a cottage. The floor plan will be a rectangle whose area is between 550 ft² and 650 ft². The cottage should have two entrance doors and at least four rooms, as described in the table.

Any hallways you include should be between three and four feet wide.

Minimum Room Areas	
Living Room	300 ft²
Bedroom	90 ft²
Kitchen	65 ft²
Bathroom	50 ft²

Arranging the Floor Plan

1. Determine at least three possibilities for the length and width of the rectangular cottage. For each possibility, make a rough sketch showing the locations of the rooms.

2. Make a detailed cottage floor plan, using one of your sketches. Draw the rectangle on graph paper or dot paper, then determine the exact dimensions and placement of the rooms. Label each room with its name, dimensions, and area.

3. Show the locations of the windows and doors. You may also want to show appliances and furniture.

Indicate the scale of your floor plan.

For nonrectangular rooms, give all the dimensions needed to find the area.

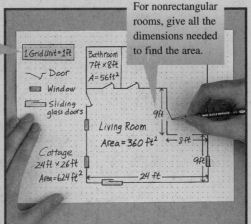

The Third Dimension

Knowing the volume of a building is important for choosing a heating system. The completed cottage will be shaped like a pentagonal prism. Sketch one of the bases, labeling all the lengths you need to find its area. Find the area of the pentagon. Then find the volume of the house.

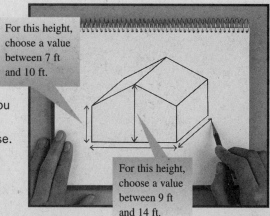

For this height, choose a value between 7 ft and 10 ft.

For this height, choose a value between 9 ft and 14 ft.

Submitting Your Plan

Create a proposal describing the cottage to its future owners. Include the detailed floor plan and explain the features of your design. Also explain how you calculated the volume of the cottage. You can extend the project by exploring one of the following ideas:

- Use a computer with drawing or CAD (Computer-Aided Design) software to help you create your plan.

- Take measurements of rooms where you live or at your school. How do they compare with those in the cottage you designed?

- How would the floor plan be different if it were based on a shape other than a rectangle? Design a floor plan that uses other shapes that you learned about in this chapter.

- Talk to an architect in your area. What other factors affect the design of a house?

Self-Assessment

How did your group decide which of the rough sketches to use for the final floor plan? If you did not have to follow the specifications given in this project, how would you change your design? Explain your reasoning.

Modeling Cavalieri's Principle

Archimedes discovered the formula for the volume of a sphere by imagining cutting a sphere, cone, and cylinder into very thin slices and comparing the slices. This method was developed further by Cavalieri, and became part of the foundation for calculus. Imagine slicing each object at the same height. How do you think the areas of the cross sections are related?

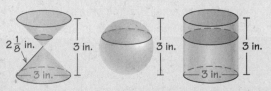

PROJECT GOAL Compare the volumes of a sphere, cylinder, and two cones by comparing cross sections of the objects.

Making the Shapes

Work with a partner to make the sphere, cylinder, and two cones with the dimensions shown above. Use modeling clay.

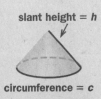

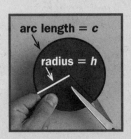

CONE To make a mold for the cone above, cut a circle out of strong plastic and draw a sector as shown. Tape the sector's edges together.

SPHERE You can check the diameter of your sphere by using a circular cutout with a diameter that is slightly larger than 3 in.

CYLINDER You might want to make your cylinder too large and then trim it carefully by using a compass and plastic knife.

Comparing Cross Sections

1. Cut each object carefully into six slices of equal thickness. Use fishing line or dental floss.

2. Combine the clay from the bottom slice of the cones and the bottom slice of the sphere to make a new disk of equal thickness.

3. Compare the new disk with the bottom slice of the cylinder. How were the cross sectional areas of the bottom slices of the objects related?

4. Repeat Steps 2 and 3 five times, comparing the cross sections of the slices at each height.

Presenting Your Project

Write a report describing your experiment. Include answers to the following questions.

- How are the areas of the cross sections of the objects related? How are the volumes of the objects related? How do you know?

- How can you use the volume formulas for a cylinder and a cone to find the volume formula for a sphere?

You may want to extend your project to include some of the ideas below:

- Look up *Cavalieri's Principle* in an encyclopedia or a mathematics dictionary. Summarize it and explain how you used it in your project.

- If *x* is the height at which you slice each object, write an expression for the area of each cross section. Show that the relationship you discovered is true for any length *x* that is less than 3 in.

Self-Assessment
What grade would you give yourself for this project? Why? If you did the experiment again, what would you do differently? Why?

Algebra 2
Explorations

EXPLORATION
COOPERATIVE LEARNING

Getting Variables onto One Side

Work with a partner.
You will need:
• algebra tiles

SET UP Use tiles to represent the equation $3x + 1 = x + 5$.

1 Remove an x-tile from each side of your tile equation. What mathematical operation does this model?

2 Finish solving the equation using the algebra tile model. What is the value of one x-tile? Check this result in the original equation.

3 Take turns using the algebra tile method introduced in the previous steps to solve each of these equations.

a. $4x + 2 = x + 5$ b. $x + 9 = 5x + 1$
c. $2x + 8 = 4x + 2$ d. $5x + 3 = 2x + 6$

4 Work together to make a generalization about the first step you should take to solve an equation with variables on both sides of it.

Explorations and Projects Book, Copyright © McDougal Littell Inc.

EXPLORATION
COOPERATIVE LEARNING

Exploring Slopes of Perpendicular Lines

Work with a partner.
You will need: • graph paper   • a straightedge
• a protractor

1 Draw a line with a slope of 1. Choose a point on the line and label the point.

2 Use a protractor to draw another line perpendicular to the first line at the labeled point.

3 Find the slope of the perpendicular line and record it in a table like the one shown.

4 Repeat Steps 1–3 at least three more times, each time starting with a new line having a different slope, such as 2.

5 Make a conjecture about the slopes of perpendicular lines. Compare your conjecture with those of other groups.

Slope of line	Slope of perpendicular line
1	?
2	?
$-\frac{1}{3}$	?

EXPLORATION
COOPERATIVE LEARNING

Measuring Water Height

Work with a group of three or four students.

You will need:

- a glass container about half filled with water
- twenty marbles of the same size
- a centimeter ruler

A narrow container with straight sides works best.

Measure the water height to the nearest **0.1 cm**. Be sure to put your eyes at the level of the water before measuring.

Number of marbles	Water height (cm)
0	?
5	?
10	?
15	?
20	?

1 Copy the table. Measure and record the water height before you add any marbles to the container.

2 Add five marbles at a time to the container. Measure and record the water height each time.

3 Make a scatter plot of your data. Put the number of marbles on the horizontal axis and the water height on the vertical axis. What do you notice about your data points?

4 Calculate the change in water height per marble.

5 Let m = the number of marbles and h = the water height. Use your data to write an equation of the form:

$$\text{water height} = \text{starting height} + \frac{\text{change in water height}}{\text{per marble}} \times \text{number of marbles}$$

Explorations and Projects Book, Copyright © McDougal Littell Inc.

EXPLORATION
COOPERATIVE LEARNING

**Measuring the
Thickness of Books**

**Work with a group of three
or four students.**
You will need:
- a set of encyclopedias
- a metric ruler
- graph paper and a pencil

1 Choose ten of the volumes from a set of encyclopedias. For each, find
the number of pages P and measure the volume's thickness T to the
nearest 0.1 cm. Record your data in a table.

2 Plot the data pairs (P, T) in a coordinate plane.

3 Use the ruler to draw a *line of fit*.

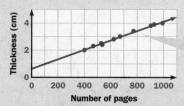

Thickness (cm) vs. Number of pages

A **line of fit** is a line
that lies as close as
possible to all the
points in a scatter plot.
It does not have to pass
through any of them.

Use your graph to answer the following questions.

1. Find the slope of your line. What does the slope represent in this situation? (*Hint:* Think about the relationship between the number of pages
and the number of pieces of paper.)

2. a. Find an equation of your line of fit. What is the significance of the
T-intercept?

   b. Measure the thickness of a volume not included in your data set.
Use the equation to predict how many pages it has. Then use the
book to check your prediction.

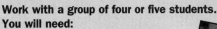

EXPLORATION

COOPERATIVE LEARNING

Guessing People's Ages

Work with a group of four or five students.
You will need:
- paper and pencil
- graph paper

1 Each person in your group should estimate the ages of the people shown. (Keep your estimates a secret; it will be more fun.)

2 Get the list of the actual ages from your teacher.

3 Make a scatter plot of your group's data. Use the horizontal axis for a = actual age and the vertical axis for e = estimated age.

Use your scatter plot to answer the following questions.

1. What does each vertical column of dots represent?

2. Do any plotted points fall on the line $e = a$? If so, what does this mean?

3. a. What does it mean if a plotted point falls below the line $e = a$? How would you represent this mathematically?

b. What does it mean if a plotted point falls above the line $e = a$? How would you represent this mathematically?

4. Overall, what pattern do you see in your group's scatter plot? Compare your scatter plot with those from other groups.

5. If people were estimating your age, would you prefer that most points fell above the line $e = a$, below the line, or on the line? Do you think everyone prefers that region?

Explorations and Projects Book, Copyright © McDougal Littell Inc.

EXPLORATION
COOPERATIVE LEARNING

Investigating Ways that Lines Intersect

Work with a partner.
You will need:
- a graphing calculator or graphing software

Be sure to use parentheses when the coefficient of x is a fraction.

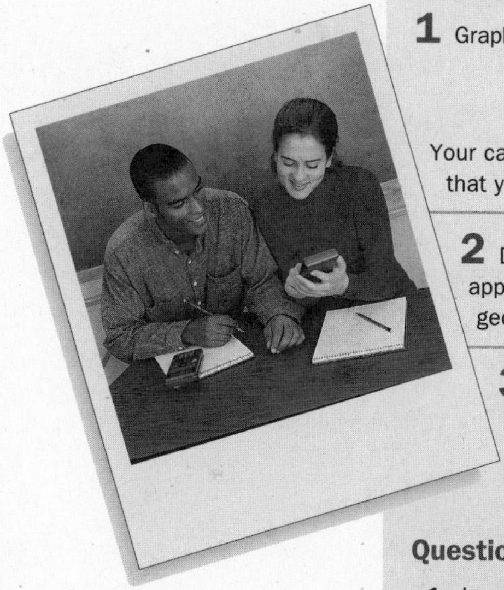

1 Graph this system:

$$2x - 3y = 5$$
$$3x + 4y = -12$$

Your calculator or software may require that you solve each equation for y first.

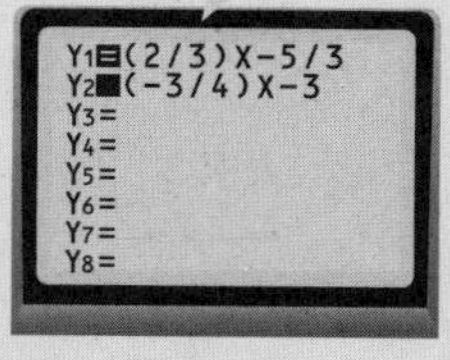
Y1=(2/3)X-5/3
Y2=(-3/4)X-3
Y3=
Y4=
Y5=
Y6=
Y7=
Y8=

2 Do the lines intersect in a single point? If so, find the approximate coordinates of the point. If not, describe the geometric relationship between the lines.

3 Repeat Steps 1 and 2 for each of the following systems of equations.

$$2x - 3y = 5 \qquad\qquad 2x - 3y = 5$$
$$4x - 6y = 1 \qquad\qquad -6x + 9y = -15$$

Questions

1. In what ways can two lines in a plane intersect? What does this mean in terms of the number of solutions that a system of linear equations can have?
2. If a system of linear equations is to have a *unique* solution, what must be true about the slopes of the lines?

Explorations and Projects Book, Copyright © McDougal Littell Inc.

EXPLORATION
COOPERATIVE LEARNING

Organizing Data in Matrices

Work with half of your class.

1 Find out which hand each person in your group uses to write. Record the results in a *matrix* like the one shown.

$$
\begin{array}{c}
 & \text{Left} \quad \text{Right} \quad \text{Both} \\
\text{Males} \\
\text{Females}
\end{array}
\begin{bmatrix}
? & ? & ? \\
? & ? & ?
\end{bmatrix}
$$

Use the "Both" column if a person writes well with both hands.

2 Give your matrix to the other group. Create a new matrix by adding the number in each position of your matrix to the number in the same position in the other group's matrix. What does the new matrix represent?

3 How many females in your class are right-handed? How many males in your class are left-handed?

4 How do you think you could use your data to predict what a similar matrix for your whole school might be?

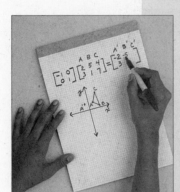

EXPLORATION
COOPERATIVE LEARNING

Reflections Using Matrix Multiplication

Work in a group of four students.
You will need:
• graph paper

1 Each member of the group should draw a different △ABC and label the coordinates of its vertices. Each of you should write a polygon matrix that represents your triangle.

2 Multiply your triangle matrix by each transformation matrix below, putting the transformation matrix on the left. Graph the image of △ABC after each multiplication.

$$\begin{bmatrix} 1 & 0 \\ 0 & -1 \end{bmatrix} \quad \begin{bmatrix} -1 & 0 \\ 0 & 1 \end{bmatrix} \quad \begin{bmatrix} 0 & 1 \\ 1 & 0 \end{bmatrix} \quad \begin{bmatrix} 0 & -1 \\ -1 & 0 \end{bmatrix}$$

3 Compare your results. Describe the effect each transformation matrix has on a triangle.

EXPLORATION

COOPERATIVE LEARNING

Matrices with Zeros on a Diagonal

Work in a group of four students. You will need:

• graph paper

1 As a group, make a list of every possible 2×2 matrix for which both elements on one diagonal are 0 and each element on the other diagonal is either 1 or -1.

$$\begin{bmatrix} ? & 0 \\ 0 & ? \end{bmatrix} \quad \text{or} \quad \begin{bmatrix} 0 & ? \\ ? & 0 \end{bmatrix}$$

Each of the missing elements is either 1 or -1.

2 Divide the list of matrices among the members of your group.

Multiply each matrix that you are assigned by $\begin{bmatrix} 3 & 4 & 7 \\ 1 & 3 & 1 \end{bmatrix}$, which represents $\triangle ABC$.

3 For each matrix product in Step 2, graph $\triangle ABC$ and its image. Describe each transformation.

4 Make a chart that shows your group's results.

Algebra 2 Exploration 10

EXPLORATION
COOPERATIVE LEARNING

Moving Parabolas Around

Work with a partner.
You will need:
- a graphing calculator or graphing software

SET UP Copy and complete the table. Then answer the questions below.

Equation 1	Equation 2	How is the graph of equation 2 geometrically related to the graph of equation 1?
$y = x^2$	$y = (x - 1)^2$	translated 1 unit to the right
$y = x^2$	$y = x^2 + 1$	?
$y = 2x^2$	$y = 2(x + 3)^2$	?
$y = 2x^2$	$y = 2x^2 - 4$	?
$y = -\frac{1}{2}x^2$	$y = -\frac{1}{2}(x + 1)^2 + 3$	?
$y = -\frac{1}{2}x^2$	$y = -\frac{1}{2}(x - 2)^2 + 1$	?

Questions

1. Predict what the graph of each equation below looks like by making a sketch. Then check your sketch by using a graphing calculator or graphing software.

   a. $y = \frac{1}{3}x^2 + 5$ **b.** $y = -4(x - 1)^2$ **c.** $y = (x + 4)^2 - 3$

2. **a.** How is the graph of $y = ax^2 + k$ geometrically related to the graph of $y = ax^2$ when k is positive? when k is negative?

   b. How is the graph of $y = a(x - h)^2$ geometrically related to the graph of $y = ax^2$ when h is positive? when h is negative?

Explorations and Projects Book, Copyright © McDougal Littell Inc.

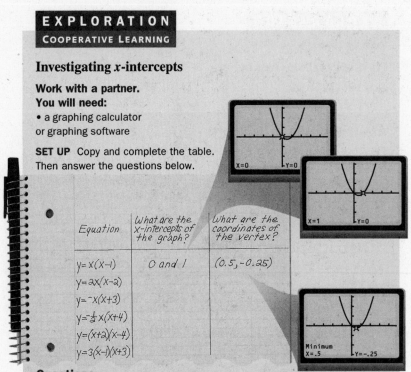

EXPLORATION
COOPERATIVE LEARNING

Investigating *x*-intercepts

Work with a partner.
You will need:
• a graphing calculator
or graphing software

SET UP Copy and complete the table.
Then answer the questions below.

Equation	What are the x-intercepts of the graph?	What are the coordinates of the vertex?
$y = x(x-1)$	0 and 1	$(0.5, -0.25)$
$y = 2x(x-2)$		
$y = -x(x+3)$		
$y = -\frac{1}{2}x(x+4)$		
$y = (x+2)(x-4)$		
$y = 3(x-1)(x+3)$		

X=0   Y=0

X=1   Y=0

Minimum
X=.5   Y=-.25

Questions

1. Predict what the graph of each equation looks like by making a sketch. Then check your sketch by using graphing technology.

   a. $y = 3x(x + 1)$ **b.** $y = 2(x + 2)(x - 4)$

   c. $y = -\frac{1}{4}(x - 1)(x - 3)$ **d.** $y = \frac{1}{2}(x - 2)(x + 2)$

2. The equations you graphed have the form $y = a(x - p)(x - q)$. In terms of a, p, and q, what are the *x*-intercepts of the graph? What is the *x*-coordinate of the vertex?

Explorations and Projects Book, Copyright © McDougal Littell Inc.

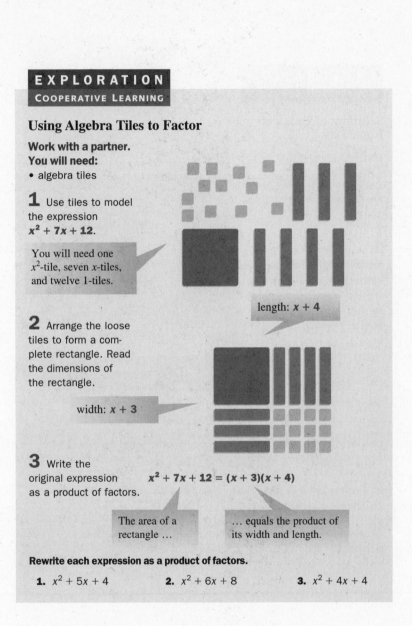

EXPLORATION
COOPERATIVE LEARNING

Using Algebra Tiles to Factor

Work with a partner.
You will need:
• algebra tiles

1 Use tiles to model the expression $x^2 + 7x + 12$.

You will need one x^2-tile, seven x-tiles, and twelve 1-tiles.

length: $x + 4$

2 Arrange the loose tiles to form a complete rectangle. Read the dimensions of the rectangle.

width: $x + 3$

3 Write the original expression as a product of factors.

$x^2 + 7x + 12 = (x + 3)(x + 4)$

The area of a rectangle …

… equals the product of its width and length.

Rewrite each expression as a product of factors.

1. $x^2 + 5x + 4$ **2.** $x^2 + 6x + 8$ **3.** $x^2 + 4x + 4$

EXPLORATION
COOPERATIVE LEARNING

Solutions of Quadratic Equations

Work in a group of 2 or 3 students.
You will need:
• a graphing calculator

1 Take turns graphing the following equations. Use a table like the one shown to record the number of solutions of each equation when $y = 0$.

a. $y = -3x^2 + 5x + 5$

b. $y = 5x^2 + 3x + 2$

c. $y = 6x^2 + 12x + 6$

d. $y = x^2 + 8x - 3$

e. $y = x^2 - 2x + 4$

f. $y = x^2 + 4x + 4$

Equation	Number of solutions	$b^2 - 4ac$
$0 = -3x^2 + 5x + 5$	?	?
$0 = 5x^2 + 3x + 2$	?	?
$0 = 6x^2 + 12x + 6$	?	?
$0 = x^2 + 8x - 3$	?	?
$0 = x^2 - 2x + 4$	?	?
$0 = x^2 + 4x + 4$	?	?

2 Find the value of $b^2 - 4ac$ for each equation in Step 1. Record the results in your table.

3 Work together to make a generalization about the value of the discriminant and the number of solutions of an equation.

Explorations and Projects Book, Copyright © McDougal Littell Inc.

EXPLORATION
COOPERATIVE LEARNING

Counting Real Zeros

Work with a partner.
You will need:
• a graphing calculator or graphing software

SET UP Adjust the viewing window for your calculator or software so that the intervals $-5 \leq x \leq 5$ and $-20 \leq y \leq 20$ are shown on the axes.

1 Graph the following functions. Tell how many real zeros each function has.

This function has **three** real zeros.

• $y = x^3 + x^2 - 7x - 5$ • $y = x^4 - 10x^2 + 9$

• $y = x^5 - 7x^3 - x^2 + 8x$ • $y = x^6 - 11x^4 + 29x^2 - x - 8$

◀ Example: $y = x^3 - 2x^2 - 5x + 6$

2 For each function in Step 1, how is the number of real zeros related to the function's degree?

3 Repeat Step 1 using these functions:

• $y = x^3 + x^2 + 3x + 5$ • $y = x^4 + 2x^3 - x^2 + 6x + 7$

• $y = x^5 - x^4 - 6x^3 + 4x^2 + 8x$ • $y = x^6 - 3x^4 - 7x^2 + 10$

Is the relationship you found in Step 2 true for these functions? Explain.

4 Graph several other polynomial functions having different degrees. If necessary, modify your answer for Step 2 so that the stated relationship between a polynomial function's degree and its number of real zeros is *always* true.

EXPLORATION
COOPERATIVE LEARNING

Looking for Patterns in Graphs

Work with a partner.
You will need: • a graphing calculator or graphing software

SET UP Adjust the viewing window for your calculator or software so that the intervals $-5 \le x \le 5$ and $-20 \le y \le 20$ are shown on the axes. Complete Steps 1 and 2 for each of these functions:

- $y = 4x^2 - 8x - 3$
- $y = x^3 - x^2 - 3x + 1$
- $y = x^4 + 2x^3 - 5x^2 - 7x + 3$
- $y = 2x^5 + 6x^4 - 2x^3 - 14x^2 + 5$
- $y = 3x^6 - 13x^4 + 15x^2 + x - 17$
- $y = x^7 - 8x^5 + 18x^3 - 6x$

1 Describe what happens to the graph as x takes on large positive and large negative values.

Example: $y = 2x^2 - 2x - 11$

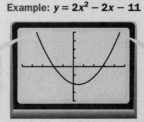

As x takes on large negative values, the graph rises.

As x takes on large positive values, the graph rises.

2 Find the number of *turning points*. Give the approximate coordinates of each turning point.

Example: $y = 2x^2 - 2x - 11$

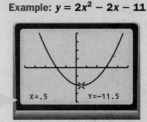

X=.5   Y=−11.5

The graph has one turning point. Its coordinates are $(0.5, -11.5)$.

Questions

1. How do the graphs of the even-degree polynomial functions behave as x takes on large positive values? as x takes on large negative values?

2. How do the graphs of the odd-degree polynomial functions behave as x takes on large positive values? as x takes on large negative values?

3. a. How is the number of turning points on the graph of each function in the Exploration related to the function's degree?

b. Decide if the relationship from part (a) is always true by graphing other polynomial functions. If necessary, modify your statement of the relationship so that it applies to *all* polynomial functions.

Explorations and Projects Book, Copyright © McDougal Littell Inc.

EXPLORATION
COOPERATIVE LEARNING

Reflecting the Graph of $y = x^2$ over the Line $y = x$

Work with a partner. You will need:
• graph paper
• a MIRA® transparent mirror, tracing paper, or a ruler

1 Graph $y = x^2$ and $y = x$ in the same coordinate plane.

2 Sketch the reflection of the graph of $y = x^2$ over the line $y = x$. Remember to reflect not only the points above the line but also the points below the line. Here are three ways of reflecting the graph:

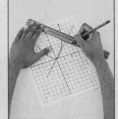

You can place a MIRA® along the line $y = x$ and sketch the reflection you see.

You can fold tracing paper along the line $y = x$ and trace on the other side of the paper.

You can hold a ruler perpendicular to the line $y = x$ and measure equal distances on each side.

Questions

1. Does the graph you get represent a function? Explain why or why not.

2. Consider the function $y = x^2$ with a restricted domain of $x \geq 0$. What does the graph look like? Is the reflection of the graph over the line $y = x$ the graph of a function?

EXPLORATION
COOPERATIVE LEARNING

Reflecting the Graph of $y = x^n$ over the Line $y = x$

Work with a partner.
You will need:
• a graphing calculator
or graphing software

SET UP Adjust the viewing window so that it shows $-3 \le x \le 3$
and $-2 \le y \le 2$.

1 Graph the line $y = x$ and the function $y = x^3$. Then draw the reflection of the function's graph over the line. Does the reflection represent a function?

2 Repeat Step 1 using the functions $y = x^4$, $y = x^5$, and $y = x^6$. (Clear the screen each time.)

> Use your calculator or software's draw-inverse feature.

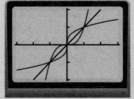

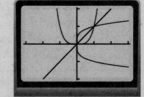

Questions

1. Describe how the graphs of $y = x^n$ when n is odd are different from the graphs when n is even. How are their reflections different?

2. Which functions of the form $y = x^n$ must have their domains restricted in order for the reflections of their graphs over the line $y = x$ to represent functions? How would you restrict the domains of the original functions?

Explorations and Projects Book, Copyright © McDougal Littell Inc.

EXPLORATION
COOPERATIVE LEARNING

Organizing Data in a Box Plot

Work with a partner.
You will need:
- scissors
- graph paper

1 Count the number of letters in your first name, in your last name, and in your first and last names combined. Share your results with your class. Write down each person's responses. Use the data for the total number of letters in a person's first and last names for this Exploration. Save the rest of the data to use in Exercises 4–6.

2 List the data in order from least to greatest on a strip of graph paper. Put one number in each square. Then cut the paper so that there are no extra squares to the left or right of the data.

3 Fold the strip of paper in half. Then fold the paper in half again. Open the paper up and draw a line on each fold.

Questions

1. What does the middle fold tell you about the data? What do the other folds represent?

2. Below what number of letters do 25% of the names fall? 75% of the names?

A person who drives 10,000 miles a year in a fuel-efficient car, rather than a gas-guzzler, will save how much in gasoline costs for one year?

A. Under $100

B. Several hundred dollars

C. About $1000

D. Several thousand dollars

EXPLORATION
COOPERATIVE LEARNING

Making a Sampling Distribution

Work with a partner.
You will need:
• a calculator with a random number generator

SET UP In 1990, the Consumer Federation of America designed a test of consumer knowledge. The group gave the test to 1139 adults at shopping centers. At the left is one of the questions on the test.

1 Write the answer that you think is correct on a piece of paper. Collect all the papers and write the responses on the board, numbering them for easy reference. Your teacher will provide the correct answer.

2 With your partner, use the random number generator on your calculator to choose 6 different random samples of 5 responses from the board. For each sample, find the proportion of correct responses. Write each sample proportion as a percent.

3 In Step 2, did you get the same proportion from each sample? Based on your results from Step 2, would you say that the percent correct for the entire class is closest to *0%, 20%, 40%, 60%, 80%,* or *100%*? Explain.

4 As a class, make a histogram of all the sample proportions. Do they tend to cluster around some value? If so, what is that value?

5 Calculate the *population proportion* (that is, the percent of correct answers for the entire class). Compare this with what you found in Step 4.

Explorations and Projects Book, Copyright © McDougal Littell Inc.

EXPLORATION
COOPERATIVE LEARNING

Modeling Exponential Decay

Work with a partner.
You will need:
- 100 pennies
- a cup
- a graphing calculator

Follow Steps 1–3. Then answer the questions below.

1 Put the pennies in the cup. Then empty them onto a desk.

2 Remove all pennies that land heads up. Record the number of pennies remaining.

3 Repeat Steps 1 and 2 until no pennies remain.

Number of times cup is emptied	Number of pennies left
0	100
1	?
2	?
3	?
4	?
5	?
6	?

Questions

1. Make a scatter plot of the data. Put the number of times the cup is emptied on the horizontal axis. Put the number of pennies remaining on the vertical axis.

2. You can expect to remove about half of the pennies each time. Use this fact to copy and complete the table at the right.

3. Write an equation that models the expected number y of pennies remaining after the cup is emptied x times. Graph the equation in the same coordinate plane as your scatter plot. What do you notice?

x = number of times cup is emptied	y = expected number of pennies remaining
0	100
1	$100\left(\frac{1}{2}\right)$
2	$\left(100 \cdot \frac{1}{2}\right)\left(\frac{1}{2}\right) = 100\left(\frac{1}{2}\right)^2$
3	?
4	?
5	?
6	?

EXPLORATION
COOPERATIVE LEARNING

Investigating Exponential Graphs

Work in a group of four students.
You will need:
• a graphing calculator

1 In the same coordinate plane, graph $y = 8^x$, $y = 4^x$, $y = 2^x$, and $y = 1^x$. Sketch the results. What do you notice about the y-intercepts?

2 In the same coordinate plane, graph $y = \left(\frac{1}{8}\right)^x$, $y = \left(\frac{1}{4}\right)^x$, and $y = \left(\frac{1}{2}\right)^x$. Sketch the results. How are they related to the graphs from Step 1?

3 Choose a positive value for b and graph $y = b^x$ and $y = \left(\frac{1}{b}\right)^x$. What do you notice about the graphs? Draw the graphs from your group on one piece of paper. Which graphs represent exponential growth? Which represent exponential decay?

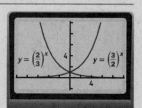

4 In the same coordinate plane, graph $y = 8 \cdot 2^x$, $y = 4 \cdot 2^x$, $y = 2 \cdot 2^x$, and $y = 1 \cdot 2^x$. Sketch the results. What do you notice?

5 Choose a positive value for a and graph $y = a \cdot 3^x$ and $y = -a \cdot 3^x$. What do you notice about the graphs? Draw the graphs from your group on one piece of paper.

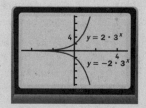

6 Discuss how the values of a and b affect the graph of $y = ab^x$.

Explorations and Projects Book, Copyright © McDougal Littell Inc.

Algebra 2 Exploration 22

Most banks offer interest that is compounded more than once a year. When interest is compounded n times per year for t years at an interest rate r (expressed as a decimal), a principal of P dollars grows to the amount A given by this formula:

$$A = P\left(1 + \frac{r}{n}\right)^{nt}$$

EXPLORATION
COOPERATIVE LEARNING

Compounding Interest

Work in a group of four students.
You will need:
- a scientific calculator

1 The table shows the value of one dollar after one year of compounding. Copy and complete the table. Each of you should complete one column for one of the interest rates.

Compounding	n	Formula	r=0.05	r=0.10	r=0.50	r=1.00
annually	1	$\left(1 + \frac{r}{1}\right)^{1}$	1.05			
semiannually	2	$\left(1 + \frac{r}{2}\right)^{2}$		1.1025		
quarterly	4	$\left(1 + \frac{r}{4}\right)^{4}$			1.6018	
monthly	12	$\left(1 + \frac{r}{12}\right)^{12}$				2.6130
daily	365	$\left(1 + \frac{r}{365}\right)^{365}$				
hourly						
every minute						
every second						

2 Describe how increasing the frequency of compounding interest affects the value of a dollar that is invested for one year.

3 If a bank compounded interest more often than every second, would this make much difference? Explain.

EXPLORATION
COOPERATIVE LEARNING

Investigating the Inverse of $f(x) = 2^x$

Work with a partner.
You will need: • a MIRA® transparent mirror
• graph paper

x	f(x)
−2	?
−1	?
0	?
1	?
2	?
3	?

1 Let $f(x) = 2^x$. Copy and complete the table.

2 Graph $y = f(x)$. Label the points on the graph corresponding to the ordered pairs in the table.

3 Graph the line $y = x$ in the same coordinate plane you used for graphing f.

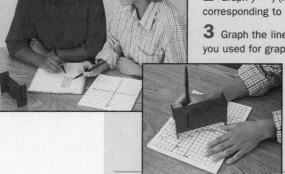

4 Graph $y = f^{-1}(x)$ by using the MIRA® to draw the reflection of the graph of f over the line $y = x$. Label the points on the graph of f^{-1} that are reflections of labeled points on the graph of f.

Questions

1. Replace each ? with the number that makes the equation true.

    a. $f^{-1}(8) = $?
    b. $f^{-1}\left(\frac{1}{4}\right) = $?
    c. $f^{-1}(1) = $?

2. Replace each ? with *exponents* or *powers of 2*.

    a. For the function f, the input values are ? and the output values are ? .

    b. For the function f^{-1}, the input values are ? and the output values are ? .

Explorations and Projects Book, Copyright © McDougal Littell Inc.

EXPLORATION
COOPERATIVE LEARNING

Investigating Properties of Logarithms

Work with a partner.
You will need:
• a scientific calculator

SET UP Copy the table. Use a calculator to complete the table. Round each logarithm to four decimal places.

N	1	2	3	4	5	6	7	8	9	10	20	30	40	50	60	70	80	90	100	1000
log N	?	?	?	?	?	?	?	?	?	?	?	?	?	?	?	?	?	?	?	?

Questions

1. a. Use your table to find log 2 + log 4.

 b. Look for a value of N in your table for which log N equals your answer to part (a). Complete this equation: $\log 2 + \log 4 = \log \underline{?}$.

2. Use your table to complete these equations.

 a. $\log 8 + \log 5 = \log \underline{?}$ **b.** $\log 4 + \log 20 = \log \underline{?}$

 c. $\log 7 + \log 10 = \log \underline{?}$ **d.** $\log 9 + \log 10 = \log \underline{?}$

3. Generalize your results from Questions 1 and 2:
$\log M + \log N = \log \underline{?}$.

4. Use your table to complete these equations.

 a. $\log 8 - \log 2 = \log \underline{?}$ **b.** $\log 50 - \log 5 = \log \underline{?}$

 c. $\log 60 - \log 10 = \log \underline{?}$ **d.** $\log 90 - \log 30 = \log \underline{?}$

5. Generalize your results from Question 4: $\log M - \log N = \log \underline{?}$.

6. Use your table to complete these equations.

 a. $2 \log 3 = \log \underline{?}$ **b.** $2 \log 10 = \log \underline{?}$ **c.** $3 \log 10 = \log \underline{?}$

7. Generalize your results from Question 6: $k \log M = \log \underline{?}$.

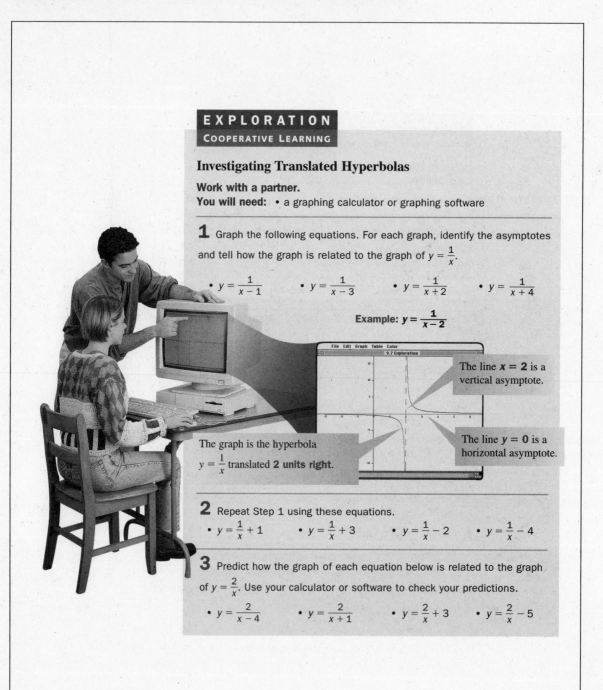

EXPLORATION
COOPERATIVE LEARNING

Investigating Translated Hyperbolas

Work with a partner.
You will need: • a graphing calculator or graphing software

1 Graph the following equations. For each graph, identify the asymptotes and tell how the graph is related to the graph of $y = \frac{1}{x}$.

- $y = \frac{1}{x - 1}$
- $y = \frac{1}{x - 3}$
- $y = \frac{1}{x + 2}$
- $y = \frac{1}{x + 4}$

Example: $y = \frac{1}{x - 2}$

File Edit Graph Table Color
9.7 Exploration

The line $x = 2$ is a vertical asymptote.

The line $y = 0$ is a horizontal asymptote.

The graph is the hyperbola $y = \frac{1}{x}$ translated **2 units right**.

2 Repeat Step 1 using these equations.

- $y = \frac{1}{x} + 1$
- $y = \frac{1}{x} + 3$
- $y = \frac{1}{x} - 2$
- $y = \frac{1}{x} - 4$

3 Predict how the graph of each equation below is related to the graph of $y = \frac{2}{x}$. Use your calculator or software to check your predictions.

- $y = \frac{2}{x - 4}$
- $y = \frac{2}{x + 1}$
- $y = \frac{2}{x} + 3$
- $y = \frac{2}{x} - 5$

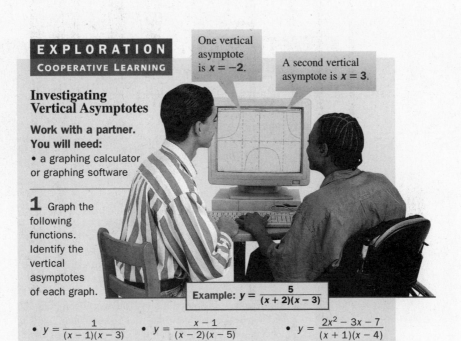

EXPLORATION
COOPERATIVE LEARNING

One vertical asymptote is $x = -2$.

A second vertical asymptote is $x = 3$.

Investigating Vertical Asymptotes

Work with a partner.
You will need:
• a graphing calculator or graphing software

1 Graph the following functions. Identify the vertical asymptotes of each graph.

Example: $y = \dfrac{5}{(x + 2)(x - 3)}$

• $y = \dfrac{1}{(x - 1)(x - 3)}$ • $y = \dfrac{x - 1}{(x - 2)(x - 5)}$ • $y = \dfrac{2x^2 - 3x - 7}{(x + 1)(x - 4)}$

• $y = \dfrac{4}{x(x + 3)(x - 3)}$ • $y = \dfrac{-x^2 - 6x + 2}{(x + 3)(x + 1)(x - 4)}$ • $y = \dfrac{x^4 + x^3 - 5x^2}{(x + 1)^2(x - 2)}$

2 Predict the vertical asymptotes of the graph of each function below. Use your calculator or software to check your predictions.

• $y = \dfrac{-3x^2}{(x + 3)(x - 2)}$ • $y = \dfrac{7x + 2}{(x + 5)(x + 1)(x - 3)}$ • $y = \dfrac{x^3}{x^2 - 16}$

3 Based on your results from Steps 1 and 2, how are the vertical asymptotes of a rational function's graph related to the function's equation?

EXPLORATION
COOPERATIVE LEARNING

Finding Distances and Midpoints

Work with a partner.
You will need:
- centimeter graph paper
- a metric ruler

1 Draw coordinate axes on a piece of graph paper. Plot the points (1, 2), (4, 2), and (4, 6). Find the distance in centimeters between (1, 2) and (4, 6). Verify your measurement using the Pythagorean theorem applied to the right triangle formed by the three plotted points.

2 Explain how you can use the Pythagorean theorem to find the distance between any two points in a coordinate plane. Then choose two points and find the distance between them.

3 On the same graph, use your ruler to estimate the coordinates of the point halfway between (1, 2) and (4, 6).

4 Find the mean of the *x*-coordinates of the points (1, 2) and (4, 6). Also find the mean of the *y*-coordinates of these points. How are these means related to the coordinates of the point you found in Step 3?

5 Explain how you can find the midpoint of the line segment connecting any two points in a coordinate plane. Then choose two points and find the coordinates of the midpoint of the line segment connecting them.

Explorations and Projects Book, Copyright © McDougal Littell Inc.

Using Focus-Directrix Paper to Draw a Parabola

Work with a partner.
You will need:
• focus-directrix paper

SET UP The circles on focus-directrix paper share a common center and the parallel lines are tangent to the circles.

1 Label as *d* the line that is tangent to the circle with radius 4 units and is *below* the center of the circle. Mark the single point where the line that is 2 units above *d* intersects the circle with radius 2 units.

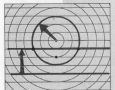

2 Mark the two points where the line 3 units above *d* intersects the circle with radius 3 units.

3 Continue marking points as in Step 2, each time increasing by 1 unit the distance above *d* and the radius of the circle.

4 All the points you marked in Steps 2 and 3 should lie on a parabola. Sketch the parabola.

Questions

1. What is special about the point you marked in Step 1?

2. Line *d* is the *directrix* of the parabola, and the common center of the circles is the *focus* of the parabola. Based on Steps 2 and 3, how is a point on a parabola related to its focus and directrix?

3. What happens if you start with a directrix that lies *above* the focus?

E X P L O R A T I O N
COOPERATIVE LEARNING

Drawing an Ellipse

Work with a partner.
You will need:
- graph paper
- a 10-inch piece of string
- two pushpins
- a piece of cardboard

1 Draw axes on a piece of graph paper. Label the points (–4, 0) and (4, 0). Place the graph paper on the cardboard. Use the pins to hold one end of the string at (–4, 0) and the other end at (4, 0).

2 Use a pencil to pull the string until it is taut. Move the pencil above and below the *x*-axis, keeping the string taut, until you have sketched a closed geometric figure called an *ellipse*.

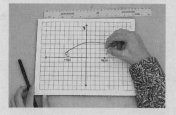

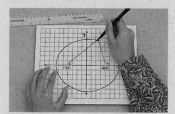

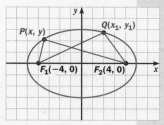

Questions

1. If *P* and *Q* are any two points on the figure you drew, how do the lengths F_1P and F_2P compare with the lengths F_1Q and F_2Q?

2. Give a definition for the figure you drew using the relationship between F_1P, F_2P, and the length of the string.

3. Move the pins closer together and repeat Steps 1 and 2. How did the ellipse change? What do you think happens to the shape of the ellipse when the pins are moved even closer together?

Explorations and Projects Book, Copyright © McDougal Littell Inc.

EXPLORATION
COOPERATIVE LEARNING

**Investigating Methods
for Cutting Paper**

**Work with a partner.
You will need:**
• scissors

SET UP Turn an $8\frac{1}{2}$ in. by 11 in. sheet of paper sideways. Cut the paper into strips about a half inch wide. One of you should use Method A, and the other should use Method B. Each time you make a cut, record the total number of cuts and the total number of pieces of paper in a table.

No. of cuts	No. of pieces	
	A	B
1	2	2
2	4	3
⋮	⋮	⋮

Method A

1 Cut the paper in half.

2 Stack the halves. Cut the stack in half.

3 Continue stacking and cutting.

Method B

1 Cut a thin strip from one end.

2 Continue cutting off strips.

Answer Questions 1–3 for each method.

1. How does the number of pieces change with each cut after the first?

2. Find the next 3 terms of the sequence of the number of pieces.

3. Write a formula for the *n*th term of the sequence in terms of *n* and the first term of the sequence.

EXPLORATION
COOPERATIVE LEARNING

Investigating Repeated Addition and Multiplication

Work with a partner.
You will need:
• graphing calculators

1 The calculator screen shows the procedure you should follow to generate a sequence. Choose various starting values and various constants (both positive and negative), and write down the first 6 terms of the sequences you generate.

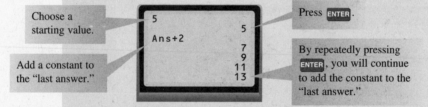

Choose a starting value.

Add a constant to the "last answer."

5	
Ans+2	5
	7
	9
	11
	13

Press ENTER.

By repeatedly pressing ENTER, you will continue to add the constant to the "last answer."

2 Repeat Step 1, but this time *multiply* by a constant instead of adding a constant. For example, use Ans * 2 instead of Ans + 2.

Questions

1. In each sequence, what is the relationship between any term (except the first) and the term before it?

2. Tell whether each sequence formed by repeatedly adding a constant is *arithmetic*, *geometric*, or *neither*.

3. Tell whether each sequence formed by repeatedly multiplying by a constant is *arithmetic*, *geometric*, or *neither*.

EXPLORATION
COOPERATIVE LEARNING

Investigating the Multiplication Counting Principle

Work with a partner.
You will need:
- paper of four different colors
- scissors

1 Cut a 1 in. by 3 in. strip from each of three colors of paper. Arrange the strips to form flags with two horizontal bars like those at the right.
   List all of the different flags you can make. How many are there? This number is the product of what two consecutive integers?

Indonesia

2 Cut a 1 in. by 3 in. strip of the fourth color. List all of the two-bar flags you can make with four colors. How many are there? This number is the product of what two consecutive integers?

Burkina Faso

3 Look for a pattern in Steps 1 and 2. If you had one strip of each of ten different colors, how many different two-bar flags could you make?

Poland

Morocco

4 Cut another strip of each of the three original colors. How many different two-bar flags can you make from three colors if the bars may be the same color (as on the Moroccan flag) or different colors? Explain. This number is the square of what integer?

5 How many two-bar flags do you think can be made from four colors if repetition of colors is allowed? Explain.

EXPLORATION
COOPERATIVE LEARNING

Making Connections

Work in a group of 2–4 students.
You will need:
- a graphing calculator

SET UP A **complete graph** has a single edge between every pair of vertices.

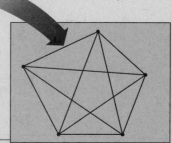

1 Draw a complete graph with 2 vertices. How many edges does it have? Draw complete graphs with 3, 4, 5, 6, and 7 vertices. How many edges does each graph have? Organize your results in a table.

Put the number of vertices on the horizontal axis.

◄2 Use a graphing calculator to make a scatter plot showing how the number of edges is related to the number of vertices. Choose a good viewing window.

3 Predict the number of edges in a complete graph with 8 vertices. Explain your reasoning. Check your prediction.

4 Write an equation for the number of edges in a complete graph as a function of the number of vertices. Explain your reasoning.

5 Graph the function from Step 4 on your scatter plot from Step 2. Does it seem to fit the data?

Explorations and Projects Book, Copyright © McDougal Littell Inc.

Lucky 3 Drawing
Three lucky winners will receive **$3000** each!

Grand Sweepstakes
1st prize: $30,000
2nd prize: $300
3rd prize: $30

In which contest would you rather be a winner? In the Lucky 3 Drawing, it matters only that you're in the top three, while in the Grand Sweepstakes, your exact position in the top three is important. There are more ways to award prizes for the Grand Sweepstakes than for the Lucky 3 Drawing.

E X P L O R A T I O N
COOPERATIVE LEARNING

Investigating Ways of Choosing Winners

Work in a group of 4 or 5 students.

Suppose only the members of your group enter the Grand Sweepstakes.

1 Each of you should list all of the ways that others in your group can win the second and third prizes if you are the first-prize winner.

2 As a group, count the number of ways to award the 3 prizes. Explain how to use permutations to check your answer. Write the answer in the form $_nP_r$.

Suppose only the members of your group enter the Lucky 3 Drawing.

3 Since each winner receives the same amount of money, the group of winners "John, Kia, and Ann," for example, is the same as "Ann, John, and Kia." In your lists from Step 1, how many times is each group of three winners listed? Explain why you can write your answer in the form $r!$.

4 Use the lists from Step 1 to count the number of ways to award the Lucky 3 prizes. How is your answer related to the answer in Step 2? Express the number of ways to choose the Lucky 3 winners in the form $\frac{_nP_r}{r!}$.

EXPLORATION
COOPERATIVE LEARNING

Simulating a Coupon Giveaway

Work with a partner.
You will need:
• a die

SET UP Suppose a music store gives each customer a discount coupon. The amount of the discount is known when a sales clerk removes the seal on the coupon to reveal either a 10%, 15%, or 30% discount.

1 Suppose there is an equal chance of getting each discount. Let each face of a die represent the type of discount you receive.

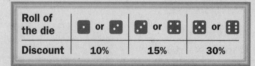

Roll of the die	or	or	or
Discount	10%	15%	30%

Roll the die until you get a 5 or a 6, and then record the number of rolls it took you to get a 5 or a 6. Repeat the simulation 10 times.

2 What was the greatest number of coupons you needed to have to get a 30% discount? What was the least number? the average number?

3 The store manager decides that in the next coupon order, she will request that half of the coupons give a 10% discount, a third give a 15% discount, and a sixth give a 30% discount. Which numbers on the die will you use to represent a discount of 10%? 15%? 30%? Why?

4 Run a simulation for the new coupon values. About how many coupons do you need to collect to get a 30% discount?

Explorations and Projects Book, Copyright © McDougal Littell Inc.

Most movies are screened by test audiences before they open at your local theater. This helps movie studios predict whether their movies will be successful. It also allows studios to target advertising toward groups (such as men or women) that seem most receptive to a particular movie.

EXPLORATION
COOPERATIVE LEARNING

Conducting a Movie Survey

Work as an entire class.
You will need:
• small slips of paper

1 Your class should choose a movie that most of you have seen.

2 Each of you should have a slip of paper. On your slip, write whether you are male or female and whether you liked or disliked the movie. If you haven't seen the movie, write "no opinion."

3 Collect all the slips of paper. Tally the results of the survey in a table like the one shown in the photo.

Questions

1. Suppose a student is randomly selected from your class. Let *A* be the event "the student is female," and let *B* be the event "the student liked the movie."

   a. Find *P(A and B)* and *P(A)* • *P(B)*.

   b. Are the events *A* and *B* independent? Explain.

2. Suppose a student is randomly selected from the *males* in your class. What is the probability that the student liked the movie? disliked the movie? had no opinion about the movie?

EXPLORATION

COOPERATIVE LEARNING

Guessing on a True/False Test

Work with your class.
You will need:
• a coin

1 Flip a coin to guess the answer to each question on the test shown. If the coin comes up heads, answer that question *True*. If it comes up tails, answer *False*.

2 What is the theoretical probability of answering the first question correctly? of answering all six correctly?

3 Your teacher will tell you the answers to the test. Find your score by counting the number of questions you answered correctly.

Esperanto Geography Test
Tell whether each statement is *True* or *False*.
1. Pli da homoj loĝas en Kalifornio ol en la tuta Aŭstralio.
2. La ĉefa rikoltaĵo en Ukrajno estas tritiko.
3. Kenjo iĝis sendependa en 1963.
4. Kalkuto estas la ĉefurbo de Bharato.
5. Ŝanhajo estas lando en Azio.
6. Malavio troviĝas sur la okcidenta bordo de granda laĝo.

4 As a class, make a relative frequency histogram of everyone's scores. What is the general shape of the histogram?

5 Based on the histogram, what is the probability of answering all of the questions correctly? Does this agree with the probability you calculated in Step 2? Why or why not?

6 Based on the histogram, what is the probability of answering four or more questions correctly? of answering three or fewer questions correctly? Is one situation theoretically more likely than the other? Why?

EXPLORATION
COOPERATIVE LEARNING

Finding Ratios of Side Lengths in Similar Right Triangles

Work with a partner.
You will need:
- graph paper
- a protractor

1 Draw a segment along a horizontal grid line on your graph paper. Label one endpoint *A*.

2 Use a protractor to draw a 60° angle at *A*.

3 Draw segments along vertical grid lines to form right triangles, such as △*ABC*, △*ADE*, and △*AFG* shown.

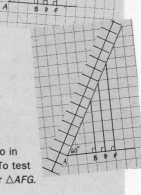

Questions

1. Why are △*ABC*, △*ADE*, and △*AFG* similar triangles?

2. Cut a strip of graph paper to use as a ruler. Use your ruler to find the value of the following ratio for △*ABC* and for △*ADE*:

$$\frac{\text{length of leg opposite } \angle A}{\text{length of hypotenuse}}$$

What do you notice?

3. Make a conjecture about the value of the ratio in Question 2 for any triangle similar to △*ABC*. To test your conjecture, find the value of this ratio for △*AFG*.

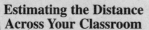

EXPLORATION
COOPERATIVE LEARNING

**Estimating the Distance
Across Your Classroom**

Work with a partner.
You will need:
• a ruler, yardstick, or meterstick

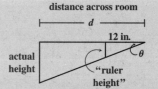

1 Stand at one end of the classroom holding the ruler. Your partner should stand at the other end of the room.

2 Hold the ruler about 12 in. in front of your eyes and line up the "0" end of the ruler with the top of your partner's head.

3 Spot the floor at your partner's feet along the ruler. What are your partner's "ruler height" and actual height?

4 Copy and complete the diagram below. Include the measurements from Step 3.

Questions

1. What is the value of tan θ using the small triangle?

2. Let d be the unknown distance across the room. Using the large triangle, write an expression involving d for the value of tan θ.

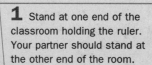

3. Use your answers from Questions 1 and 2 to write an equation. Solve for d. (You may want to use the ruler to find the actual distance across the room and compare it with your calculated result.)

Explorations and Projects Book, Copyright © McDougal Littell Inc.

Making a Radian String

Work with a partner.
You will need:

- a cylinder
- a string
- tape
- a ruler
- a marker
- a protractor

SET UP Measure the diameter of a circular cross section of the cylinder and then calculate the radius. Cut a piece of string so that it is about 14 times as long as the radius. Mark the midpoint of the string, and make marks at one radius (one *radian*) intervals to the left and right of the midpoint. You may want to use a different color in each direction.

−1 radius −1 radius +1 radius +1 radius

1 Attach the midpoint of your "radian string" to your cylinder. This is the origin.

2 Wrap the string around the cylinder. The counterclockwise direction is positive, and the clockwise direction is negative.

Questions

Use your string and cylinder to answer the following questions.

1. About how many radians are in a full circle?

2. Compare your answer to Question 1 with the answer found by a group that used a different sized cylinder. Does the size of the cylinder affect the answer? Explain.

3. How are the points at 2 radians and −2 radians geometrically related to each other? Does this relationship hold for any two points that are at ±r radians from the origin?

Algebra 2 Exploration 41

EXPLORATION
COOPERATIVE LEARNING

Constructing a Triangle

Work with a partner.
You will need:
- a ruler
- a protractor
- a compass

1 Draw $\overrightarrow{AX}$ at least 15 cm long. Then draw $\overline{AC}$ so that $\angle CAX = 30°$ and $AC = b = 8$ cm.

2 Place the compass point at C. Choose a radius from the table below and draw an arc as shown.

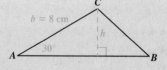

3 Each point (if any) where the arc meets $\overrightarrow{AX}$ should be labeled B to complete a $\triangle ABC$. Determine the number of such triangles that can be drawn with the given radius.

4 Copy and complete the table by repeating Steps 1–3 for each radius r.

Radius r (cm)	Number of triangles
2	?
4	?
6	?
8	?
10	?

Questions

1. Find the height h of $\triangle ABC$ when $\angle A = 30°$ and $b = 8$ cm. Do all the triangles you constructed have the same height? Explain.

2. How many triangles are possible when $\overrightarrow{AX}$ is tangent to the arc drawn with the compass? For which value(s) of r does this happen?

3. a. For which value(s) of r does the arc intersect $\overrightarrow{AX}$ twice?

   b. Express your answer to part (a) as an inequality in terms of b, h, and r.

4. How many triangles are possible when the arc intersects $\overrightarrow{AX}$ exactly once? For which value(s) of r does this happen?

5. Repeat Steps 1–4 above using $\angle A = 120°$. Under what circumstances do you get a triangle? don't you get a triangle?

Explorations and Projects Book, Copyright © McDougal Littell Inc.

EXPLORATION
COOPERATIVE LEARNING

Landing a Plane

Work with a partner.
You will need:
• a graphing calculator
with parametric mode

SET UP Imagine you are
piloting a small airplane at
12,000 ft, preparing to
land. Once you begin your
descent to the runway, your
altitude changes at a rate
of **–15 ft/s**. Your horizontal
speed is **200 ft/s**.

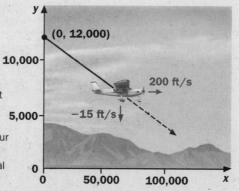

1 The plane is initially at the point (0, 12,000). Complete the
equations for x and y.

The plane's horizontal position at time t (in seconds) is given by:

$$x = 0 + \underline{\ ?\ }\, t$$

The plane's vertical position at time t (in seconds) is given by:

$$y = \underline{\ ?\ } + \underline{\ ?\ }\, t$$

2 Enter your equations from Step 1 into a graphing calculator set
in parametric mode. Then graph the equations, adjusting the viewing
window and t-values so you can see where the graph crosses the
x-axis.

3 Use your calculator's trace feature to determine how long it takes
the plane to reach ground level. What is the value of x at this time? At
what horizontal distance from the airport should the airplane begin its
descent? (*Note:* 1 mi = 5280 ft)

EXPLORATION
COOPERATIVE LEARNING

Graphing Sine and Cosine as Functions

Work with a partner.
You will need:
- a scientific calculator
- graph paper

1 Copy the table. Use a calculator to complete the table.

2 Use the table to graph the sine function $y = \sin \theta$ for $0° \leq \theta \leq 360°$. With θ on the horizontal axis and y on the vertical axis, plot the points (θ, y). Then connect the points with a smooth curve.

Angle θ	sin θ	cos θ
0°	?	?
30°	?	?
60°	?	?
90°	?	?
120°	?	?
150°	?	?
180°	?	?
210°	?	?
240°	?	?
270°	?	?
300°	?	?
330°	?	?
360°	?	?

3 Use the table to graph the cosine function $y = \cos \theta$ for $0° \leq \theta \leq 360°$. With θ on the horizontal axis and y on the vertical axis, plot the points (θ, y). Connect the points with a smooth curve.

Questions

1. How are the two graphs alike? How are they different?

2. How many values of θ for $0° \leq \theta \leq 360°$ satisfy each of the following?

   a. $\sin \theta = 0.5$ **b.** $\cos \theta = 0.5$

   c. $\cos \theta = -1$ **d.** $\sin \theta = -0.8$

Algebra 2
Projects

PORTFOLIO PROJECT

Stretching a Rubber Band

When you put fruit on a grocery store scale, the scale's dial tells you the weight. If you could look inside the scale, you would see a spring that controls the movement of the dial. This spring stretches as you add more fruit.

A rubber band behaves in a similar way: the harder you pull on it, the longer it stretches. These situations both involve a pulling force that increases length. Have you ever wondered how the force used to stretch a spring or a rubber band is related to its length?

PROJECT GOAL   Perform an experiment to study the relationship between pulling force and rubber band length.

Conducting an Experiment

Work with a partner. Here are a few suggestions for carrying out the experiment.

1. **GATHER** a rubber band, 2 large paper clips, a paper cup, 20 marbles, a ruler (preferably transparent), graph paper, and a pencil.

2. **SET UP** the equipment. Bend the paper clips to make S-shaped hooks. Using the hooks and rubber band, suspend the paper cup from the edge of a desk or table as shown.

3. **MEASURE** the length of the rubber band to the nearest 0.1 cm. After one partner adds marbles to the cup four at a time and measures the rubber band's length, the other partner records the data. Copy and complete the table.

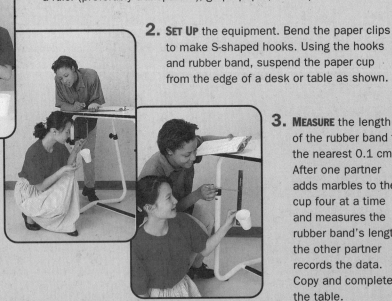

m = number of marbles in cup	0	4	8	12	16
l = length of rubber band (cm)	?	?	?	?	?

Explorations and Projects Book, Copyright © McDougal Littell Inc.

Analyzing the Data

- **DRAW** a scatter plot of the data pairs (m, l) in a coordinate plane. The plotted points should almost line up. Use the ruler or a graphing calculator to obtain a line of fit.

- **WRITE** an equation for your line. Use the equation to find l when $m = 20$.

- **CHECK** the prediction by putting 20 marbles in the cup and measuring the rubber band length. How did your predicted value for $m = 20$ compare to your experimental value?

Writing a Report

Write a report about your experiment. Include a paragraph on each of these points:

- goals of the experiment
- descriptions of your procedure
- tables and graphs of your data
- conclusions based on your results

You may want to extend your report by investigating and reporting on some other ideas.

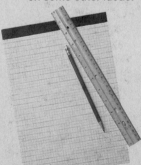

- Use your graph from the project to sketch a predicted graph for this experiment: You start with 20 marbles in the cup and remove four at a time. Then conduct the experiment to check your graph.

- Repeat the project using various types of rubber bands. Do some rubber bands stretch more than others? What factors do you think contribute to the stretchability of the rubber bands?

- Research Hooke's law from a physics book and explain how it applies to this project.

Self-Assessment
Were you satisfied with your prediction of rubber band length based on your line of fit? If so, what factors influenced your success? If not, how can you adjust your methods to improve your results?

PORTFOLIO PROJECT

Creating Fractals

Like many fractals, this *Sierpinski Triangle* is *self-similar*. It is made up of smaller pieces which are geometrically similar to the whole fractal. Each of these pieces is made up of even smaller pieces that are also similar to the whole.

PROJECT GOAL   Work with another student to analyze fractals and generate them on your graphing calculator.

Analyzing the Sierpinski Triangle

The Sierpinski Triangle contains three half-size copies of itself. Each copy is the image of the whole triangle after a transformation.

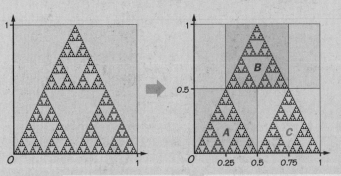

Transformation A is a dilation with center (0, 0) and scale factor 0.5.

Transformation B is a dilation followed by a translation to the right 0.25 units and up 0.5 units.

This *similarity diagram* shows how the three transformations that describe the Sierpinski Triangle affect the unit square.

Transformation C is a dilation followed by a translation to the right 0.5 units.

Explorations and Projects Book, Copyright © McDougal Littell Inc.

Finding Values for the Transformations

Each transformation used to create the Sierpinski Triangle can be represented by two matrix operations. For point $P(a, b)$:

$$\overset{P}{\begin{bmatrix} p & q \\ s & t \end{bmatrix} \begin{bmatrix} a \\ b \end{bmatrix}} + \begin{bmatrix} r \\ u \end{bmatrix} = \overset{P'}{\begin{bmatrix} ? \\ ? \end{bmatrix}}$$

For each of the three transformations, you can use algebra to find the values of p, q, r, s, t, and u.

To find the values for transformation B, use the similarity diagram to see how transformation B affects the points $(0, 0)$, $(0, 1)$, and $(1, 0)$.

The image of $(0, 0)$ is **(0.25, 0.5)**.

The image of $(0, 1)$ is **(0.25, 1)**.

Step 1 Use the image of $(0, 0)$ to solve for r and u.

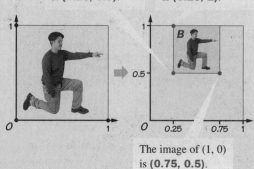

The image of $(1, 0)$ is **(0.75, 0.5)**.

$$(0, 0) \rightarrow \textbf{(0.25, 0.5)}$$

$$\begin{bmatrix} p & q \\ s & t \end{bmatrix} \begin{bmatrix} 0 \\ 0 \end{bmatrix} + \begin{bmatrix} r \\ u \end{bmatrix} = \begin{bmatrix} 0.25 \\ 0.5 \end{bmatrix}$$

$$\begin{bmatrix} p \cdot 0 + q \cdot 0 \\ s \cdot 0 + t \cdot 0 \end{bmatrix} + \begin{bmatrix} r \\ u \end{bmatrix} = \begin{bmatrix} 0.25 \\ 0.5 \end{bmatrix}$$

$$\begin{bmatrix} 0 + r \\ 0 + u \end{bmatrix} = \begin{bmatrix} 0.25 \\ 0.5 \end{bmatrix}$$

So $r = 0.25$ and $u = 0.5$.

Step 2 Use the images of $(0, 1)$ and $(1, 0)$ to solve for p, q, s, and t. Substitute the values of r and u that you found in Step 1.

$$(0, 1) \rightarrow \textbf{(0.25, 1)}$$

$$\begin{bmatrix} p & q \\ s & t \end{bmatrix} \begin{bmatrix} 0 \\ 1 \end{bmatrix} + \begin{bmatrix} r \\ u \end{bmatrix} = \begin{bmatrix} 0.25 \\ 1 \end{bmatrix}$$

$$\begin{bmatrix} p \cdot 0 + q \cdot 1 \\ s \cdot 0 + t \cdot 1 \end{bmatrix} + \begin{bmatrix} \textbf{0.25} \\ \textbf{0.5} \end{bmatrix} = \begin{bmatrix} 0.25 \\ 1 \end{bmatrix}$$

$$\begin{bmatrix} q + 0.25 \\ t + 0.5 \end{bmatrix} = \begin{bmatrix} 0.25 \\ 1 \end{bmatrix}$$

So $q = 0$ and $t = 0.5$.

$$(1, 0) \rightarrow \textbf{(0.75, 0.5)}$$

$$\begin{bmatrix} p & q \\ s & t \end{bmatrix} \begin{bmatrix} 1 \\ 0 \end{bmatrix} + \begin{bmatrix} r \\ u \end{bmatrix} = \begin{bmatrix} 0.75 \\ 0.5 \end{bmatrix}$$

$$\begin{bmatrix} p \cdot 1 + q \cdot 0 \\ s \cdot 1 + t \cdot 0 \end{bmatrix} + \begin{bmatrix} \textbf{0.25} \\ \textbf{0.5} \end{bmatrix} = \begin{bmatrix} 0.75 \\ 0.5 \end{bmatrix}$$

$$\begin{bmatrix} p + 0.25 \\ s + 0.5 \end{bmatrix} = \begin{bmatrix} 0.75 \\ 0.5 \end{bmatrix}$$

So $p = 0.5$ and $s = 0$.

Use the same method to find the values of p, q, r, s, t, and u for transformation A and for transformation C.

```
PROGRAM: FRACTAL
:PlotsOff
:AxesOff
:FnOff
:ClrDraw
{3,1} →dim [D]
:[[0][0][1]]→[D]
:0→K
:0→Xmin
:1→Xmax
:0→Ymin
:1→Ymax
:ZSquare
:While (K<2000)
:int (rand∗3+1)→R
:If R=1
:[A]∗[D]→[E]
:If R=2
:[B]∗[D]→[E]
:If R=3
:[C]∗[D]→[E]
:[E](1,1)→[D](1,1)
:[E](2,1)→[D](2,1)
:Pt-On([E](1,1),[E](2,1))
:K+1→K
:End
```

Displaying the Fractal

Using the program at the left and a TI-82 graphing calculator, you can display the Sierpinski Triangle using the three transformations that you found.

1. Enter the program into your graphing calculator directly, or download it from another calculator or computer. See your graphing calculator manual for more information on entering or transmitting programs.

2. Store the values you found for transformation B into matrix B on your graphing calculator. Enter the six values into a 2×3 matrix in this order:

$$\begin{bmatrix} p & q & r \\ s & t & u \end{bmatrix}$$

For transformation B, store this matrix in your graphing calculator.

3. Store the values you found for transformation A and transformation C into matrices A and C, respectively.

4. Execute the program to display the fractal. It may take several minutes for the program to finish. If you entered the correct values into the matrices, your graphing calculator screen should look like this:

Explorations and Projects Book, Copyright © McDougal Littell Inc.

Generating Other Fractals

Choose one of the fractals shown below. Use the corresponding similarity diagram to find the values of p, q, r, s, t, and u for each transformation. Store these values in your graphing calculator as matrices A, B, and C. Then run the program to display the fractal.

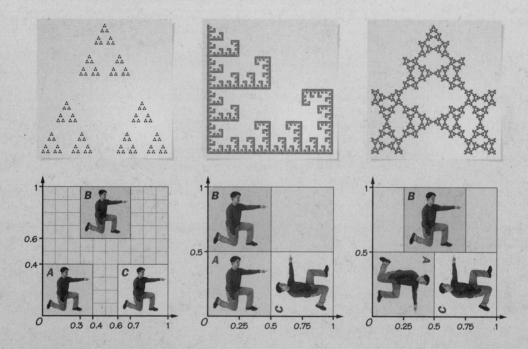

Writing a Report

In your report, give the values that you found for transformations A and C in the Sierpinski Triangle, and show the steps that you used to find them. Give the values for all three transformations in one of the fractals above, and show the steps that you used to find them. Describe how the image on your graphing calculator screen compares to the picture of the fractal above. If possible, include printouts of your calculator screen. To extend the project, draw a new similarity diagram and use your graphing calculator to display the fractal it describes.

Self-Assessment

In this project, you used some techniques that were not emphasized in the chapter. What was the most difficult part of the project? Explain.

PORTFOLIO PROJECT

Investigating the Flow of Water

Often you will see a town using a tall water tower as a means of creating enough pressure to deliver water throughout the town. The water tower functions on the simple principle that as the height of a column of water increases, the weight of the water in the column increases, which in turn causes the pressure at the base of the column to increase.

You can model this situation using a can filled with water. As you let water flow out of a hole in the bottom, the pressure at the hole decreases. What effect do you think decreasing pressure will have on the time it takes the water to flow out of the can?

PROJECT GOAL Conduct an experiment to find out how the water level in a can affects the time it takes the water to flow from a hole in the can's bottom.

Conducting an Experiment

1. PUNCH a hole in the bottom of the can.

Work with a partner to plan and perform an experiment in which you measure the height of water in a can as the water flows from a hole in the bottom. You will need a large can (like a coffee can), a nail, a hammer, a metric ruler, and a watch. Here are some guidelines for conducting your experiment.

3. RECORD the water's initial height, h_0, in millimeters.

2. COVER the hole in the can's bottom with your finger and fill the can with water.

Testing a Quadratic Model

A theoretical model based on physics applies to the situation you have investigated. The model involves the following constants (all measured in millimeters): h_0, the water's initial height; D, the diameter of the can; and d, the diameter of the hole. The model says that the water's height h, in millimeters, is a quadratic function of the time t, in seconds, after the water begins running out of the container:

$$h(t) = \left(\sqrt{h_0} - \frac{70d^2}{D^2}t\right)^2$$

- **MEASURE** the diameters of the can and the hole.

- **SUBSTITUTE** your values of D, d, and h_0 into the model.

- **CALCULATE** $h(t)$ for the t-values in your data table. Compare your calculated water-height values with the actual data from your experiment. Are there differences? What might explain them?

- **GRAPH** the function $h(t)$ along with your data using a graphing calculator or graphing software. Is the graph a good model for your data?

4. **UNCOVER** the hole for 10 s and then cover it with your finger again. Re-measure the height of the water. Repeat this until the can is nearly empty.

Writing a Report

Write a report about your experiment. Describe your procedures, and present a comparison of your data to the model's predictions. Include the following:

- a statement of the goal of your project

- a data table that compares your experimental water-height data to the values predicted by the quadratic model

- an evaluation of how well the quadratic model predicts water height

- any ideas you may have that could explain differences between the data and the model

To extend your project, you may wish to investigate other factors that could affect the flow of liquid from a container. For example, what if you used a wider can or made a smaller hole? What if you used a different liquid, like pancake syrup?

Self-Assessment

In your report, include a description of any difficulties you had. For example, was it difficult to get precise measurements? How might you alter the experiment to improve the results?

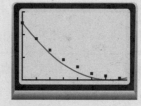

5. **ORGANIZE** your data in a table. Then make a scatter plot. Put time on the horizontal axis and water height on the vertical axis.

PORTFOLIO PROJECT

Walk This Way

Try walking across a flat, open space at an increasing speed. You'll notice that at some point you'll feel the urge to switch to a run. Your body recognizes when it's more efficient to run than to walk.

Now think about a small child trying to keep up with an adult who's walking briskly. With shorter legs than the adult, the child often has to run. Obviously, how fast someone can walk (without breaking into a run) has something to do with leg length.

PROJECT GOAL Examine the relationship between leg length and walking speed.

Doing an Experiment

Work with a partner to design and carry out an experiment in which you measure the leg length, in inches, of ten subjects, and then time the subjects as they walk. Be sure to choose subjects with a variety of leg lengths. You will need a tape measure and a stopwatch. Here are some guidelines for doing your experiment.

1. MEASURE each subject's leg length from hip to heel.

2. CHOOSE a straight, flat, 60 ft course that is free of obstacles.

3. INSTRUCT each subject to walk the 60 ft course as fast as he or she can. With each step, the walker must be sure that the rear foot does not leave the ground before the forward foot lands.

4. TIME each subject as he or she walks the course. Divide the distance traveled (60 ft) by each subject's time to calculate his or her speed in feet per second.

Explorations and Projects Book, Copyright © McDougal Littell Inc.

Using a Model

A person's maximum walking speed s, in feet per second, is given by the following model:

$$s = \frac{\sqrt{gl}}{12}$$

where g, the acceleration due to gravity, is 384 in./s², and l is leg length in inches.

• **CALCULATE** the predicted maximum speed for each of your subjects according to the model. You may find a spreadsheet helpful.

	Walking Speed Data			
	A	**B**	**C**	**D**	**E**
1	Name	Leg length (in.)	Time (s)	Actual speed (ft/s)	Predicted speed (ft/s)
2	Lester	40	5.9	10.2	10.33
3	Cindy	34	6.4	9.38	9.52
4	Gena	31	6.7	8.96	9.09

• **PLOT** the predicted speeds on the same graph as the actual values. Use different colors or symbols for each data set.

• **COMPARE** the actual values with the predicted values. Are there differences? What might explain them?

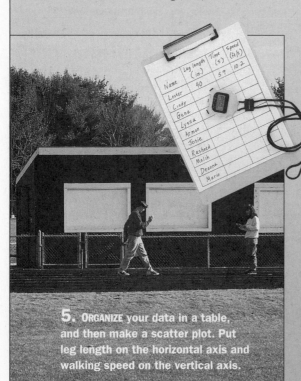

5. ORGANIZE your data in a table, and then make a scatter plot. Put leg length on the horizontal axis and walking speed on the vertical axis.

Writing a Report

Write a report summarizing your results. It should include all your data as well as a comparison of the data with the predictions of the model. You can also extend your project to explore one of these ideas:

• The acceleration due to gravity varies from planet to planet. Suppose you were walking on Mars or on the moon. How fast could you walk? How does gravity affect walking speed?

• The model above is based on the assumption that the *centripetal force* acting on a walker's hips cannot exceed the walker's weight.

Centripetal force is given by $\frac{ms^2}{l}$, and weight is given by mg, where m is mass. Derive the model from this information. (You'll need to take units of measurement into account.)

Self-Assessment

In your report, describe any difficulties you had gathering data for this project. Did you feel that your data were in agreement with the model? If not, what might have gone wrong?

PORTFOLIO PROJECT

Predicting Basketball Accuracy

In 1979 the National Basketball Association instituted a *three-point rule*. According to this rule, a basket shot from a point outside the three-point "line" is worth three points, while a basket shot from a closer distance is worth two points. Why do you think the rules were changed?

The **three-point line** is two inches wide. A shot counts for only two points if a player's foot touches the three-point line.

PROJECT GOAL Do an experiment to find how your ability to make a basket changes with distance.

Investigating Your Basketball Ability

For this investigation, you will need a piece of wadded-up paper to be your ball, a wastebasket, a yardstick, and graph paper. You may find it helpful to have a graphing calculator or graphing software.

1. STAND 0 yards from the wastebasket. Shoot your paper ball into the basket 10 times and record the number of shots that go into the basket.

2. STEP back one yard and record your results for 10 shots from this distance. Continue stepping back one yard until you reach a distance where none of your 10 shots go into the basket.

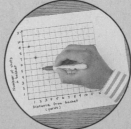

3. MAKE a scatter plot of your data. Let the horizontal axis show the distance from the basket, and let the vertical axis show the number of shots that went into the basket.

Making a Model

• **DESCRIBE** your graph. Do you think the data decreases *linearly*? *exponentially*? At what distance did the number of shots that went into the basket decrease the most?

• **ORGANIZE** your data in a table like the one shown. Find the average change and the average percent change.

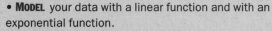
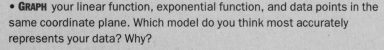

Distance from basket (yd)	Number of shots that went into basket	Change	Percent change
0	?	—	—
1	?	?	?
2	?	?	?
⋮	⋮	⋮	⋮

• **MODEL** your data with a linear function and with an exponential function.

• **GRAPH** your linear function, exponential function, and data points in the same coordinate plane. Which model do you think most accurately represents your data? Why?

Writing a Report

Write a report about your experiment that includes your data, graphs, models, and explanations. You may also want to investigate and report on these things:

• How do you think your results would change if you repeated the experiment 5 times? 10 times? 50 times? Explain your reasoning. Then repeat the experiment at least 5 times. How do your results compare to your prediction?

• Repeat the experiment using a real basketball and hoop. How could a basketball player use this experiment to decide whether to try for a two-point shot or a three-point shot?

• Why do you think the three-point rule was created? What other sports have rules that take the *likelihood* of scoring points into account? Describe the method of scoring for each sport.

Self-Assessment
Describe any difficulties you had in finding a linear and an exponential model to fit your data. How did you resolve these difficulties?

PORTFOLIO PROJECT

The Way a Ball Bounces

Have you ever watched a ball bounce repeatedly? Due to the loss of energy each time a bouncing ball hits the floor, the ball never rebounds to the same height from which it fell.

The bounciness, or "bounce factor," of a ball can be determined by comparing the ball's rebound height to the original height from which the ball was dropped. Then, using the bounce factor of the ball, you can predict the height of the ball after any number of bounces.

PROJECT GOAL Create a model that relates the bounce height of a ball to the number of times the ball has bounced.

Conducting an Experiment

Work with a partner to design and carry out an experiment in which you measure the bounce height of a ball after dropping the ball from varying heights. You will need a ball and two metersticks or a tape measure. Here are some guidelines for conducting your experiment.

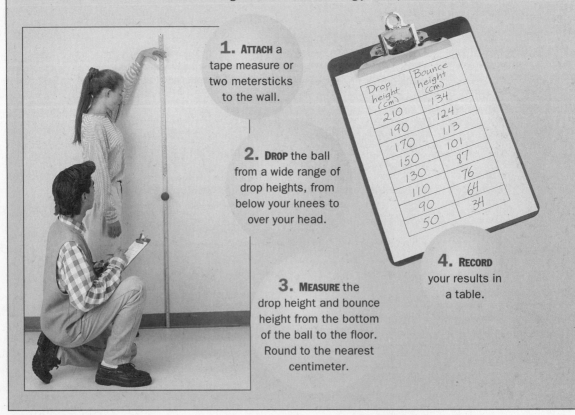

1. ATTACH a tape measure or two metersticks to the wall.

2. DROP the ball from a wide range of drop heights, from below your knees to over your head.

3. MEASURE the drop height and bounce height from the bottom of the ball to the floor. Round to the nearest centimeter.

4. RECORD your results in a table.

Drop height (cm)	Bounce height (cm)
210	134
190	124
170	113
150	101
130	87
110	76
90	64
50	34

Bounce Factor		
C10		= SUM (C2:C9)/8
	A	**B**	**C**
1	Drop height (cm)	Bounce height (cm)	Bounce factor
2	210	134	0.64
3	190	124	0.65
4	170	113	0.66
5	150	101	0.67
6	130	87	0.67
7	110	76	0.69
8	90	64	0.71
9	50	34	0.68
10	Mean bounce factor:		0.67

Analyzing the Data

• **CALCULATE** the bounce factor of your ball for each drop height. The bounce factor of your ball is equal to the ratio $\dfrac{\text{bounce height}}{\text{drop height}}$.

• **FIND** the mean of the bounce factors. Use this figure as the average bounce factor of your ball.

Predicting Exponential Decay

Suppose you dropped your ball from the height of the top of your head, and watched it fall and rebound, over and over.

• **MAKE** a table of predicted rebound heights. Start with the ball's initial height, and calculate the ball's height after one bounce, after two bounces, and so on. Continue for several bounces.

• **FIND** an equation that describes rebound height as a function of the number of bounces. Determine the proper values for *a* and *b* to substitute into the exponential decay model $y = ab^x$. What does *a* stand for in your model? What does *b* stand for?

• **PREDICT** how many bounces it will take until the ball's rebound height is less than the height of your knee. Test your prediction.

Writing a Report

Write a report about your experiment. State the project goal, describe your procedures, and present data that support the conclusions you make. Be sure to explain the role that drop height and bounce factor have in your model and evaluate how well your exponential decay model predicts bounce height.

   You may wish to extend your report to include data about other types of balls, or do some research about the official rules concerning the bounciness of a ball in a sport like tennis, basketball, or football.

Self-Assessment

Does the model that you developed for this project make sense to you? If so, in what ways? If not, where did you get confused? What would help make things clearer for you?

Comparing
Olympic Performances

In some Olympic events where both men and women compete against the clock, women's times, although not as fast as men's times, have improved more rapidly. This suggests that women may someday surpass men's times in these events. By choosing an appropriate model, you can make reasonable predictions about the future performances of men and women in comparable events.

PROJECT GOAL Use a system of equations to model men's and women's performance data in an Olympic event.

Collecting the Data

Work in a group of three students. You will need a graphing calculator or statistical software, and access to an Olympic data source, such as a sports almanac.

Find an event in which both men and women compete. Choose a timed event like swimming or running, or an event like the high jump or long jump, where distance is used to measure performance.

Olympic 100 m Freestyle		
	Winning time (s)	
Year	**Men**	**Women**
1948	57.3	66.3
1952	57.4	66.8
1956	55.4	62.0
1960	55.2	61.2
1964	53.4	59.5
1968	52.2	60.0
1972	51.2	58.6
1976	50.0	55.7
1980	50.4	54.8
1984	49.8	55.9
1988	48.6	54.9
1992	49.0	54.6

Using Linear Models

Make a scatter plot of your data. Fit a line to each set of points, and find equations of the lines. For example, using data for the 100 m freestyle (see the table) with $x =$ years since 1948 and $y =$ winning times, you get the results shown.

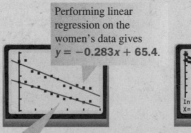

Performing linear regression on the women's data gives $y = -0.283x + 65.4$.

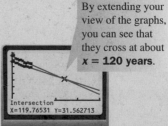

By extending your view of the graphs, you can see that they cross at about $x = 120$ years.

Intersection
X=119.76531 Y=31.562713

Performing linear regression on the men's data gives $y = -0.214x + 57.2$.

What does your model predict? Why might a linear equation be a poor model for athletic performance?

Explorations and Projects Book, Copyright © McDougal Littell Inc.

Using Exponential Models

Suppose you want to model winning times using an exponential decay equation of the form $y = ab^x$ (where $0 < b < 1$). You know y approaches 0 as x increases. Since you wouldn't expect performance times to decrease to 0, it makes sense to choose a reasonable lower bound for the data.

Try using a decay equation of the form $y = ab^x + c$, where the number c is the lower bound. (If you think your data have an upper bound, use a model of the form $y = c - ab^x$.) Suppose, for instance, that you don't expect men's or women's times for the 100 m freestyle to go below 40 s.

STEP 1 Find an exponential model that fits the data points (x, y') where $y' = y - 40$.

STEP 2 In the equation from Step 1, substitute $y - 40$ for y' and solve for y to obtain a model that fits the data points (x, y).

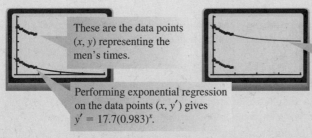

These are the data points (x, y) representing the men's times.

Performing exponential regression on the data points (x, y') gives $y' = 17.7(0.983)^x$.

The function $y = 17.7(0.983)^x + 40$ models the original data points. The graph does not fall below the line $y = 40$.

STEP 3 Repeat Steps 1 and 2 for the women's times, and graph the models for both data sets to see if they intersect.

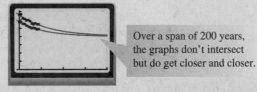

Over a span of 200 years, the graphs don't intersect but do get closer and closer.

Would you get different results if you changed the lower bound? What if you used different lower bounds for men and women?

Writing a Report

Write a report summarizing your results. Include these items: a table and a scatter plot of your data sets, graphs of your linear and exponential models, a comparison of future performances based on your models, and an evaluation of the limitations of each model. To extend your project, you may wish to compare results with other groups, or investigate the topic of human limits in sports.

Self-Assessment

Describe how comfortable you are modeling data and making predictions. What aspects of modeling are you unclear or unsure about?

PORTFOLIO PROJECT

The Shape of Things

Grocery store shelves are filled with containers having many different sizes and shapes, and made of many different materials. When designing containers, food packagers must consider serving size, the cost of materials, and other factors. Packages must be durable, attractive, and easy to handle.

For liquid products that can assume the shape of any container, selecting the shape with the least surface area for a specified volume may reduce the cost of the material used to make the container.

PROJECT GOAL Determine the best shape and dimensions of a container that will hold a specified volume of liquid.

Designing an Efficient Container

Work in groups of three. Suppose you are part of a package design team assigned to design a container that will hold 500 cm^3 of tomato sauce. The most desirable package design will minimize material costs, yielding the most efficient container. Here's a possible plan of action for your team:

1. CONSIDER a cylindrical can. Since many food containers are cylindrical, this is a logical shape to consider first. Your team must determine the radius and height of a 500 cm^3 cylindrical can with the least surface area.

STEP 1 Express surface area as a function of base radius only. (*Hint:* The fact that the volume must be 500 cm^3 will allow you to replace h with an expression involving r.)

STEP 2 Find the dimensions of the cylinder that minimizes surface area. One method is to examine a graph using a graphing calculator or graphing software. Another method is to examine a table of values using a spreadsheet like the one shown.

Cylinder Surface Areas

	A	B	C
	Radius	Height	Surface area
1			
2	3.00	17.684	389.684
3	3.10	16.570	382.931
4	3.20	15.542	376.649
5	3.30	14.615	371.266

Explorations and Projects Book, Copyright © McDougal Littell Inc.

2. INVESTIGATE other shapes for your tomato sauce container. Are there other geometric shapes that can hold 500 cm³ using less surface area than the cylinder you identified in Part 1?

With other team members, discuss the advantages and disadvantages of using unusual container shapes, such as a cone, pyramid, prism, or sphere. Analyze their surface areas as you did in Part 1.

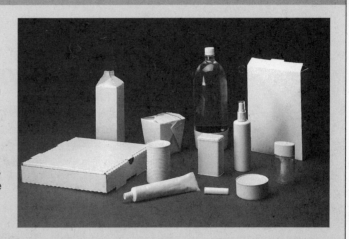

Presenting a Report

Present your report as a recommendation to the management of your company. Describe your procedures, and provide data that support the conclusions you make. You may also wish to extend your project. Here are a few ideas:

• Based on your findings for a cylindrical can with a volume of 500 cm³, make a generalization about the ratio of radius to height for a cylindrical can of any specified volume if the surface area is to be minimized.

• Visit a grocery store. Can you find cylindrical containers that have the radius-to-height ratio described above? Based on the examples you see in the store, what are some other factors that should be considered in packaging a product?

• Consider the problems of packaging objects with unusual shapes. How would you package a football, a boomerang, or a dozen coat hangers?

• Most products are shipped in large quantities after packaging. What issues need to be considered when making larger packages from smaller ones? For example, how would you package 24 cans of tomato sauce so that they can be shipped?

Self-Assessment

How did the team divide up the tasks? What problems, if any, did you have setting up and analyzing the equations you used for the project? In what ways, if any, did the results of the project surprise you?

PORTFOLIO PROJECT

Designing a Logo

Do you recognize the logo shown? It's the symbol for the Olympic Games, which include thousands of participants from around the world.

The five rings symbolize Africa, Asia, Australia, Europe, and the Americas.

The interlocking of the rings symbolizes the meeting of athletes from all over the world.

At least one of the colors of the Olympic logo appears in the flag of every nation.

A *logo* is a symbol that visually represents an organization, such as a club, a charity, or a company. A good logo will often suggest or explain something about the organization it represents. In this project, you will design a logo for an organization that interests you.

PROJECT GOAL   Use a graphing calculator or graphing software to design a logo composed of conic sections.

Drawing with a Graphing Calculator

Paloma is designing a logo for her mother's company, *Orbital Transmissions*, which sells satellite dishes. For her design, Paloma decides to feature a planet with an orbiting satellite. These are the steps she takes to make her logo.

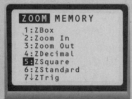

1. **USE** a square window so that circles are not distorted.

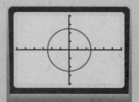

2. **ENTER** equations to draw a circle, leaving enough room for the rest of the drawing.

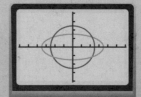

3. **ENTER** equations to draw an ellipse with a minor axis that is shorter than the radius of the circle and a major axis that is longer.

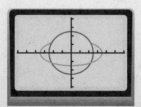
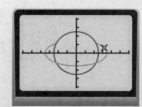

4. RESTRICT the domain of the equation for the upper half of the ellipse so that the ellipse appears to go behind the circle.

5. PLOT a point on the ellipse to give the appearance of an orbiting satellite.

Making Your Own Logo

Describe the organization for which you will design a logo. Then use a graphing calculator or graphing software to create the logo using conic sections. Include points and lines if you wish. Your logo should meet these criteria:

• The logo should be simple and easy to read.

• It should be distinctive and easily understood.

• It should feature information about the organization's functions, services, or products.

Transfer your logo to a poster. Use color to highlight parts of your logo.

Presenting Your Design

Present your logo to the class. Explain what the parts of your logo represent and how you created your design. Show all the equations you used as well as any restrictions on the variables. Explain how your logo meets the criteria given above.

You can extend your project by exploring these ideas:

• Try using a graphing calculator or graphing software to duplicate an actual logo for which conic sections are part of the design.

• Make a list of places where simple visual symbols like the ones shown are used as a substitute for words.

• Try using a graphing calculator or graphing software to draw simple pictures (not necessarily logos) that include conic sections.

Self-Assessment

Describe any problems that you had while creating your logo. How has your understanding of conic sections improved as a result of doing this project?

PORTFOLIO PROJECT

The Future Is Now

A college education can be expensive, and the cost continues to rise as time passes. Planning ahead makes the task of providing the money needed to pay for college much easier. Paying for a college education can be difficult if you wait too long before starting a savings program.

Based on today's costs, you can estimate the cost of a college education at some point in the future. You can then explore various savings and investment plans to see how they can help pay for college.

PROJECT GOAL Estimate the future cost of a college education, and test the effectiveness of several plans for saving this amount of money.

Collecting the Data

Suppose you had 20 years to save enough money to pay for a college education. How could you determine the best method for achieving this goal?

Work in groups of three to collect the data necessary to develop good models. Each group member should do research in one of these areas:

- **Current college costs**

    Research the cost of going to various 4-year colleges and universities. You can use either an average cost for all public or private institutions or the cost for a college of your choice.

- **Average annual percent increase in college costs**

    Find data on college costs over the past 10–15 years. Determine the average annual percent increase in total college costs.

- **Interest rates for various investments**

    Find out the average annual rate of return for various investments, such as savings accounts, certificates of deposit, and mutual funds.

    Two good sources for college data are the *Digest of Educational Statistics* and the *Statistical Abstract of the United States*. For investment data, try calling a bank or brokerage firm.

Projecting Costs and Savings

Use a spreadsheet to project future college costs and to explore different methods of saving for college. For example, the spreadsheet below shows college costs growing at 5.9% per year. It also shows a savings plan in which annual deposits of $1200 earn 10% annual interest. Will this plan yield enough savings to pay for college in 20 years?

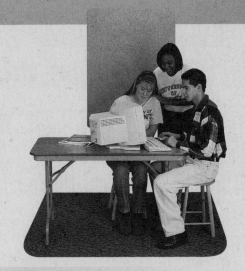

College Planning		
	A	**B**	**C**
1	Year	College cost	Savings
2	1	24876	1200
3	2	B2*1.059	C2*1.1+120

Enter the **current college cost** in the first cell of this column. Use a recursive formula to calculate costs for future years.

Enter the amount of **money saved annually** in the first cell of this column. Use a recursive formula to calculate the effect of annual savings and deposits.

Use a spreadsheet to investigate scenarios like the one above, as well as other savings and investment programs, including those that involve:

• making only a large initial investment

• increasing your annual investment each year

• waiting until the final few years before starting to save

You can extend your project by investigating the cost differences between public and private institutions.

Writing a Report

Write a report summarizing your results. Include the following:

• all your data, estimates, and sources

• a description of each scenario you investigated and a printout of each spreadsheet you created

• a discussion of the feasibility of each scenario and which one makes the most sense for most people

Self-Assessment

What do you think are the limitations of the models you used in this project? Did you have any trouble setting up your spreadsheet models? What insights did you gain from this project?

PORTFOLIO PROJECT

Playing the Game

For centuries, people in Africa and Asia have been developing strategies for winning games that involve moving counters around a board. Some versions of this ancient game are *mancala, adi, kala,* and *oware.* Finding strategies for winning many different kinds of games is an important part of a field of mathematics known as *game theory.*

PROJECT GOAL Develop strategies for winning a game of wari from Ghana, a country in Africa.

How to Play Wari

MATERIALS The Wari board has 12 playing cups, in two rows of six, and two scoring cups. The game is played with 48 counters—stones or seeds are often used.

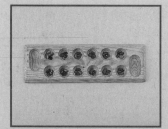

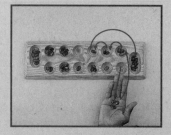

1. SET UP Work with a partner. Each of you should choose one side of the board. Your scoring cup is on your right. Place 4 stones in every cup but the scoring cups.

2. PLAY On your turn, choose any cup on your side of the board. Take all the stones out of this cup. Moving counterclockwise drop one stone in each cup (not including the scoring cups) until you run out of stones.

3. CAPTURE If the last stone is placed in one of your partner's cups and makes the total number of stones in that cup 2 or 3, capture those stones and put them in your scoring cup.

If your partner's side of the board is empty, you must play so that you drop *at least one stone* into your partner's cups. If you cannot, you capture all remaining stones.

WINNING The game ends when no captures are possible. The player who has captured the most stones is the winner.

Explorations and Projects Book, Copyright © McDougal Littell Inc.

Developing Strategies

Play several games of *wari*. Take turns going first. While you are playing try different strategies for collecting as many stones as possible. Discuss your strategies. Which seem to work best? Do any of your strategies depend on whether you play first?

You may want to use an egg carton for your board. You may want to use dried beans or pumpkin seeds instead of stones.

Presenting Your Results

Give an oral report on this project to your class. Demonstrate the strategies you developed. Explain how they work and how you developed them.

You may want to extend your report to explore other ideas:

• Research and explore some of the variations of this game. Develop a strategy for winning a different version of the game. How does this new strategy compare with the strategy that you developed for *wari?*

• Research the history and directions for another game. Where and when was the game developed? Explore the game and develop a strategy for winning that game. Present your findings to your classmates. Some games you might research are *Go, Nim, Senet,* and *Nyout.*

Self-Assessment

What general advice would you give someone who is trying to develop strategies for winning a new game? How did you and your partner work together to develop strategies? Based on your experience playing wari, does the same strategy for winning always work? How do your partner's moves affect your strategy?

Senet

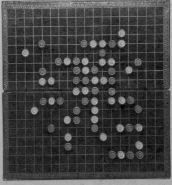

Go

Exploring the Possibilities

The average day presents many situations that call for choices. Various options and combinations present themselves. "Does the blue sweater go with this outfit?" "Would I rather have the entree with a baked potato or rice? And what type of dressing for the salad?" "Should I buy the two-door or the four-door model of this car?"

You can examine your options by writing them all down, but sometimes it helps to see the possibilities. By making a flip book, you can visualize all the combinations of choices.

PROJECT GOAL Make a flip book to show all the possibilities for a real-world situation involving choices.

Making Your Own Flip Book

Choose a real-world situation that has many options and where the options are divided into at least four categories. Make a flip book that displays every possible combination of the options. You will need a pad of paper, posterboard, and scissors.

The flip book below illustrates the choices for someone planning a dinner. Assemble your flip book in a similar manner.

1. USE a pad of paper or several sheets of paper stapled together.

2. DIVIDE the pad by cutting the paper so that there is a section for each category of options. Be sure to leave a border on the side where the sheets of paper are bound together.

Fruit and cheese platter	Roasted chicken	Rice pilaf	Strawberries
Appetizer	Entree	Side dish	Dessert

3. MOUNT the pad on posterboard and put the name of each category on the side opposite the binding.

4. DRAW pictures (or clip and paste photos from magazines) to illustrate the options for each category. Remove any unused pieces of paper.

Explorations and Projects Book, Copyright © McDougal Littell Inc.

Writing a Report

Write a report about your flip book. Consider these questions:

• How many different combinations of options does your flip book display? How do you know?

• What are the advantages and drawbacks of using a flip book to display options?

• How might other people, such as a police sketch artist, a landscaper, or a fashion designer, use a flip book? Can you think of other areas in which a flip book might be useful?

Extend your investigation by doing related projects that involve combinations. For example:

• Make drawings on strips of paper that you can put next to each other and slide back and forth to change, say, the expressions on a face or the clothes on a model.

• Make drawings on clear plastic overlays to explore options such as toppings on a pizza or disguises for a face.

• Create a colorful toy or game that a young child can play with to explore combinations.

Self-Assessment

Describe your understanding of combinations. In what ways do you feel that you are better able to recognize and examine situations involving choices?

PORTFOLIO PROJECT

A Matter of Taste

If you've ever gone grocery shopping, you know that generic foods are generally less expensive than their brand-name counterparts. However, many shoppers believe that "buying generic" means sacrificing quality. Is there really a difference? You can find out by doing some market research.

PROJECT GOAL Determine whether people can distinguish a generic beverage from one or more brand-name beverages.

Performing an Experiment

1. CHOOSE a beverage, such as cola or orange juice, that you want to test. Buy a generic version and one or more brand-name versions of the beverage.

2. FIND a person to survey. Have the person taste each beverage *without* letting him or her see the beverage containers. You may want to use small paper cups to hold beverage samples.

3. ASK the person to identify the generic beverage. Record whether the person is correct.

4. REPEAT Steps 2 and 3 with other people. You should survey a total of 20 people.

Explorations and Projects Book, Copyright © McDougal Littell Inc.

Evaluating Your Results

If the responses of the people you surveyed were totally random (that is, if the people were only guessing when they tried to identify the generic beverage), then the probability that r of the 20 people responded correctly is

$$P(r) = {}_{20}C_r \cdot p^r \cdot (1 - p)^{20 - r}$$

where p is the probability of a correct guess.

1. What kind of probability distribution does the formula for $P(r)$ determine?

2. What is the value of p for your experiment? How is this value related to the number of beverages you tested? Explain.

In a binomial experiment like this one (with more than just a few trials), the value of $P(r)$ is small for any value of r. So $P(r)$ alone is not a good indicator of the likelihood that the experiment's outcome is due to chance. A better indicator is the probability of getting *at least r* correct responses:

$$P(\text{at least } r) = P(r) + P(r + 1) + \cdots + P(20)$$

3. Calculate the value of $P(\text{at least } r)$ for the value of r from your experiment. Does this probability suggest that chance determined the outcome of the experiment? Explain your reasoning.

Being very cautious, scientists and mathematicians *presume* that chance determines the outcome of an experiment unless there is strong evidence to the contrary. In this case, "strong evidence" might mean that the value of $P(\text{at least } r)$ is less than 0.1 or even 0.05 (for extra-cautious types).

4. Given the requirement for strong evidence stated above, can you conclude that people really can distinguish the generic beverage from the brand-name beverage(s)?

Writing a Report

Write a report summarizing your results. Include the data from your experiment and your answers to the questions above. If you wish, you can extend your project by conducting a survey that compares generic and brand-name versions of a different product, such as peanut butter or paper towels.

Self-Assessment

After completing this project, how comfortable are you with the ideas of probability as they relate to a scientific experiment? What ideas do you understand well? What ideas are still unclear?

PORTFOLIO PROJECT

How High Is Up?

A surveyor can determine positions and elevations with the help of a tool called a *transit*, which can be used to measure angles. After taking some measurements, a surveyor uses trigonometry to calculate distances that would be impractical or impossible to measure directly.

In this project, you will make a type of transit. Then you will explore and evaluate two trigonometric methods of calculating the height of a tall object.

PROJECT GOAL Determine the height of a tall object using two trigonometric methods.

Making and Using a Transit

Work with a partner. You will need a protractor, a drinking straw, a piece of string, a small weight (such as a key or a washer), and masking tape. Assemble your transit as shown.

To measure the angle of elevation to some high point, view the point through the straw. Have your partner record the angle of elevation while you view the point.

For each of the following methods, you will need a tape measure.

Tape a straw to the base of a protractor.

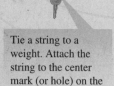

Tie a string to a weight. Attach the string to the center mark (or hole) on the base of the protractor.

The angle of elevation is equal to the measure of the angle formed by the string and the 90° mark.

Method 1: The Direct Approach

Choose a tall object whose height you wish to measure. Stand some distance away from the object, and look through your transit at the top of the object. Draw a diagram of the situation, and record your data on the diagram.

1. MEASURE and record the angle of elevation of the top of the object.

2. MEASURE and record your distance from the bottom of the object.

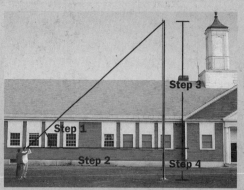

Step 1
Step 2
Step 3
Step 4

3. USE a trigonometric ratio to calculate the object's height above eye level.

4. ADD the height at eye level to the height in Step 3 to find the object's total height.

Explorations and Projects Book, Copyright © McDougal Littell Inc.

Method 2: The Indirect Approach

Even when it's not possible to measure the distance between observer and object, it's still possible to measure the height of the object. To do this, you must measure the angle of elevation from two points, *A* and *B*, that lie on a line running directly to the object. Draw a diagram like the one shown, and record your data on the diagram.

1. MEASURE and record the angle of elevation of the top of the object from each of points *A* and *B*.

2. MEASURE and record the distance between *A* and *B*.

3. CALCULATE the measure of ∠*ABC*.

4. CALCULATE the measure of ∠*ACB*.

5. USE the law of sines to find *BC*.

6. USE a trigonometric ratio to calculate *CD*, and add the height at eye level to find the total height of the object.

Writing a Report

Write a report summarizing your results. Include your data, calculations, and a completed diagram for each method used. Compare your results from the first and second methods, and try to account for any differences. Why might someone prefer to use one method rather than the other?

Here are some ideas for extending your project:

- Give a geometric argument to explain why the angle between the 90° mark on the protractor and the position of the string on your transit is the same as the angle of elevation.

- Apply the methods of this project to calculate the height of a tall object whose height is already known from some reliable source, and compare your results with the known height.

Self-Assessment

Describe any problems that you had completing the project. How well were you able to apply the trigonometric formulas needed to calculate some of the distances? What formulas, if any, still give you trouble?

PORTFOLIO PROJECT

Modeling Ups and Downs

Suppose a weight is attached to a spring, pulled down, and released. As you can see from the diagram below, the position of the weight as it moves up and down is a periodic function of time.

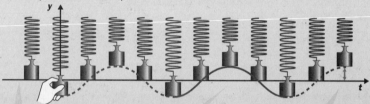

The line $y = 0$ represents the weight's **equilibrium position**, that is, its position before being pulled down and released.

One **oscillation** of the weight is one complete motion up and down.

The **amplitude** of the weight's motion is the maximum displacement of the weight from its equilibrium position.

The motion of the weight is an example of *simple harmonic motion*. An object undergoes simple harmonic motion if its displacement from its equilibrium position can be modeled by a function of the form

$$y = a \cos bt$$

where a and b are constants.

PROJECT GOAL   Use a cosine function to model the motion of a weight as it oscillates on a spring.

Experimenting with a Spring

Suspend a weight from a spring, and find an equation modeling the motion of the weight when it is pulled down and released. Work in a group of four students. Your group will need a spring, a paper clip, some masking tape, a 1 lb weight, some string, a meterstick, and a stopwatch.

1. BEND a paper clip and tape it to the edge of a desk. Hook one end of the spring to the paper clip and use string to tie the weight to the other end.

2. TAPE the meterstick next to the spring and weight as shown.

Explorations and Projects Book, Copyright © McDougal Littell Inc.

3. STRETCH the spring some distance *d*, using the meterstick to measure the distance stretched.

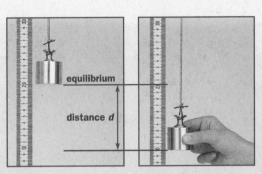

equilibrium

distance *d*

4. RELEASE the weight and use the stopwatch to measure the time it takes the weight to complete five oscillations. Divide this time by 5 to calculate the time of one oscillation.

5. REPEAT Step 4 two more times using the same stretch distance *d*. Find *T*, the average of your three oscillation times.

Modeling Oscillation

1. What is the relationship between your values of *d* and *T* and the values of *a* and *b* in the equation $y = a \cos bt$?

2. Write an equation of the form $y = a \cos bt$ for the oscillating weight.

3. Graph your equation from Question 2, and use your graph to predict the time required for the weight to complete four oscillations. Test your prediction.

4. What does your equation assume about the amplitude of the oscillating weight as time passes? Do you think this assumption is accurate?

Writing a Report

Write a report about your experiment. Describe your procedures, and present your data and the equation of your model. Also include these items:

- a graph of your model

- a comparison of your model with your experimental results

- an evaluation of your model's strengths and weaknesses

An equation of the form $y = ae^{-kt} \cos bt$ (where $k > 0$) more accurately models the weight's displacement as a function of time. This is because the factor e^{-kt} *damps*, or decreases, the amplitude of the oscillations as time passes. You can extend your report by finding an equation of the form $y = ae^{-kt} \cos bt$ for your oscillating weight.

Self-Assessment

Describe your understanding of the usefulness of trigonometric functions in modeling. What is it about the graphs of these functions that makes them useful? What are some other types of situations that might be modeled by trigonometric functions?

Algebra 1 Explorations
Teacher Notes

Algebra 1 Exploration 1 Note

Purpose
The purpose of this Exploration is to have students discover what happens to a number as it is multiplied by itself repeatedly.

Materials/Preparation
Each group should have a sufficient amount of rice to fill at least the first five squares of a chessboard.

Procedure
Before beginning, make sure that each pair of students knows how to use the exponent key on a calculator. Students should record their answers to each step.

Closure
Groups can share their results with each other. All students should arrive at an understanding that a whole number multiplied by itself repeatedly increases very rapidly.

Algebra 1 Exploration 2 Note

Purpose
The purpose of this Exploration is to have students understand why an order of operations is needed.

Materials/Preparation
Students should have as many different types of calculators available as possible.

Procedure
Before beginning, make sure that each pair of students has two different calculators and that one of the calculators has parentheses keys. Students should record their answers to each step.

Closure
Groups can share their answers and results with each other. All students should arrive at an understanding that when simplifying a numerical expression, an order of operations is essential so that the expression has only one value.

Algebra 1 Exploration 3 Note

Purpose
The purpose of the Exploration is to have students discover a number pattern and then relate that pattern to a variable expression.

Materials/Preparation
Each group of two students should have 30 or more toothpicks.

Procedure
Students should copy the table shown in the Set Up. Using all of their toothpicks, students should make as many triangles as they can. Using their triangles, they can then extend the table.

Closure
Discuss the answers to all three questions. In particular, students should discuss question 3 in detail so they are sure they understand the meaning of the variable expression needed to make *n* triangles.

Explorations and Projects Book, Copyright © McDougal Littell Inc.

Algebra 1 Exploration 4 Note

Purpose

The purpose of this Exploration is to have students learn how to write an algorithm, in this case, one that explains how to sit down in a chair.

Materials/Preparation

Students should first choose a chair. The algorithms for sitting in an armchair, a straight-back chair without arms, or a chair that is attached to a desk would be slightly different.

Procedure

Students should number each step in their algorithm. As one student in the group fol-lows the algorithm, have another student check off each step completed successfully. Students should begin revising their algorithm at the first step that did not receive a checkmark.

Closure

Discuss the similarities and differences in the different algorithms. Ask students which algorithm they think gives the best instructions in the least number of steps.

Algebra 1 Exploration 5 Note

Purpose

The purpose of this Exploration is to explore the concept of probability by conducting an experiment of rolling a die 24 times.

Materials/Preparation

You may wish to organize students into groups of six. Each group of students should have one die and a place where they can roll it and record their results. Alternatively, students can use the *Probability Constructor* software to simulate the experiment.

Procedure

Students in each group should take turns rolling the die. One student can be chosen to draw the group's graph and show it to the other groups. If students are working in groups of six, each student can be responsible for finding the ratio for a particular number on the face of the die.

Closure

Students should understand that each number has the same probability of occurring on any one roll of the die and that this probability is approached as more rolls are made.

Algebra 1 Exploration 6 Note

Purpose

The purpose of the Exploration is to use algebra tiles to help students see the steps involved in solving two-step equations.

Materials/Preparation

Each group should have at least five *x*-tiles and twenty 1-tiles in order to solve equations 1–4.

Procedure

Students should first solve the equation $2x + 3 = 11$ by following the steps shown. Then they can solve equations 1–4.

Closure

Volunteer groups can demonstrate their solutions to equations 1–4 and answer questions from their classmates.

Algebra 1 Exploration 7 Note

Purpose

The purpose of this Exploration is to introduce students to the idea of graphing the coordinates that make an equation true. Students see that the solutions to this equation form a straight line.

Materials/Preparation

Students should be arranged in class as shown. If any students are absent, or a desk has not been assigned to a student, move other students to fill those positions. In other words, every position in the grid should be occupied by a student.

Procedure

You can begin by asking each student to state verbally his or her coordinates. Then follow Steps 2 and 3. Other equations you can use are $y = x + 1$, $y = -x - 1$, and $y = -x + 1$. After each equation is used, ask students what they see about the people standing up.

Closure

Ask students to describe what they have learned through this Exploration about graphing equations.

Algebra 1 Exploration 8 Note

Purpose

The purpose of this Exploration is to have students explore a direct variation situation and to write an equation to describe it.

Materials/Preparation

Each group needs one meterstick and graph paper or a graphing calculator.

Procedure

Students should record their data in a table. They may use calculators to express ratios as decimals. Suggest that all decimals be rounded to the nearest hundredth. Groups should compare their results and discuss what they have found.

Closure

Ask students if they think that regardless of how many people were used, the ratio of kneeling height of a person is $\frac{3}{4}$ the person's standing height.

Algebra 1 Exploration 9 Note

Purpose

The purpose of this Exploration is to help students discover that the graph of an equation in the form $y = mx + b$ has slope m and y-intercept b.

Materials/Preparation

Before students begin graphing, help them choose the *standard window* from the ZOOM menu.

Procedure

As students work with their partners, one person should write down the answers to each activity. In Step 3, students can check their predictions by drawing a graph of $y = 2x + 6$. In Step 4, they should make up an equation in the form $y = mx + b$ and graph it.

Closure

Ask pairs of partners to share their results. You can then have a whole-class discussion of the fact that the graph of $y = mx + b$ has slope m and y-intercept b. Some students may also discover that equations with the same value for m but different values for b have graphs that are parallel lines.

Explorations and Projects Book, Copyright © McDougal Littell Inc.

Algebra 1 Exploration 10 Note

Purpose
The purpose of this Exploration is to have students gather data from a simple experiment and model it by a linear equation. The equation is then used to make a prediction.

Materials/Preparation
After students are organized into groups, provide each group with the materials listed.

Procedure
Discuss briefly the sequence of steps students are to follow. For best results, suggest that students add the marbles to the cup

gently. Discuss why dropping the marbles into the cup from too great a height is not a good idea.

Closure
Groups can compare their data and the equations they obtained. Ask if their results are different in any major way. If so, they should try to explain why this is the case.

Algebra 1 Exploration 11 Note

Purpose
The purpose of this Exploration is to have students discover how to find and graph the solutions to an inequality.

Materials/Preparation
Each pair of students should have colored pencils and a ruler.

Procedure
Students should circle *all* points where grid lines intersect that are solutions of the inequality and discuss what they notice.

Closure
Have a class discussion of the results of this Exploration. Students should notice that the region of the coordinate plane shaded in color shows all points on the line $x - y = 1$ and all points *below* the line.

Algebra 1 Exploration 12 Note

Purpose
The purpose of this Exploration is to introduce students to the concept of a weighted average.

Materials/Preparation
Plastic cups and bowls can eliminate the possibility of accidental breakage. If more than one group is doing the Exploration at the same time, it would be desirable for each group to have the same size cups and bowls to facilitate a discussion and comparison of results.

Procedure
One student in each group should be assigned the task of recording the results. All students should compute their own average.

Closure
Discuss why the computation in Step 4 gives a better way of comparing the players' aims than the computation in Step 3. Be sure students understand that a higher average means a better aim.

Algebra 1 Exploration 13 Note

Purpose
The purpose of this Exploration is to have students use tables and graphs to explore and solve the same problem in order to have them compare and contrast the two methods.

Materials/Preparation
Have graphing calculators or graph paper available for the groups to use.

Procedure
Each team uses a table or a graph to decide whether it is more economical to buy CDs through a club or at a discount store. Each team should work independently on its table or graph. Some teams may need help in writing the equation for Step 5.

Closure
After Step 9 has been completed, all groups should participate in a general discussion about using tables or graphs to compare cost options. Students should conclude that either a table or a graph may be used as a problem-solving strategy and understand the advantages and disadvantages of each method.

Algebra 1 Exploration 14 Note

The purpose of this Exploration is to have students discover how to solve a system of equations by using multiplication.

Materials/Preparation
Each member of a group should have two or three pieces of graph paper and a ruler. Allow students to organize themselves into groups.

Procedure
Group members should agree in advance on the scales for the x- and y-axes. This will make it easier to compare their graphs.

Closure
Groups should compare their results and discuss how they can be used to solve systems of equations.

Algebra 1 Exploration 15 Note

Purpose
The purpose of this Exploration is to have students study a pattern in order to determine a rule for multiplying and dividing expressions involving powers.

Materials/Preparation
Each group should have a calculator. You may wish to have students review the procedures for entering exponents and for displaying numbers in scientific notation on their calculators.

Procedure
Students should look for a relationship between the exponents of the numbers being multiplied or divided and the exponent of the corresponding product or quotient.

Closure
Students should see that the rules they wrote are a shortcut method for multiplying and dividing powers having the same base.

Algebra 1 Exploration 16 Note

Purpose

The purpose of this Exploration is to have students understand how certain radical expressions can be written in simpler form.

Materials/Preparation

Each pair of students should have a sheet of graph paper with squares that are large enough for the drawing activity. Centimeter grid paper would serve this purpose.

Procedure

Suggest that students make a table to show the two ways of expressing the length of the hypotenuse of each triangle.

Closure

Call on several partners to describe their results to the class. Discuss the patterns observed in Step 3 of the activity. All students should be able to answer the questions in Step 4 correctly.

 ## Algebra 1 Exploration 17 Note

Purpose

The purpose of this Exploration is to have students discover that a relationship between two variables can be nonlinear.

Materials/Preparation

Each group should have graph paper and a graphing calculator.

Procedure

Groups should complete the table in Step 1 and answer the questions in Step 2. Then one student in each group can be in charge of drawing the graphs for Steps 3 and 4.

Closure

After completing Step 4, groups can share their results with each other. The class should conclude that the graph of the area of a rectangle as a function of the length of a side is not a straight line.

 ## Algebra 1 Exploration 18 Note

Purpose

The purpose of this Exploration is to have students explore equations of the form $y = ax^2$ to see what happens to the graphs as a increases from 0 to 1 and beyond and decreases from 0 to −1 and beyond.

Materials/Preparation

Each group needs graph paper and a graphing calculator.

Procedure

Students graph parabolas and make predictions about the graphs of $y = ax^2$. Students should discuss their generalizations in Steps 5 and 6 to verify them. Students should

understand that changing the viewing window on a calculator changes the appearance of the parabola being graphed but not the actual parabola.

Closure

Groups can share results with each other. They should conclude that the graph of $y = ax^2$ gets wider as |a| decreases and narrower as |a| increases. If a is positive, the graph opens up. If a is negative, the graph opens down.

Algebra 1 Exploration 19 Note

Purpose
The purpose of this Exploration is to have students use algebra tiles to find the product of two algebraic expressions.

Materials/Preparation
Each pair of partners will need at least 4 x^2-tiles, 12 x-tiles, and 11 1-tiles.

Procedure
Mention to students that it is important to make sure the lines they draw are perpendicular. Also, they should be careful in marking off the dimensions $2x$ and $x + 3$.

Closure
Have students share with the class their ideas about how to find a correct arrangement of the tiles. Explore with students how they might find the products $2x(x + 3)$ and $3x(x + 2)$ without using algebra tiles.

Algebra 1 Exploration 20 Note

Purpose
The purpose of this Exploration is to have students build a box from a rectangular piece of paper and write polynomial expressions for its dimensions.

Materials/Preparation
Each group should have a ruler and rectangular pieces of paper that are not square.

Procedure
Each group of students first folds a rectangular piece of paper into 16 equal parts and then folds it again in different ways to form a box. Groups then unfold their boxes and write expressions for the length, width, and height of the box in terms of the variable x. Students then compare their box dimensions within their groups and discuss how they are alike and how they are different.

Closure
Groups can share their results with each other. Students should conclude that if the corners of an a in. by b in. piece of paper are folded up x units to make a box, its new dimensions are x, $a - 2x$, and $b - 2x$.

Algebra 1 Exploration 21 Note

Purpose
The purpose of this Exploration is to have students discover the relationship between the factored form of a polynomial equation and the x-intercepts of its graph in terms of finding solutions when the equation equals 0.

Materials/Preparation
Students should have a graphing calculator.

Procedure
Students graph polynomials in standard form and in factored form. They then match the equations that have the same graph. Students look at the factored form of an equation and tell how the x-intercepts of the graph are relat-ed to the factors. Have students use the Zoom 8:ZInteger feature for each graph so that tracing gives exact values for the x-intercepts.

Closure
Students should realize the x-intercepts of the graph of the polynomial function are the numbers that make each factor of the factored form equal to 0 and that these numbers represent the solutions of the equation when it equals 0.

Explorations and Projects Book, Copyright © McDougal Littell Inc.

Algebra 1 Exploration 22 Note

Purpose
The purpose of this Exploration is to have students discover how to use a pair of ratios to estimate quantities that are difficult to count.

Materials/Preparation
You may wish to ask students to bring their own cans and dried beans to school if they are not available in the classroom. All groups should begin their work at the same time.

Procedure
As students work through Steps 1–4, one partner should have the responsibility of recording the number of beans marked in Steps 2 and 4. The other partner can record the answers to the questions.

Closure
Ask students to write a brief description of the procedure they used to estimate the number of beans in the can. Students should understand how a sample of beans allows them to estimate the total number of beans in the can. Ask students why they think this method is called the capture-recapture method.

 ## Algebra 1 Exploration 23 Note

Purpose
The purpose of this Exploration is to have students use rectangles with a constant area to discover the graph and equation for inverse variation.

Materials/Preparation
Each pair of partners needs graph paper and 36 algebra unit tiles.

Procedure
Students should record the dimensions of their rectangles as they form them. Students should then graph the data pairs and answer questions 4–6, adjusting their graphs as necessary.

Closure
Students should understand that if the area of a rectangle is a constant, then the length and width have an inverse relationship, that is, as one increases, the other decreases. Students should also come to the conclusion that this relationship is not linear.

 ## Algebra 1 Exploration 24 Note

Purpose
The purpose of this Exploration is to have students discover a pattern for subtracting successive unit fractions and then to extend that pattern to subtract successive rational expressions with numerators of 1.

Materials/Preparation
Each student should have his or her own ruler and graph paper.

Procedure
Partners should first study the diagram and understand what it shows. Then they can complete Step 2 and answer the questions.

Closure
Students should come to the conclusion that the same procedures used to subtract fractions can be used to subtract rational expressions. You may wish to ask students if they think this applies to addition as well.

Algebra 1 Exploration 25 Note

Purpose

The purpose of this Exploration is to have students discover the properties of similar triangles.

Materials/Preparation

Each group should have all the materials listed. Students may need a review of measuring angles with a protractor.

Procedure

Make sure students label their triangles correctly. Suggest that different groups fold along different parallel lines.

Closure

Have students discuss their results for questions 1–4. Because of measuring inaccuracies, not all students will have equal measures for corresponding angles or equal ratios for corresponding sides. By examining all the results, however, students should understand that corresponding angles of similar triangles have the same measure and that the three ratios of the pairs of corresponding sides are all equal.

Explorations and Projects Book, Copyright © McDougal Littell Inc.

Algebra 1 Projects
Teacher Notes

Project Notes

Mathematical Goals

- Collect and organize data using a spreadsheet or table.
- Calculate a percent of change in the data.
- Display the percent of change results in a graph.

Planning

Materials

- Newspapers, magazines, or almanac
- Graph paper

Project Teams

Students can choose a partner to work with and then discuss how they wish to proceed.

Guiding Students' Work

Suggest that each partner research at least two statistics and calculate their percent of change. Each student should calculate his or her own percent of change. One partner can then make the graph showing their results visually, while the other partner begins to write a report or make a poster. Both partners should work to complete this analysis of their results and participate in explaining their results.

Second-Language Learners

Students learning English may not be familiar with the term "in-line skaters." Explain that in-line skates are a specific kind of rollerskate with three to four wheels, one behind the other, or "in-line."

Rubric for Chapter 2 Project

4 Students collect four statistics and calculate their percents of change correctly. They make an accurate graph that clearly shows which quantities increased or decreased. The written analysis includes all six items listed under *Remember to*, and is well organized and easy to read.

3 Students collect their statistics and compute the percents of change accurately. Their graphs present the results correctly. Their presentation, however, has a few flaws and is incomplete in at least one of the ways listed under *Remember to*.

Explorations and Projects Book, Copyright © McDougal Littell Inc.

2 Students collect four statistics but make a mathematical mistake in calculating a percent of change. Their graph does not show clearly which quantities increased and which decreased. Their final report is not well organized, contains some errors or omissions, and is difficult to understand.

1 Students fail to collect all four statistics and do not calculate the percents of change correctly. No graphs are made or those made are poorly done. A final analysis is attempted but falls short in explaining the results. Students should be encouraged to speak with the teacher as soon as possible to review their work and to make a new start on the project.

For the Student

Rubric for Chapter 2 Project

4 You collect four statistics and calculate the percents of change correctly. You make an accurate graph that clearly shows which quantities increased or decreased. Your written analysis includes all six items listed under *Remember to*, and is well organized and easy to read.

3 You collect four statistics and compute the percents of change accurately. Your graphs present the results correctly. Your presentation, however, has a few flaws and is incomplete in at least one of the ways listed under *Remember to*.

2 You collect four statistics but make a mathematical mistake in calculating a percent of change. Your graph does not show clearly which quantities increased and which decreased. Your final report is not well organized, contains some errors or omissions, and is difficult to understand.

1 You fail to collect all four statistics and do not calculate the percents of change correctly. You do not make a graph or the one that you do make is not very well done. Your final analysis falls short in explaining the results. You should speak with your teacher as soon as possible to review your work and to make a new start on the project.

Project Notes

Mathematical Goals

- Collect data that represent a function.
- Graph the data.
- Describe the domain and range of the function.

Planning

Materials

- Graph paper
- Books or magazines

Project Teams

Students should choose a partner to work with and discuss which event they would like to investigate and how they can divide up the work.

Guiding Students' Work

You may wish to begin this project by having the whole class brainstorm things that change over time. Then each pair of students can discuss further what they wish to investigate. As students choose an event to investigate, you can check with each group to see that their event is easy to measure. This will ensure that all groups get off to a good start. Students should complete all aspects of the project as a team and decide for themselves how to divide up the work.

Second-Language Learners

A peer tutor or aide might help students learning English discuss and organize their ideas for the presentation or written report.

Rubric for Chapter 4 Project

4 Students investigate a function and record their data accurately. They make a neatly drawn graph that correctly represents the data. Their presentation of ideas explains the graph, describes what they observed, and correctly describes the domain and range of their function. They use library sources to find other data to compare with the data they investigated. Their final report is interesting and well organized.

3 Students complete their collection of data and present the data accurately in a graph. They identify a pattern and work together to present their ideas. Some details of the final report are not entirely satisfactory. For example, the title of the graph may not be clear or the graph may be labeled incorrectly.

 Explorations and Projects Book, Copyright © McDougal Littell Inc.

2 Students' data are somewhat incomplete and so is their graph. A pattern is difficult to see. A report is prepared, but it has some serious omissions and errors. For example, the domain and the range of the function are identified incorrectly. The report, poster, or oral presentation is not well organized and shows a lack of serious effort.

1 Students collect some data, but they do not exhibit a pattern. A graph is attempted but is drawn incorrectly. No attempt is made to explain the graph in a final report. Students should be encouraged to speak with the teacher as soon as possible to review their work and to make a new start on the project.

For the Student

Rubric for Chapter 4 Project

4 You investigate a function and record your data accurately. You make a neatly drawn graph that correctly represents the data. Your presentation of ideas explains the graph, describes what you observed, and correctly describes the domain and range of your function. You use library sources to find other data to compare with the data you investigated. Your final report is interesting and well organized.

3 You complete your collection of data and present the data accurately in a graph. You identify a pattern and work together to present your ideas. However, some details of your final report are not entirely satisfactory. For example, the title of your graph may not be clear or the graph may be labeled incorrectly.

2 Your data are somewhat incomplete and so is your graph. The pattern in the data is difficult to see. A report is prepared, but it has some omissions and errors. For example, the domain and the range of the function may not be identified correctly. Your report, poster, or oral presentation is not well organized.

1 You collect some data, but the data do not exhibit a pattern. Your graph is drawn incorrectly and no attempt is made to explain the graph in a final report. You should speak with your teacher as soon as possible to review your work and to make a new start on the project.

Mathematical Goals

- Write an equation of a line in slope-intercept form.
- Write an inequality for a line segment that identifies its endpoints.

Planning

Materials

- Graph paper
- Loose-leaf notebook

Project Teams

For teams as large as five or six students, you should work with the class to help organize the groups. Students having a mix of abilities working together can be advantageous to the development of the project goal.

Guiding Students' Work

All students should participate in each activity involved in creating a book of linear puzzles, following Steps 1–3. You can circulate among the groups and provide help to individual students as needed. As students check their work, they should feel free to discuss what they are doing with other group members. To assemble their puzzle book, each group should discuss who will do the different tasks and then organize the work accordingly.

Second-Language Learners

Students learning English may benefit from working with an English-proficient partner to plan their instructions for solving and creating puzzles.

Rubric for Chapter 5 Project

4 Students create shapes and write correct equations in slope-intercept form for each line in their design. The inequalities that describe the endpoints of each line segment are also correct. Students check their work and assemble their puzzle book. The book is clearly organized, the puzzles and their solutions are accurate, and the names of the puzzle designers, instructions for solving, and an answer key are included.

3 Students proceed to create shapes for their puzzles, write equations for each line segment, and write inequalities that describe the endpoints. In checking their work, not all mathematics errors are found and corrected. A puzzle book is assembled, but there are some mistakes in the answer key.

   Explorations and Projects Book, Copyright © McDougal Littell Inc.

2 Students have some difficulties getting started. Not all members of the group can write correct equations in slope-intercept form or correct inequalities. Group members work together to help one another, but the final puzzle book has some serious mathematical errors.

1 Students do not always follow the instructions for designing their puzzles. Some drawings do not have endpoints that are on grid intersections. Many equations and inequalities are wrong. The checking procedure is incomplete and the puzzle book does not include instructions for solving the puzzles or an answer key. Students should be encouraged to speak with the teacher as soon as possible to review their work and to make a new start on the project.

For the Student

Rubric for Chapter 5 Project

4 You create shapes and write correct equations in slope-intercept form for each line in your design. The inequalities that describe the endpoints of each line segment are also correct. You check your work and assemble your puzzle book. The book is clearly organized, the puzzles and your solutions are accurate, and the names of the puzzle designers, instructions for solving, and an answer key are included.

3 You proceed to create shapes for your puzzles, write equations for each line segment, and write inequalities that describe the endpoints. In checking your work, however, not all mathematics errors are found and corrected. A puzzle book is assembled, but there are some mistakes in the answer key.

2 Your group has some difficulties getting started, and not all members can write correct equations in slope-intercept form or correct inequalities. Group members work together to help one another, but your final puzzle book has a number of mathematical errors.

1 You do not always follow the instructions for designing your puzzles. Some drawings do not have endpoints that are on grid intersections. A large number of equations and inequalities are wrong. Your checking procedure is incomplete and your puzzle book does not include instructions for solving the puzzles or an answer key. You should speak with your teacher as soon as possible to review your work and to make a new start on the project.

Project Notes

Mathematical Goals

- Calculate expenses and income for making a batch of cookies.
- Use a table and graph to model expenses and income as functions of the number of batches sold.
- Use the table and graph to find the point at which a profit is made.
- Write and solve an inequality to find the point at which a profit is made.

Planning

Materials

- Cookie recipe
- Graph paper
- Writing paper

Project Teams

Allow students to choose their own partners. They should then read the project's goal and decide how they want to proceed.

Guiding Students' Work

Suggest that each student bring one cookie recipe to class. You may also wish to have a few recipes available for use by students who cannot find their own. Students can share the cost of a bag of sugar, but they should determine themselves the number of cups per bag. Students should share evenly the other tasks involved in doing the project. For example, one student can make a table while the partner creates the graph. Both students should write parts of the final report.

Second-Language Learners

Students learning English may benefit from working with a peer tutor to plan, write, and refine their report and their self-assessment paragraph.

Rubric for Chapter 6 Project 1

4 Students calculate their expenses and income accurately and charge a reasonable price for their cookies. They construct correct tables and graphs and determine their profit-making point. They are successful in writing and solving an inequality that also finds the profit-making point. The final report includes all the features listed in the text and is clearly organized, well written, and interesting to read.

3 Students complete the initial activities involving the financial plans and analysis of data correctly. Their final report, however, has a few minor errors and is incomplete in some way, for example, the discussion of the decisions made concerning ingredients, labor costs, and pricing.

2 Students complete all of the activities, but some errors and misconceptions permeate the entire project. Their table or graph does not clearly show the profit-making point. They do not write an inequality to show another method of finding the profit-making point. The final written report is hastily written and has some serious omissions.

1 Students start the project but are confused about how to set a price to make a profit. Their table and graph reflect this confusion and no profit-making point is determined. They cannot write a correct inequality and no report is attempted. Students should be encouraged to speak with the teacher as soon as possible to review their work and to make a new start on the project.

For the Student

Rubric for Chapter 6 Project 1

4 You calculate your expenses and income accurately and charge a reasonable price for your cookies. You construct correct tables and graphs and determine your profit-making point. You are successful in writing and solving an inequality that also finds the profit-making point. Your final report includes all the features listed in the text and is clearly organized, well written, and interesting to read.

3 You complete the initial activities involving the financial plans and analysis of data correctly. Your final report, however, has a few minor errors and is incomplete in some way, for example, the discussion of the decisions made concerning ingredients, labor costs, and pricing.

2 You complete all of the activities, but there are some errors and misconceptions throughout the project. Your table or graph does not clearly show the profit-making point. You do not write an inequality to show another method of finding the profit-making point. Your final report is hastily written and has a number of omissions.

1 You start the project but are not sure about how to set a price to make a profit. Your table and graph reflect this confusion and no profit-making point is determined. You do not write a correct inequality and your report is not very clear or informative. You should speak with your teacher as soon as possible to review your work and to make a new start on the project.

Mathematical Goals

- Collect riser and tread data for at least five different stairways and decide on an ideal riser/tread ratio.

- Design a stairway and make a scale drawing of it.

- Make a graph that shows all the riser/tread data collected and that meets the generally accepted rules for stairway construction.

Planning

Materials

- Ruler
- Graph paper

Project Teams

Students can choose a partner to work with and then discuss how they wish to proceed.

Guiding Students' Work

Suggest that students collect their riser and tread data in different public buildings, apartment houses, schools, homes, and so on. This will ensure a variety of data. Students should then work together to carry out the goals of the project.

Second-Language Learners

Students learning English may benefit from a conference with an aide or peer tutor after they complete the first draft of their report.

Rubric for Chapter 6 Project 2

4 Students collect their data, decide on an ideal riser/tread ratio, and design their own stairway. They graph the data that meet the generally accepted rules for stairway construction and the data collected for the project. They present their results in a report that includes their graph, table, and scale drawing. They give their recommendations for riser/tread ratios. All work is accurate and the report is well organized, clearly written, and interesting to read. There are no mathematical errors in the report.

3 Students complete all aspects of the project and present their results in a report. Overall, the work is well done with some minor exceptions. The graphs, for example, are not entirely clear or the scale drawing could have been drawn better. The paragraph comparing local stairways' dimensions with the accepted rules for stairs is somewhat hard to understand.

2 Students design a stairway, analyze stairway standards, and present their results in a report. Most of the work is carelessly done and shows little effort. There are errors in the scale drawing and the graphs of the four inequalities. The report is incomplete and poorly written.

1 Students collect some data and decide on an ideal riser/tread ratio but cannot satisfactorily design their own stairway nor graph the data they collected. A report is attempted but is not completed. Students should be encouraged to speak with the teacher as soon as possible to review their work and to make a new start on the project.

For the Student

Rubric for Chapter 6 Project 2

4 You collect your data, decide on an ideal riser/tread ratio, and design your own stairway. You graph the data that meet the generally accepted rules for stairway construction and the data collected for the project. You present your results in a report that includes your graph, table, and scale drawing. You give your recommendations for riser/tread ratios. All work is accurate and the report is well organized, clearly written, and interesting to read. There are no mathematical errors in the report.

3 You complete all aspects of the project and present your results in a report. Overall, the work is well done with some minor exceptions. The graphs, for example, are not entirely clear or the scale drawing could have been drawn better. The paragraph comparing local stairways' dimensions with the accepted rules for stairs is somewhat hard to understand.

2 You design a stairway, analyze stairway standards, and present your results in a report. Most of the work, however, is not well done. There are errors in the scale drawing and the graphs of the four inequalities. Your report is incomplete and not well written.

1 You collect some data and decide on an ideal riser/tread ratio but do not satisfactorily design your own stairway nor graph the data you collected. A report is attempted but is not completed. You should speak with your teacher as soon as possible to review your work and to make a new start on the project.

Project Notes

Mathematical Goals

- Measure the distance d_1 in millimeters from the center of the spiral in a nautilus shell to the outside corner of the first chamber.

- Calculate the ratio of the distance for each chamber to the distance for the previous chamber.

- Calculate the mean, r, of the ratios found.

- Substitute values found for d_1 and r into the equation $d_n = d_1 \cdot r^n$ to create an equation for d_n.

Planning

Materials

- Photograph of a nautilus shell
- Ruler
- Graph paper
- Protractor

Project Teams

Students can choose partners to work with and then discuss how they wish to proceed.

Guiding Students' Work

Suggest that students try to find a photograph of a nautilus shell to bring to class. Make sure they understand what measurements they should make and what ratios they are to calculate, and that they are to organize their results in a table or spreadsheet. You may wish to show students having difficulties creating their equation for d_n how to do this. Each student should finish the project by creating his or her own spiral.

Rubric for Chapter 8 Project

4 Students bring a photograph of a nautilus shell to class. They make the appropriate measurements and accurately calculate the necessary ratios. They also create an equation for d_n, make a scatter plot of their data, and graph their equation with the scatter plot. They accurately describe their results. Each partner creates a spiral following Steps 1–5. The spiral looks natural. Students answer the questions following Step 5 fully and correctly.

3 Students work through all aspects of the project and their work is generally accurate and well done. Some students have difficulty in actually creating their own spirals. Their spirals do not look fully natural with a smooth curve connecting all the points. The questions following Step 5 are answered correctly.

2 Students' measurements are not as accurate as they could be. Their ratios are not representative of the shell measured. The equation they create gives calculated values for d_n that are not very close to the distances measured. Students create their own spirals, but they are not very natural looking. The curve connecting all the points is a series of line segments that are not smooth.

1 Students start the project by making measurements and calculating ratios. Many errors are made in both the measurements and the calculations. An equation is created, but it does not give values close to those measured. Students cannot create their own spirals. Students should be encouraged to speak with the teacher as soon as possible to review their work and to make a new start on the project.

For the Student

Rubric for Chapter 8 Project

4 You bring a photograph of a nautilus shell to class. You make the appropriate measurements and accurately calculate the necessary ratios. You also create an equation for d_n, make a scatter plot of your data, and graph your equation with the scatter plot. You accurately describe your results. Each partner creates a spiral following Steps 1–5. The spiral looks natural. You answer the questions following Step 5 fully and correctly.

3 You work through all aspects of the project and your work is generally accurate and well done. You have some difficulty in actually creating your own spirals. Your spirals do not look fully natural with a smooth curve connecting all the points. The questions following Step 5 are answered correctly.

2 Your measurements are not as accurate as they could be. Your ratios are not representative of the shell measured. The equation you create gives calculated values for d_n that are not very close to the distances measured. You create your own spirals, but they are not very natural looking. The curve connecting all the points is a series of line segments that are not smooth.

1 You start the project by making measurements and calculating ratios. However, there are errors in both the measurements and the calculations. An equation is created, but it does not give values close to those measured. You do not create your own spirals. You should speak with your teacher as soon as possible to review your work and to make a new start on the project.

Mathematical Goals

- Collect data on how long it takes a ball to reach the end of a ramp that forms a 10° angle with the floor.

- Make a scatter plot of the data.

- Use the equation $d = 0.61t^2$ to calculate how long it would take a ball to roll 55 cm.

Planning

Materials

- Two meter sticks
- Tape
- Protractor
- Solid heavy ball or marble
- Stopwatch
- Graph paper

Project Teams

Students should choose their own partners and collect the materials they need to do the project.

Guiding Students' Work

Suggest that students share all aspects of collecting their data, drawing graphs, and writing the report. Help groups to locate places in the classroom where they can work without interfering with other groups. As the ball rolls down the ramp, one student in each group should be responsible to see that it is stopped after leaving the ramp.

Second-Language Learners

Students learning English may have difficulty understanding the sentence *Since Earth is the biggest thing around, it pulls objects (like skiers) toward it.* Explain to students that since Earth has a greater mass than any other object on it, all other objects are drawn to its surface.

Rubric for Chapter 9 Project

4 Students follow the key steps stated in the text to collect their data. They make an accurate scatter plot of the data, use the formula $d = 0.61t^2$ to calculate how long it would take a ball to roll 55 cm, and compare this value to the one estimated by using their scatter plot. They then sketch a graph of the equation $d = 0.61t^2$ and compare it to their scatter plot. All calculations and graphs are accurate and explanations are clear and correct. A complete and well-written report summarizes the experiment and states the relationship between distance and time correctly.

3 Students collect their data, make the necessary plots, calculations, and graphs, and write a report of their work. Each aspect of the work is done correctly, but the graphs could have been drawn more neatly and the description of the procedure in the report is too brief. Students describe the relationship between distance and time correctly.

2 Students complete the experiment by collecting their data, drawing and comparing graphs, and writing a report. The differences in the estimate value from the scatter plot and the calculated value from the equation $d = 0.61t^2$ for a ball to roll 55 cm are hard to reconcile.

1 Students set up their ramps but do not record the time and distance for ten starting points accurately. The scatter plot of the data is not representative of the real situation. Students have difficulty comparing their results to those given by the formula $d = 0.61t^2$. A report is not written. Students should be encouraged to speak with the teacher as soon as possible to review their work and to make a new start on the project.

For the Student

Rubric for Chapter 9 Project

4 You follow the key steps stated in the text to collect your data. You make an accurate scatter plot of the data, use the formula $d = 0.61t^2$ to calculate how long it would take a ball to roll 55 cm, and compare this value to the one estimated by using your scatter plot. You then sketch a graph of the equation $d = 0.61t^2$ and compare it to your scatter plot. All calculations and graphs are accurate and explanations are clear and correct. A complete and well-written report summarizes the experiment and states the relationship between distance and time correctly.

3 You collect your data, make the necessary plots, calculations, and graphs, and write a report of your work. Each aspect of the work is done correctly, but the graphs could have been drawn more neatly and your description of the procedure in the report is too brief. You describe the relationship between distance and time correctly.

2 You complete the experiment by collecting your data, drawing and comparing graphs, and writing a report. The differences in the estimate value from your scatter plot and the calculated value from the equation $d = 0.61t^2$ for a ball to roll 55 cm are hard to reconcile, however.

1 You set up your ramps but do not record the time and distance for ten starting points accurately. Your scatter plot of the data is not representative of the real situation. You have difficulty comparing your results to those given by the formula $d = 0.61t^2$. You should speak with your teacher as soon as possible to review your work and to make a new start on the project.

Project Notes

Mathematical Goals

- Measure the volume of water displaced by a model of a doll or an action figure and convert the volume to liters.
- Calculate the scale factor s of a person's height to the model's height.
- Calculate the volume of the person using the formula $V_p = V_m s^3$.
- Calculate how much the person would weigh using the formula Weight = Volume $\times$ Weight density.

Planning

Materials

- Doll or action figure
- Ruler
- Large pitcher
- Large pot
- Water
- Tape
- Measuring cups and spoons

Project Teams

Students can choose partners to work with and then discuss how they wish to proceed.

Guiding Students' Work

Students can share the use of pitchers and pots to do this project. Have a large pot of water available that can be reused by each pair of students. Make sure that hollow models do not have any openings that would allow water to leak inside them. Provide students with tape to cover any openings.

Second-Language Learners

Students learning English may need help from a peer tutor or aide to write an analysis of results.

Rubric for Chapter 10 Project

4 Students measure the volume of water accurately and convert the volume to liters. All subsequent calculations are done correctly and all questions are answered. A report is written that includes a complete and accurate summary of the experiment. The results are analyzed and reasonable answers are given to the questions asked under *Writing a Report*.

3 Students perform all aspects of the experiment in an orderly manner and make the required calculations correctly. The written report covers all the points required, but some parts are too brief or not entirely clear. The results are analyzed and the questions answered, but more thought would have produced a better analysis overall.

2 Students take the necessary measurements but are a little careless in their measurements of the volume of the water. They also have errors in their calculations of the volume and weight of the real person. A report is written, but there are shortcomings in both the summary and the analysis.

1 Students attempt to start the experiment but are very careless in measuring the volume of the water. Subsequent calculations are incorrect and no report is written. Students should be encouraged to speak with the teacher as soon as possible to review their work and to make a new start on the project.

For the Student

Rubric for Chapter 10 Project

4 You measure the volume of water accurately and convert the volume to liters. All subsequent calculations are done correctly and all questions are answered. A report is written that includes a complete and accurate summary of the experiment. Your results are analyzed and reasonable answers are given to the questions asked under *Writing a Report*.

3 You perform all aspects of the experiment in an orderly manner and make the required calculations correctly. The written report covers all the points required, but some parts are too brief or not entirely clear. Your results are analyzed and the questions answered, but more thought would have produced a better analysis overall.

2 You take the necessary measurements but are a little careless in your measurements of the volume of the water. You also have errors in your calculations of the volume and weight of the real person. A report is written, but there are shortcomings in both the summary and the analysis.

1 You attempt to start the experiment but are careless in measuring the volume of the water. Subsequent calculations are incorrect and you cannot write a report because of this. You should speak with your teacher as soon as possible to review your work and to make a new start on the project.

Project Notes

Mathematical Goals

- Choose a set of statistical data to illustrate with a cartogram.
- Select three to five neighboring states with relevant data and organize the data in a table.
- Choose a convenient size and scale to make squares that can be used to form the shapes of the states chosen.

Planning

Materials

- Computer drawing program or graph paper
- Poster board

Project Teams

Work with students to organize the class into groups of two or three students. Each team should discuss the goal of the project and decide how to proceed.

Guiding Students' Work

You may wish to discuss the project with the whole class before the groups are organized. Ask the class for suggestions about possible topics for gathering data. This would provide a source of ideas for students to get started. Suggest that the groups explore reference materials in their school or public libraries or use reference books they may have at home.

Second-Language Learners

Students learning English may not be familiar with the expression *neighboring states*. Explain that this phrase refers to states that have borders in common.

Rubric for Chapter 11 Project 1

4 Students work cooperatively in their group to choose an interesting set of statistical data for their cartogram and find relevant data for three to five states. They choose an appropriate scale for the squares and are successful in forming the shapes of their states. The states are placed in their correct respective positions, a poster is made, and the correct information is placed on the poster.

3 Students are successful in collecting the necessary data, and they organize it properly to make their cartogram. The size and scale chosen for the squares could have been better, but it works. A poster is made and labeled, but a little more effort would have made it visually more attractive.

2 The statistical data students choose are difficult to work with and are somewhat incomplete. States are chosen and relevant data collected. The size and scale chosen for the squares is not a convenient one and the resulting cartogram does not come out very well and is misleading. A poster is made, but labels are incorrect or missing altogether.

1 Students have difficulty getting started and cannot find appropriate data to begin constructing their cartograms correctly. Squares are drawn, but they are not representative of the data. No attempt is made to construct a poster. Students should be encouraged to speak with the teacher as soon as possible to review their work and to make a new start on the project.

For the Student

Rubric for Chapter 11 Project 1

4 You work cooperatively in your group to choose an interesting set of statistical data for your cartogram and find relevant data for three to five states. You choose an appropriate scale for the squares and are successful in forming the shapes of your states. The states are placed in their correct respective positions, a poster is made, and the correct information is placed on the poster.

3 You are successful in collecting the necessary data, and you organize it properly to make your cartogram. The size and scale chosen for the squares could have been better, but it works. A poster is made and labeled, but a little more effort would have made it visually more attractive.

2 The statistical data you choose are difficult to work with and are somewhat incomplete. States are chosen and relevant data collected. The size and scale chosen for the squares is not a convenient one and the resulting cartogram does not come out very well and is misleading. A poster is made, but labels are incorrect or missing.

1 Your group has difficulty getting started and cannot find appropriate data to begin constructing your cartograms correctly. Squares are drawn, but they are not representative of the data. Because of these difficulties no attempt is made to construct a poster. You should speak with your teacher as soon as possible to review your work and to make a new start on the project.

Project Notes

Mathematical Goals

- Collect real-world data and make a scatter plot of the data.
- Write an equation that relates distance as a function of the number of marbles in a bag.
- Explore rational expressions that involve real-world data.
- Write and simplify a variable expression.

Planning

Materials

- String
- Plastic bags
- Binder clip
- Marbles
- Yardstick
- Tape
- Graph paper

Project Teams

Students can choose partners to work with and then discuss how they wish to proceed. Partners can share in the collection of the materials needed to do the project.

Guiding Students' Work

Students will need a place from which to hang their balance. You can set up the working areas prior to the beginning of the project. Try to have some extra materials available if students need them. These steps will facilitate the project work by all groups.

Second-Language Learners

Before writing a summary of their results, students learning English may benefit from explaining their experiment orally to an aide or peer tutor.

Rubric for Chapter 11 Project 2

4 Students make a balance, collect their data, make a scatter plot of the data, and write an equation that shows the distance b as a function of the number of marbles in bag B. The work is well organized and correctly done. Students also complete Steps 4–7 and draw the correct conclusions from the

---

Explorations and Projects Book, Copyright © McDougal Littell Inc.

calculations in their table. They summarize their results in a report that is complete, well written, and mathematically correct.

3 Students complete all steps of the experiment. The final report is complete but has a few mathematical errors. The explanations are correct but could have been stated more clearly. Diagrams are not used to clarify the explanations.

2 Students make a balance and collect their data to explore inverse variation. The balance and data collection are done correctly, but the work to explore rational expressions has some serious problems involving the data collection, the calculations, and the variable expression written. Students attempt to write a report, but it is incomplete and the explanations given are confusing.

1 Students have difficulty making a balance and collecting data for exploring inverse variation. They do not proceed beyond this point in the experiment. Students should be encouraged to speak with the teacher as soon as possible to review their work and to make a new start on the project.

For the Student

Rubric for Chapter 11 Project 2

4 You make a balance, collect your data, make a scatter plot of the data, and write an equation that shows the distance b as a function of the number of marbles in bag B. Your work is well organized and correctly done. You also complete Steps 4–7 and draw the correct conclusions from the calculations in your table. You summarize your results in a report that is complete, well written, and mathematically correct.

3 You complete all steps of the experiment. Your final report is complete but has a few mathematical errors. Your explanations are correct but could have been stated more clearly. You do not use diagrams to clarify the explanations.

2 You make a balance and collect your data to explore inverse variation. The balance and data collection are done correctly, but your work to explore rational expressions has some problems involving the data collection, the calculations, and the variable expression written. You attempt to write a report, but it is incomplete and the explanations given are not very clear.

1 You have difficulty making a balance and collecting data for exploring inverse variation and you cannot proceed beyond this point in the experiment. You should speak with your teacher as soon as possible to review your work and to make a new start on the project.

Project Notes

Mathematical Goals

- Collect data relating the period of a pendulum to its length and make a scatter plot of the data.
- Use the formula $P = 0.2\sqrt{L}$ that relates the period P of a pendulum to its length L to calculate P for different values of L.
- Graph $P = 0.2\sqrt{L}$ on a graphing calculator.
- Use the formula $P = 0.2\sqrt{L}$ to find L when P is one second.

Planning

Materials

- String
- Coins
- Pencil
- Graph paper
- Ruler
- Graphing calculator
- Watch

Project Teams

Students can choose a partner to work with and then discuss how they wish to proceed. They should choose a convenient place to conduct the experiment and record their results.

Guiding Students' Work

Make sure students have a sufficient number of tables to use for their experiments. Suggest that they share the work of timing the pendulum for 10 swings and recording the results. Both students in each group should do the work stated under *Using a Formula*. They should also share in writing the report about their experiment.

Second-Language Learners

Make sure students learning English recognize that the term *period* (of a pendulum) is defined as *the amount of time it takes the pendulum to swing from point A to point B and back to point A.*

Explorations and Projects Book, Copyright © McDougal Littell Inc.

Rubric for Chapter 12 Project

4 Students complete all aspects of the experiment successfully. Their report describes all procedures clearly and states the relationship between the length of a pendulum and its period correctly. Pictures, graphs, and tables are used to support statements made in the report. The report is well organized, neat, and does not contain any mathematical errors.

3 Students are successful in conducting their experiment. They collect the results and write a report. There are a few problems with the report, but none of them are serious. For example, the pictures and graphs could have been drawn better. Students' conclusions are correct and the report is complete.

2 Students do not use 10 different lengths of string and their measurements of 10 full swings are sometimes inaccurate. A report is written, but it does not contain a full description of the procedures followed. The conclusions reached are correct but not fully supported by pictures, graphs, and tables.

1 Students have difficulty setting up their experiments. They make a few measurements of 10 full swings but do not collect sufficient data to make a meaningful scatter plot. Students should be encouraged to speak with the teacher as soon as possible to review their work and to make a new start on the project.

For the Student

Rubric for Chapter 12 Project

4 You complete all aspects of the experiment successfully. Your report describes all procedures clearly and states the relationship between the length of a pendulum and its period correctly. Pictures, graphs, and tables are used to support statements made in the report. The report is well organized, neat, and does not contain any mathematical errors.

3 You are successful in conducting your experiment. You collect the results and write a report. There are a few problems with the report, but none of them are serious. For example, the pictures and graphs could have been drawn better. Your conclusions are correct and the report is complete.

2 You do not use 10 different lengths of string and your measurements of 10 full swings are sometimes inaccurate. A report is written, but it does not contain a full description of the procedures followed. Your conclusions are correct but not fully supported by pictures, graphs, and tables.

1 You have difficulty setting up your experiments. You make a few measurements of 10 full swings but do not collect sufficient data to make a meaningful scatter plot. You should speak with your teacher as soon as possible to review your work and to make a new start on the project.

Geometry Explorations
and Projects
Teacher Notes

Geometry Exploration 1 Note

Purpose
The purpose of this Exploration is to have students discover that by identifying a pattern in several examples of a geometric figure, they can use the pattern to make predictions about the subsequent figures.

Materials/Preparation
No special materials are required.

Procedure
Students copy the figures shown in Steps 1–3 and continue the pattern by following the directions in Step 4. They copy and extend their table with information about the figures. Finally, they examine the figures and the data in the table to find patterns and make predictions about subsequent figures.

Closure
Discuss the results of Steps 6–8. Discuss the idea that by analyzing several examples of a situation to determine a pattern, the pattern can then be used to make predictions about the situation.

Geometry Exploration 2 Note

Purpose
The purpose of this Exploration is to have students observe the possible relationships between two lines, between a line and a plane, and between two planes.

Materials/Preparation
Each pair of students needs three trays or pieces of stiff paper, tape, scissors, and several pieces of uncooked spaghetti.

Procedure
Students should join the trays or pieces of paper as shown in the diagram. They then follow the instructions in Steps 1–5 to explore possible relationships between various lines and planes.

Closure
Students should see that for any two points, there is one line through them; two lines intersect in a point; and that in a plane, lines can have no points or a single point in common. They should also see that two lines in different planes do not share any points, and if two planes intersect, then their intersection is a line.

Geometry Exploration 3 Note

Purpose
The purpose of this Exploration is to have students discover the possible relationships of lines and planes in space.

Materials/Preparation
Each pair of students needs three index cards, scissors, and two toothpicks.

Procedure
Students use index cards to represent planes and toothpicks to represent lines. They use these physical models to investigate the following situations: three parallel planes, two parallel planes intersected by a third plane, three intersecting planes, and lines perpendicular to a plane.

Closure
Students should see that when two parallel planes are intersected by a third plane, the lines of intersection are parallel, and that two lines perpendicular to a plane are parallel.

Explorations and Projects Book, Copyright © McDougal Littell Inc.

Geometry Exploration 4 Note

Purpose

The purpose of this Exploration is to have students discover a rule that can be used to tell whether a network is traceable.

Materials/Preparation

No special materials are required.

Procedure

Students copy the five networks shown in Step 1 and work together to see which networks can be traced without lifting their pencils or retracing an edge. They copy and complete a table showing the number of odd vertices of a network and if it is traceable.

They then look for a pattern that can be used to predict whether a network is traceable.

Closure

Discuss the rules that students write for Step 6. Help students understand that if a network has more than two odd vertices, it is not traceable.

Geometry Exploration 5 Note

Purpose

The purpose of this Exploration is for students to discover that if two lines are intersected by a transversal and corresponding angles are congruent, then the lines are parallel.

Materials/Preparation

Each group of students needs a straightedge or ruler and an index card.

Procedure

Students cut an index card on the diagonal to form two right triangles. They use their triangles to draw two lines that intersect a transversal so that the corresponding angles are congruent.

Closure

Students should understand that when a transversal intersects a pair of lines so that the corresponding angles are congruent, then the lines are parallel.

Geometry Exploration 6 Note

Purpose

The purpose of this Exploration is to have students discover the relationship between the slopes of parallel lines and the relationship between the slopes of perpendicular lines.

Materials/Preparation

Each group of students needs geometry software or graph paper, and a straightedge.

Procedure

Students graph pairs of parallel lines, calculate their slopes, and make a conjecture about the slopes of parallel lines. They then graph pairs of perpendicular lines, calculate their slopes, and make a conjecture about the slopes of perpendicular lines.

Closure

Students should see that the slopes of parallel lines are equal, and that the product of the slopes of perpendicular lines is -1.

Geometry Exploration 7 Note

Purpose
The purpose of this Exploration is to have students discover five rules that can be used to sort or classify a triangle by considering its sides or its angles.

Materials/Preparation
Each group of students needs paper or cardboard cutouts of the triangles shown.

Procedure
One student in the group writes a rule for sorting the triangles. A second student uses the rule to choose those triangles that fit it. The other two students try to guess the rule that determined how the triangles were sorted. All students participate in writing a rule, sorting the triangles, and guessing a rule.

Closure
Use a class discussion to compare the sorting rules that students discover. Students should see that angle relationships and side relationships are two ways of sorting any group of triangles.

Geometry Exploration 8 Note

Purpose
The purpose of this Exploration is to have students discover that the measure of an exterior angle of a triangle is equal to the sum of the measures of the two interior angles that are not adjacent to it.

Materials/Preparation
Each pair of students needs geometry software or a ruler and protractor.

Procedure
Students draw a triangle and an exterior angle at one vertex. They then find the measures of the interior angles, the exterior angle, and the sum of the nonadjacent interior angles, and record the data in a table. They repeat this process for several triangles and then make a conjecture about the measures of the interior and exterior angles of any triangle.

Closure
Students should see that the measure of an exterior angle equals the sum of the measures of the interior angles that are not adjacent to it.

Geometry Exploration 9 Note

Purpose
The purpose of this Exploration is to have students discover how two congruent triangles can be combined to form other shapes and, thus, to prepare students to find congruent triangles in diagrams associated with proofs.

Materials/Preparation
Each group of students needs a pair of scissors.

Procedure
Students use reflection to make a pair of congruent right triangles. They then arrange them to form different shapes and name the congruent triangles in each one.

Closure
Ask various groups to draw the five new shapes they formed in Step 5 on the board and to list the congruent triangles in each one. Discuss the results with the class.

Explorations and Projects Book, Copyright © McDougal Littell Inc.

Geometry Exploration 10 Note

Purpose
The purpose of this Exploration is for students to learn that the perpendicular bisectors of the sides of a triangle intersect in a point which is the center of the circle that can be circumscribed about the triangle.

Materials/Preparation
Each pair of students needs patty paper, a compass, and a straightedge.

Procedure
Students draw a triangle on patty paper and fold it to form the perpendicular bisectors of each side of the triangle. They use the point of intersection of the three perpendicular bisectors to draw a circle whose radius is equal to the distance from the center to one of the vertices.

Closure
Discuss the results of Steps 5 and 6 so students understand that the circle intersects all three vertices of the triangle.

 Geometry Exploration 11 Note

Purpose
The purpose of this Exploration is to have students discover how the lengths of the sides of a triangle are related.

Materials/Preparation
Each group needs geometry software.

Procedure
Students graph two concentric circles and draw a radius for each. The ends of the radii are connected to form a triangle. Students then calculate the sum and difference of the radii and compare these to the length of the third side. The points on the circle are moved and the length of the third side is compared to the sum and difference of the lengths of the other two sides. Although the circles are hidden, students should realize that AB and BC remain constant because they are on the circles.

Closure
Students should see that the length of one side of a triangle is less than the sum of the lengths of the other two sides and greater than the difference of the lengths of the other two sides.

 Geometry Exploration 12 Note

Purpose
The purpose of this Exploration is to have students discover some properties of a parallelogram.

Materials/Preparation
Each group needs lined paper, patty paper or tracing paper, a ruler, and a protractor.

Procedure
Students trace parallel lines from a sheet of lined paper in order to draw several parallelograms. For each parallelogram, they measure the sides and angles, draw a diagonal and mark its midpoint, and then draw the other diagonal. Students then observe how the measures of opposite sides and angles are related and where the diagonals intersect. They then conjecture what must be true about these parts of parallelograms.

Closure
Have students discuss their conjectures about the parts of a parallelogram. Students should observe that the opposite sides are congruent, the opposite angles are congruent, and the diagonals bisect each other.

Geometry Exploration 13 Note

Purpose
The purpose of this Exploration is to have students discover that properties of geometric figures are not affected by the placement of the figure on a coordinate plane.

Materials/Preparation
Each group of students needs graph paper, scissors, and a straightedge.

Procedure
Each student places a congruent quadrilateral in a different location on the coordinate plane so that all four vertices have integer coordinates. Students then use these coordinates to show that the quadrilateral is a parallelogram, and that its diagonals bisect each other.

Closure
Discuss the fact that although the coordinates for the midpoints and the slopes of the sides of the quadrilateral are different for each placement, the basic properties that the quadrilateral is a parallelogram and that the diagonals bisect each other are not affected by the placement of the quadrilateral on a coordinate plane.

Geometry Exploration 14 Note

The purpose of this Exploration is to have students discover that the diagonals of a rhombus are perpendicular and that the adjacent angles at each vertex have equal measures.

Materials/Preparation
Each group needs four drinking straws, a protractor, and a piece of string that is about 8 times as long as one of the straws.

Procedure
Students thread the string through the straws to form a movable rhombus. They thread the string once more through the first straw. The ends of the string are then used as the diagonals. Students move the rhombus into different positions, and each time measure the angles that are formed by the diagonals.

Closure
Students should see that the diagonals of a rhombus are perpendicular and that each diagonal bisects the angles at the vertices of the rhombus.

Geometry Exploration 15 Note

Purpose
The purpose of this Exploration is to have students discover the area formulas for a triangle, a parallelogram, and a trapezoid.

Materials/Preparation
Each group needs a rectangular sheet of paper and scissors.

Procedure
Students cut the paper into two noncongruent rectangles, one of which is then cut along the diagonal to form two congruent right triangles. Students observe that the area of one triangle is half the area of the rectangle from which it was cut. The remaining rectangle and two triangles are then arranged to form a parallelogram and a trapezoid that have the same area as the original sheet of paper. Students then analyze and use these figures to describe their areas in terms of their bases and heights.

Closure
Students should have discovered the area formulas for a triangle, a parallelogram, and a trapezoid.

Explorations and Projects Book, Copyright © McDougal Littell Inc.

Geometry Exploration 16 Note

Purpose

The purpose of this Exploration is to have students discover that the result of two reflections across a pair of parallel lines is the same as a translation.

Materials/Preparation

Each group of students needs geometry software or patty paper and a ruler.

Procedure

Students draw a pair of vertical parallel lines that intersect a horizontal line. A triangle is drawn to the left of the left-most vertical line. This triangle is then reflected across the vertical line, and its image is reflected across the other vertical line. Students then examine the distances between the vertices of the original triangle and its image after both reflections.

Closure

Discuss the results of Steps 3–5 so students understand that the two reflections create a translation and that the shift or distance of the translation is twice the distance between the parallel lines.

Geometry Exploration 17 Note

Purpose

The purpose of this Exploration is to discover that in a right triangle, the sum of the squares of the lengths of the legs equals the square of the length of the hypotenuse.

Materials/Preparation

Each group of students needs paper, scissors, and a ruler.

Procedure

Students cut out four identical right triangles and arrange them to form two squares. They then find the area of the large square and the sum of the areas of the right triangles.

Next, they subtract the sum of the areas of the triangles from the area of the large square to find the area of the central square. Groups compare their results and then use algebra to show that in any right triangle, the sum of the squares of lengths of the legs equals the square of the length of the hypotenuse.

Closure

Discuss the algebraic results to be sure students understand the Pythagorean theorem.

Geometry Exploration 18 Note

Purpose

The purpose of this Exploration is to discover whether a triangle is right, obtuse, or acute.

Materials/Preparation

Each group needs graph paper and scissors.

Procedure

Students cut ten squares out of graph paper, using different side lengths. They select three squares and place them to make a triangle. They should order the side lengths from shortest to longest and complete the table. Students repeat this procedure and then conjecture how the side lengths can be used to predict whether the triangle is right, obtuse, or acute.

Closure

Students should see that if c is the length of the longest side and a and b are the lengths of the other two sides, then the triangle is a right triangle when $c^2 = a^2 + b^2$, obtuse when $c^2 > a^2 + b^2$, and acute when $c^2 < a^2 + b^2$.

Geometry Exploration 19 Note

Purpose
The purpose of this Exploration is to have students investigate the values of the sine and cosine ratios for various acute angles.

Materials/Preparation
Each group of students needs geometry software or a ruler and protractor.

Procedure
Students draw right triangles that contain various acute angles and find the ratio of the side opposite the angle to the hypotenuse, and the ratio of the side adjacent to the angle and the hypotenuse. They con-sider what happens to the values of these ratios as the angle measures increase and as the angle measures approach 0. They also consider what value of $m\angle A$ will make the two ratios equal.

Closure
Call upon various students to answer the questions in Steps 2–4. Students should understand that as the angle measures increase, the sine ratio approaches 1 and the cosine ratio approaches 0. The opposite effect is seen as the angle measures approach 0°.

 Geometry Exploration 20 Note

Purpose
The purpose of this Exploration is for students to discover how areas can be used to determine probabilities.

Materials/Preparation
Each group needs paper and dried beans.

Procedure
Students draw and shade several shapes for which they can find the areas on their paper. They then use this paper as a target and toss a bean until it lands on the paper 50 times. Students then calculate the percent of tosses that land on shaded areas and compare this percent with the percent of the paper that is shaded. After this comparison, students make a conjecture about the probability of a bean landing in a shaded area if it lands on the paper.

Closure
Students should realize that the probability of a bean landing on the shaded area of the target is equal to the ratio of the shaded area to total area of the target.

 Geometry Exploration 21 Note

Purpose
The purpose of the Exploration is to have students discover that the radius of a cylinder has more effect on its volume than does the height.

Materials/Preparation
Each group needs rectangular pieces of paper that are the same size, tape, and popcorn or dried beans.

Procedure
Students tape together the long sides of one sheet of paper and the short sides of another to form two different sized tubes. They fill the taller tube with popcorn or beans, and then transfer them to the shorter tube. This procedure is repeated with paper of different dimensions.

Closure
Discuss students' responses to Step 6. Students should agree that the radius of a cylinder has more effect on its volume than does the height.

 Explorations and Projects Book, Copyright © McDougal Littell Inc.

Geometry Exploration 22 Note

Purpose
The purpose of this Exploration is to have students investigate triangles on a sphere in order to discover that the sum of the measures of the interior angles is greater than 180°.

Materials/Preparation
Each group of students needs a basketball, globe, or other sphere-shaped object, five long strips of paper, tape, and a protractor.

Procedure
Students tape three of the strips of paper on a sphere to form a triangle. The other two strips are used to form one of the angles, taped at the vertex, then laid flat to be measured. The sum of the three angles is then calculated. This process is repeated at least three other times.

Closure
Students should discover that the sum of the measures of a triangle formed on a sphere is greater than 180°.

Mathematical Goals

- Make and use a classification system.
- Develop a system for classifying a group of objects.
- Draw a diagram for a classification system.

Planning

Materials

- objects collected by students, items needed to make a display

Project Teams

You may wish to have students work in pairs or in groups of three to complete this project. When working in groups, the objects collected should be of interest to all members of the group. Group members can discuss how they want to proceed and who will record the results of their work.

Guiding Students' Work

If students have difficulty following the given classification system, have them review Exs. 12–14 on page 128 and Exs. 5–9 on page 133. If necessary, work through these exercises with students. Also, it may be difficult for some students to draw a diagram to classify their system. If students are having difficulty in this area, have them discuss their classification system first, using words to describe how it works. Then they can attempt to write down their ideas and use them to create the diagram.

Second-Language Learners

If necessary, invite volunteers to describe what purpose a classifying system serves, and then give additional examples of common classifying systems such as card catalogs or record store sections. You may also want to have students learning English look up *musical instruments* in an encyclopedia to read about the different classes of instruments (*stringed*, *wind*, *percussion*, *keyboard*). This should help them associate instruments and categories with their English names.

Rubric for Chapter 6 Project

4 Students correctly classify the guitar and other instruments using the diagram. They also make good suggestions for rearranging the diagram. Students develop a system for classifying their objects and draw an accurate diagram. They also correctly classify at least five items from their system. Students make a display for their system and provide a clear explanation of what it classifies. Students make an analysis of one of the other displays and give a copy to the group that made the display. Students also extend the project in one of the ways given, and perform an insightful self-assessment.

Explorations and Projects Book, Copyright © McDougal Littell Inc.

3 Students correctly classify the guitar and other instruments using the diagram, but their ideas on rearranging the diagram are not clear. Students develop a system for classification, but there are some errors in their diagram. Five items are classified using their diagram. Students analyze another system correctly and provide the group who designed the system with a copy of their analysis. Students extend the project and complete an accurate self-assessment.

2 Students classify the guitar and other instruments but make several mistakes. Also, students do not find ways to rearrange the given diagram. Students select a group of objects to classify but do not draw a correct diagram and do not correctly classify five items. An attempt is made to analyze another system, but the analysis is incomplete. An attempt is made to extend the project, but it is also not complete. Students complete a self-assessment but do not answer all of the questions.

1 Students attempt to classify the guitar and other instruments but do it incorrectly. No effort is made to rearrange the diagram, and a diagram for their system is incomplete or not done. Students do not analyze another group's diagram. No attempt is made to extend the project or complete a self-assessment. Students should be encouraged to speak with the teacher as soon as possible to review their work and to make a new start on the project.

For the Student

Rubric for Chapter 6 Project

4 You correctly classify the guitar and other instruments. You make good suggestions for rearranging the diagram. You develop a system for classifying your objects and draw an accurate diagram. You correctly classify at least five items. You make a display for your system and provide a clear explanation of what it classifies. You make an analysis of one of the other displays and give a copy to the group that made the display. You also extend the project in one of the ways given, and perform an insightful self-assessment.

3 You correctly classify the guitar and other instruments but your ideas on rearranging the diagram are not clear. You develop a system for classification, but there are some errors in your diagram. Five items are classified using your diagram. You analyze another system correctly and provide the group who designed the system with your analysis. You extend the project and complete an accurate self-assessment.

2 You classify the guitar and other instruments but make several mistakes. You do not find ways to rearrange the diagram. You select a group of objects to classify but do not draw a correct diagram and do not correctly classify five items. An attempt is made to analyze another system, but it is incomplete. An attempt is made to extend the project, but it is also not complete. You complete a self-assessment but do not answer all the questions.

1 You attempt to classify the guitar and other instruments but do it incorrectly. No effort is made to rearrange the diagram, and a diagram for your system is incomplete or not done. You do not analyze another group's diagram. No attempt is made to extend the project or complete a self-assessment. You should speak with your teacher as soon as possible to review your work and to make a new start on the project.

Project Notes

Mathematical Goals

- Identify objects that have symmetry.
- Analyze transformations that preserve shapes and sizes.

Planning

Materials

- ruler, protractor, paper and pencil, poster board (if necessary)

Project Teams

Students can work individually to collect their objects and make their drawings. If they decide to work in pairs, every aspect of the project should be completed as a team.

Guiding Students' Work

Before students begin, make sure they understand the terminology involved with this project. Terms such as *reflection*, *translation*, *rotation*, *symmetry*, and *transformation* should be clearly understood by every student. If students cannot find an object that exhibits a type of symmetry (especially objects in nature), have them find a picture of an object and then draw a sketch of it for the project. Also, students may need help selecting points on an object to illustrate a type of symmetry. If this is the case, have them make some rough sketches of the object and experiment with selecting different points to decide which ones are best to illustrate the symmetry of the object. This approach can also help students understand and investigate some of the questions in the project.

Second-Language Learners

Allowing students to make a poster instead of writing a report, or to give an oral presentation, is an excellent alternative for second-language learners. You may need to make sure that all students fully understand the directions given, so that they can complete the activity correctly.

Rubric for Chapter 7 Project

4 Students collect the required number of objects and accurately draw them on paper. Choices of points on the objects are made as are the measurements for the transformations on the sketches. The presentation of the results is well done, and it addresses the ideas and questions presented for the project. Students extend the project in one of the two ways listed and give an accurate and complete self-assessment of their work.

3 Students collect the required number of objects and accurately draw them on paper. Choices of points are made, but one of the transformations is not completed correctly or is missing some information regarding how it was done. Students make a presentation, but it does not completely convey all of the information about the project. Students extend the project in one of the two ways described and give a good self-assessment of their work.

2 Students collect the objects but make several mistakes in the sketches. Also, some of the information about the transformations is missing on the sketches. Students make a presentation, but it is evident they do not completely understand the mathematical ideas of the project because their presentation is incomplete or unclear. Students do not extend the project but do make an attempt at self-assessment.

1 Students collect only a few of the objects. They attempt to make sketches but do not complete them and the transformation being described is not evident. If a presentation is made, it is not complete and shows a lack of understanding of the mathematics of the project. No attempt is made to extend the project or make a self-assessment. Students should be encouraged to speak with the teacher as soon as possible to review their work and to make a new start on the project.

For the Student

Rubric for Chapter 7 Project

4 You collect the required number of objects and accurately draw them on paper. Your choices of points on the objects are made as are the measurements for the transformations on the sketches. Your presentation of the results is well done, and it addresses the ideas and questions presented for the project. You extend the project in one of the two ways listed and give an accurate and complete self-assessment of your work.

3 You collect the required number of objects and accurately draw them on paper. Your choices of points are made, but one of the transformations is not completed correctly or is missing some information regarding how it was done. You make a presentation, but it does not completely convey all of the information about the project. You extend the project in one of the two ways described and give a good self-assessment of your work.

2 You collect the objects but make several mistakes in the sketches. Also, some of the information about the transformations is missing on the sketches. You make a presentation, but it is evident you do not completely understand the mathematical ideas of the project because your presentation is incomplete or unclear. You do not extend the project but do make an attempt at self-assessment.

1 You collect only a few of the objects. You attempt to make sketches but do not complete them and the transformation being described is not evident. If a presentation is made, it is not complete and shows a lack of understanding of the mathematics of the project. No attempt is made to extend the project or make a self-assessment. You should speak with your teacher as soon as possible to review your work and to make a new start on the project.

Project Notes

Mathematical Goals

- Collect and organize data in a spreadsheet.
- Choose an appropriate scale for the solar system model.
- Create scale models of the sun and planets.

Planning

Materials

- tape measure, materials for making planetary models

Project Teams

Students can work alone or in groups of two or three to complete the project. If students work in groups, make sure they work together, and everyone contributes equally to the project.

Guiding Students' Work

When students are selecting a scale, they may need to make several calculations before deciding upon a scale to use for their model. Creating three-dimensional models may be difficult and time consuming for some students who are working alone. However, group members can share in this activity to create a realistic model of the solar system. Suggest that all members of a group participate in presenting the group's report.

Second-Language Learners

Students may want to look up the word scale in a dictionary to find out what meaning this word has in various contexts.

Rubric for Chapter 8 Project

4 Students find correct diameters for the sun and planets and organize them in a spreadsheet or table. The scale chosen is convenient. The actual scale model is neatly done, and the locations and sizes of the planets are correct. Students write a detailed report about their project that includes all necessary information. The presentation made to the class is clear and well organized. Students extend the project in one of the ways listed and answer the self-assessment questions.

3 Students find correct diameters for the sun and planets and organize them in a spreadsheet or table. The scale chosen is convenient. Students construct a scale model but make some mistakes in the location of the planets. Students write a report, but from their presentation to the class, it is clear that they do not have a complete understanding of the mathematics of the project.

Students extend the project in one of the ways listed and complete a self-assessment.

2 Students find the diameters of the sun and planets and organize them in a spreadsheet or table. Students do not select a convenient scale for the model and this is evident in their actual model. In the model, many planets are not correctly spaced and distances are not calculated correctly. Students write a report, but it is incomplete. From the presentation, it is clear the students do not have an understanding of the mathematics of the project. Students do not extend the project but complete a self-assessment.

1 Students do not find all of the diameters for the sun and planets nor do they correctly calculate the distances for the planets they have. Students do not select a scale, and if an actual model is made, the planets are placed at random distances. If students prepare a report, it is incomplete and not well done. Students make no effort to extend the project or complete a self-assessment. Students should be encouraged to speak with the teacher as soon as possible to review their work and to make a new start on the project.

For the Student

Rubric for Chapter 8 Project

4 You find correct diameters for the sun and planets and organize them in a spreadsheet or table. The scale chosen is convenient. The actual scale model is neatly done, and the locations and sizes of the planets are correct. You write a detailed report about your project that includes all necessary information. The presentation made to the class is clear and well organized. You extend the project in one of the ways listed and answer the self-assessment questions.

3 You find correct diameters for the sun and planets and organize them in a spreadsheet or table. The scale chosen is convenient. You construct a scale model but make some mistakes in the location of the planets. You write a report, but from your presentation to the class, it is clear that your understanding of the mathematics of the project is less than complete. You extend the project in one of the ways listed and complete a self-assessment.

2 You find the diameters of the sun and planets and organize them in a spreadsheet or table. You do not select a convenient scale for the model and many planets are not correctly spaced and distances are not calculated correctly. You write a report, but it is incomplete. From the presentation, it is clear your understanding of the mathematics of the project needs improvement. You do not extend the project but complete a self-assessment.

1 You do not find all of the diameters for the sun and planets nor do you correctly calculate the distances for the planets you have. You do not select a scale, and if an actual model is made, the planets are placed at random distances. If you prepare a report, it is incomplete and not well done. You do not extend the project or complete a self-assessment. You should speak with your teacher as soon as possible to review your work and to make a new start on the project.

Project Notes

Mathematical Goals

- Use a formula to calculate the angle of the sun.
- Use trigonometry to design a solar roof.

Planning

Materials

- paper and pencil, ruler, protractor, drawing supplies (if necessary)

Project Teams

Students can work in pairs to complete the project. Each partner should do all of the calculations independently and then partners should compare results with one another.

Guiding Students' Work

If students are having difficulty with the initial steps for the project, have them label angles and lengths in the figure. Remind them that the chapter is about applying right triangles, and ask them if they can find a right triangle in the drawing. Then have them copy and label the right triangle. When drawing their designs, students may need to make one or two rough drafts before drawing their final versions.

Second-Language Learners

You may need to explain the meaning of *greenhouse effect* to students learning English. You can describe it as "trapping sunlight, so as to hold its warmth." You might also want to mention that the term *greenhouse effect* is often used to describe the phenomenon in which Earth traps the sun's heat.

Rubric for Chapter 9 Project

4 Students calculate and find all measurements described in the project correctly. Students also make a complete design for their roof. The diagrams, photographs, or models that students use to illustrate their results are appropriate, and the answers to the questions indicate an understanding of the mathematical concepts involved. Students extend the project by completing one of the four tasks and write a clear self-assessment of the project.

3 Students calculate and find all measurements described in the project, but a few of the calculations are not done correctly. Students make a design of their roof and use diagrams, photographs, or models to illustrate their results. Students answer most of the questions but do not show a complete

understanding of the concepts of the project. Students extend the project by completing one of the tasks listed and also write a self-assessment of the project.

2 Students do not complete all of the calculations and measurements, and some of the calculations are not correct. The design of the roof and the diagrams, photographs, and models that are done appear to have been done quickly and neatness was not attempted. Some of the project questions are answered but not all of them. Students do not extend the project or complete a self-assessment.

1 Students make little effort to calculate the measurements asked for in the project. The diagrams, photographs, or models that are used are not complete. If students answer any of the questions, they are poorly written, incorrect, and incomplete. Students do not extend the project or write a self-assessment. Students should be encouraged to speak with the teacher as soon as possible to review their work and to make a new start on the project.

For the Student

Rubric for Chapter 9 Project

4 You calculate and find all measurements described in the project correctly. You also make a complete design for your roof. The diagrams, photographs, or models that you use to illustrate your results are appropriate, and the answers to the questions indicate an understanding of the mathematical concepts involved. You extend the project by completing one of the four tasks and write a clear self-assessment of the project.

3 You calculate and find all measurements described in the project, but a few of the calculations are not done correctly. You make a design of your roof and use diagrams, photographs, or models to illustrate your results. You answer most of the questions but your understanding of the concepts of the project could be improved. You extend the project by completing one of the tasks listed and also write a self-assessment of the project.

2 You complete all of the calculations and measurements, and some of the calculations are not correct. The design of the roof and the diagrams, photographs, and models that are done appear to have been done quickly and neatness was not attempted. Some of the project questions are answered but not all of them. You do not extend the project or complete a self-assessment.

1 You do not calculate the measurements asked for in the project. The diagrams, photographs, or models that are used are not complete or your calculations are incorrect. Your answers to the questions are not well written and are incorrect and incomplete. You do not extend the project or write a self-assessment. You should speak with your teacher as soon as possible to review your work and to make a new start on the project.

Mathematical Goals

- Draw a regular triangle, a square, a regular pentagon, and a regular hexagon.
- Construct the Platonic solids.
- Draw nets for the Platonic solids.

Planning

Materials

- paper and pencil, ruler, tape, scissors, protractor

Project Teams

Students should select a partner and complete all phases of the project together, especially the construction of the solids where four hands are sometimes necessary. It may also be helpful for students to discuss their ideas before constructing the solids.

Guiding Students' Work

Some students may have difficulty visualizing and creating three-dimensional solids. If this is the case, work with them on the first solid to get them started. Also, have students draw their triangles, squares, pentagons, and hexagons so they are large enough to work with as three-dimensional shapes. It may take a while for students to realize that the hexagon is not used in constructing the solids and that the equilateral triangle is used three times. When students have completed making their solids, they should see that the tetrahedron has 4 triangular faces, the cube has 6 square faces, the octahedron has 8 triangular faces, the dodecahedron has 12 pentagonal faces, and the icosahedron has 20 triangular faces.

Second-Language Learners

Students learning English may need an explanation of what the term *closed three-dimensional vertex* means. Make sure that students fully understand the term before they begin Step 2.

Rubric for Chapter 12 Project 1

4 Students draw the triangles, squares, pentagons, and hexagons accurately, and construct the five solids. Students correctly draw the nets for the icosahedron and dodecahedron by taking them apart, and they draw correct nets for the other three solids without taking them apart. Students demonstrate an understanding for the mathematics involved in the project, extend the project using one of the ideas listed, and complete a self-assessment that is well written and clear.

3 Students draw the triangles, squares, pentagons, and hexagons accurately but are not able to construct one of the solids. Students may also have some difficulty in drawing the nets for the three smallest solids without taking them apart. Students extend the project by completing one of the ideas given but do not convey a thorough knowledge of the mathematics involved. Students complete an accurate self-assessment of their work on the project.

2 Students draw the triangles, squares, pentagons, and hexagons accurately but are not able to complete the construction of two or more of the solids. Students also have difficulty drawing the nets for the solids and there are mistakes in the nets they do create. An attempt is made to extend the project, but because their work on the solids is incomplete, the extension of the project is also incomplete. Students submit part of the self-assessment but is not well written.

1 Students do not accurately draw the triangles, squares, pentagons, and hexagons. As a result, they do not complete the construction of the solids and do not draw correct nets for them. Students do not attempt to extend the project and do not submit any self-assessment. Students should be encouraged to speak with the teacher as soon as possible to review their work and to make a new start on the project.

For the Student

Rubric for Chapter 12 Project 1

4 You draw the triangles, squares, pentagons, and hexagons accurately, and construct the five solids. You correctly draw the nets for the icosahedron and dodecahedron by taking them apart, and you draw correct nets for the other three solids without taking them apart. You demonstrate an understanding for the mathematics involved in the project, extend the project using one of the ideas listed, and complete a self-assessment that is well written and clear.

3 You draw the triangles, squares, pentagons, and hexagons accurately but are not able to construct one of the solids. You also have some difficulty in drawing the nets for the three smallest solids without taking them apart. You extend the project by completing one of the ideas given but do not convey a thorough knowledge of the mathematics involved. You complete an accurate self-assessment of your work on the project.

2 You draw the triangles, squares, pentagons, and hexagons accurately but are not able to complete the construction of two or more of the solids. You also have difficulty drawing the nets for the solids and there are mistakes in the nets you do create. An attempt is made to extend the project, but because your work on the solids is incomplete, the extension of the project is also incomplete. You submit part of the self-assessment but is not well written.

1 You do not accurately draw the triangles, squares, pentagons, and hexagons. As a result, you do not complete the construction of the solids and do not draw correct nets for them. You do not attempt to extend the project and do not submit any self-assessment. You should speak with your teacher as soon as possible to review your work and to make a new start on the project.

Project Notes

Mathematical Goals

- Design a floor plan using specified guidelines.
- Find the area of a pentagon.
- Find the volume of a pentagonal prism.

Planning

Materials

- pencil and paper, ruler, graph paper or dot paper, calculator, tape measure

Project Teams

Students form groups of three and work together to complete the project. When ideas are discussed and decisions are made, all team members should be involved. You may wish to suggest that each student make a drawing of a detailed floor plan and then use the best one for the group's final proposal.

Guiding Students' Work

At the beginning of the project, students can work together to decide on three different dimensions of the cottage, then each student can draw one of the rough sketches. If possible, show students an example of a floor plan for a house or other building so they can see how to mark doors and windows. You may also want to explain how this is done before students begin the project. For example, students need to indicate on their floor plan which way each door opens. Students should use a ruler when drawing the plan and graph or dot paper. If students are placing appliances and furniture in the room, it may be helpful to have them cut scale models of each piece out of paper. These can then be moved about to decide where they will be located.

Second-Language Learners

Encourage students learning English to look up in a dictionary the words with which they are unfamiliar. Possibilities include *cottage*, *constraints*, *restrictions*, and *guidelines*.

Rubric for Chapter 12 Project 2

4 Students draw at least three rough sketches for their cottage and then design a detailed floor plan. Their final floor plan shows exact dimensions. Windows, doors, furniture, and appliances are clearly labeled. Students make a three-dimensional sketch of the cottage and correctly calculate its volume. Students create a detailed proposal that describes the cottage for the future owners, and extend the project in one of the four ways listed. A self-assessment is completed that addresses all of the questions asked.

3 Students draw three rough sketches and a detailed floor plan for their cottage. Their final floor plan shows exact dimensions, but some of them are incorrect. Students make a three-dimensional sketch of the cottage and calculate its volume. A proposal describing the cottage is created and explains the features of the cottage; however, it lacks some detail. Students extend the project in one of the four ways listed. Students also complete a self-assessment of the project and address the questions asked.

2 Students draw rough sketches and a detailed floor plan for the cottage, but the sketches are not complete and the detailed plan is poorly done. Students do not label the dimensions of the room, but windows and doors are shown. A three-dimensional sketch is not drawn and the volume is calculated incorrectly. Students attempt to create a proposal describing their cottage, but it is incomplete. Students do not extend the project, and if a self-assessment is done, it answers only some of the questions asked.

1 Students try to make a detailed floor plan, but it is incomplete and does not show dimensions, windows, or doors. The volume of the cottage is not calculated. Students do not create a proposal to describe their cottage and do not extend the project or complete a self-assessment. Students should be encouraged to speak with the teacher as soon as possible to review their work and to make a new start on the project.

For the Student

Rubric for Chapter 12 Project 2

4 You draw at least three rough sketches for your cottage and then design a detailed floor plan. Your final floor plan shows exact dimensions. Windows, doors, furniture, and appliances are clearly labeled. You make a three-dimensional sketch of the cottage and correctly calculate its volume. You create a detailed proposal that describes the cottage for the future owners, and extend the project in one of the four ways listed. A self-assessment is completed that addresses all of the questions asked.

3 You draw three rough sketches and a detailed floor plan for your cottage. Your final floor plan shows exact dimensions, but some of them are incorrect. You make a three-dimensional sketch of the cottage and calculate its volume. A proposal describing the cottage is created and explains the features of the cottage; however, it lacks some detail. You extend the project in one of the four ways listed. You also complete a self-assessment of the project and address the questions asked.

2 You draw rough sketches and a detailed floor plan for the cottage, but the sketches are not complete and the detailed plan is not well done. You do not label the dimensions of the room, but windows and doors are shown. A three-dimensional sketch is not drawn and the volume is calculated incorrectly. You attempt to create a proposal describing your cottage, but it is incomplete. You do not extend the project, and if a self-assessment is done, it answers only some of the questions asked.

1 You try to make a detailed floor plan, but it is incomplete and does not show dimensions, windows, or doors. The volume of the cottage is not calculated. You do not create a proposal to describe your cottage and do not extend the project or complete a self-assessment. You should speak with your teacher as soon as possible to review your work and to make a new start on the project.

Project Notes

Mathematical Goal

- Make a sphere, cylinder, and two cones of a specified size.

- Find the cross sectional areas of a sphere, cylinder, and two cones.

- Compare the volumes of a sphere, cylinder, and two cones by comparing their cross sectional areas.

Planning

Materials

- modeling clay, strong plastic, scissors, compass, plastic knife, tape, fishing line or floss

Project Teams

Students select a partner and divide the tasks for the project evenly. Each student should mold at least one of the shapes and cut the cross sections at least once. Students should work together to write the report.

Guiding Students' Work

Constructing the cone is probably the most difficult part of the project for many students. You may need to work with the class explaining the measurements. Students should begin with a circle that has a radius of $2\frac{1}{8}$ in., or a diameter of $4\frac{1}{4}$ in. Students cut along the radius to the center and fold the circle until the diameter of the base of the cone is 3 in. To make the cylinder, students may find it easier to create a tube with a diameter of 3 in. out of a sturdy but bendable plastic and use it to cut through a piece of clay.

Second-Language Learners

You may want to give the following definitions for terms contained in this section: *slices* (thin pieces cut from a larger amount), *calculus* (a branch of mathematics), *cross sections* (a section formed by a plane cutting through an object).

Rubric for Chapter 12 Project 3

4 Students perform all tasks involved with the project correctly. They also repeat the comparison five times. Students write a clear and well-organized report describing their work and answer all of the questions correctly. It is evident that the mathematics of the project is clearly understood. Students extend the project in one of the two ways described and complete an insightful self-assessment.

3 Students perform the tasks involved with the project correctly, but they do not repeat the comparison five times. Students write a report about their work and explain most of their ideas well. For the most part, students understand the concepts involved but do not understand some of the relationships of the volumes. Students extend the project in one of the two ways listed and provide a self-assessment.

2 Students attempt the project but complete the comparison only once. Students try to write a report describing their work, but because they do not understand the ideas involved, the report is incomplete and contains many errors. Students do not extend the project but attempt a self-assessment.

1 Students attempt to create the solids but do not complete the project correctly. No report is written, and students do not extend the project. No self-assessment is made. Students should be encouraged to speak with the teacher as soon as possible to review their work and to make a new start on the project.

For the Student

Rubric for Chapter 12 Project 3

4 You perform all tasks involved with the project correctly. You also repeat the comparison five times. You write a clear and well-organized report describing your work and answer all of the questions correctly. It is evident that the mathematics of the project is clearly understood. You extend the project in one of the two ways described and complete an insightful self-assessment.

3 You perform the tasks involved with the project correctly, but you do not repeat the comparison five times. You write a report about your work and explain most of your ideas well. For the most part, you understand the concepts involved but do not understand some of the relationships of the volumes. You extend the project in one of the two ways listed and provide a self-assessment.

2 You attempt the project but complete the comparison only once. You try to write a report describing your work, but the report is incomplete and contains a number of errors. You do not extend the project but attempt a self-assessment.

1 You attempt to create the solids but do not complete the project correctly. No report is written, and you do not extend the project. No self-assessment is made. You should speak with your teacher as soon as possible to review your work and to make a new start on the project.

Algebra 2 Explorations
Teacher Notes

Algebra 2 Exploration 1 Note

Purpose

The purpose of this Exploration is to help students understand how to solve an equation with variables on both sides.

Materials/Preparation

Have sets of algebra tiles available.

Procedure

Students begin by representing the equation $3x + 1 = x + 5$ with algebra tiles. They then remove an x-tile from both sides to simulate subtracting a variable term. Students should discuss how they arrived at the solutions to each equation in Step 3. Some students

may need to record their steps as they go along. The class should reach a consensus about the generalization in Step 4.

Closure

Groups can compare results with one another. Students should understand that removing an x-tile from each side of an algebra-tile model for an equation is equivalent to subtracting x from both sides of an equation. This method gives an equivalent equation with the variable on one side.

 Algebra 2 Exploration 2 Note

Purpose

The purpose of this Exploration is to have students discover that the slopes of two perpendicular lines are negative reciprocals.

Materials/Preparation

Each pair of students needs graph paper, a protractor, and a straightedge.

Procedure

Students draw a line with slope of 1, label a point, and then use a protractor to draw another line perpendicular to the first line at the labeled point. They find the slope of the perpendicular line and record it. They then

repeat the procedure several times until they can make a conjecture about the relationship between the slopes of perpendicular lines.

Closure

Students should understand that the slopes of two perpendicular lines are negative reciprocals of each other.

 Algebra 2 Exploration 3 Note

Purpose

The purpose of this Exploration is to have students discover that the water level in a container is a linear function of the number of marbles added.

Materials/Preparation

Each group needs a glass container, water, 20 marbles, a centimeter ruler, and graph paper.

Procedure

Students record the initial height of water in a container. They then add 5 marbles at a time to the container and measure and

record the water height each time, adding a total of 20 marbles. They make a scatter plot of their data and use it to write an equation that represents the water height as a function of the number of marbles added.

Closure

Students should understand that the height of the water in a glass container increases by a fixed amount for each marble added.

Explorations and Projects Book, Copyright © McDougal Littell Inc.

Algebra 2 Exploration 4 Note

Purpose
The purpose of this Exploration is to introduce students to a *line of fit*.

Materials/Preparation
A set of encyclopedias, metric rulers, and graph paper are needed.

Procedure
Students record the number of pages and the thickness for each of ten books as data pairs. They then plot the data pairs and draw a line of fit through the points. From their graph, they find the slope and an equation of the line. Students should understand that since the data are generated experimentally, the data pairs and the line of fit may vary.

Closure
Students should conclude that the thickness of a book can be represented by a linear model $y = ax + b$, where x is the number of pages in the book, a is half the thickness of a sheet of paper (two pages per sheet), and b is the thickness of both covers combined.

Algebra 2 Exploration 5 Note

Purpose
The purpose of this Exploration is to have students discover how points in a plane above or below a line can be located by using inequalities.

Materials/Preparation
Each group needs paper, pencil, and a sheet of graph paper.

Procedure
Students estimate the ages of the people shown and make a scatter plot of the group's data, including the actual ages you provide. It may help for one student to be in charge of listing all the estimates for his or her group. Students then use their scatter plots to answer five questions about their estimated ages and the actual ages.

Closure
Have groups share their graphs with the class. Students should see how the line $e = a$ separates the plane into two regions and that points above or below the line can be represented by inequalities.

Algebra 2 Exploration 6 Note

Purpose
The purpose of this Exploration is to have students investigate systems of linear equations in standard form in order to discover how the graphs of the equations may be related to the number of solutions of the system.

Materials/Preparation
Each pair of students needs a graphing calculator or graphing software.

Procedure
Students graph a system of equations and describe the geometric relationship between the lines. They repeat this procedure for two more systems.

Closure
Have students share their answers to Questions 1 and 2. All students should understand what the relationship between the graphs of two lines implies for the number of solutions to the related system.

Algebra 2 Exploration 7 Note

Purpose
The purpose of this Exploration is to show students how to organize data in a matrix, to have students understand how to add two matrices, and to have students discover how to multiply a matrix by a number and use the data to make predictions.

Materials/Preparation
No special materials are required.

Procedure
For Step 1, have each group draw a matrix like the one shown. One student can tally the data for the group, or the page can be passed around for students to place tally marks in the appropriate boxes. When all the tally marks have been recorded, have the group make a new matrix using numbers instead of tally marks. The two groups can use their final matrices for Steps 2–4.

Closure
Discuss Steps 2–4. Be sure all students understand how to find the sum in Step 2 and the product in Step 4.

Algebra 2 Exploration 8 Note

Purpose
The purpose of this Exploration is to have students discover how reflections can be represented by using matrices.

Materials/Preparation
Each group needs graph paper.

Procedure
Each member of the group draws a different triangle and writes a matrix for it. They then multiply the triangle matrix by four different transformation matrices and graph each image.

Closure
Students should realize that each transformation matrix produces a specific reflection.

Algebra 2 Exploration 9 Note

Purpose
The purpose of this Exploration is to have students discover the matrices for rotation.

Materials/Preparation
Each group needs graph paper.

Procedure
Students write down all the different 2×2 matrices for which both elements on one diagonal are 0 and each element on the other diagonal is either 1 or −1. They divide these four matrices among group members, use them to transform a given triangle matrix, and graph the triangle and its image.

These graphs are examined to find the type of transformation produced by each matrix.

Closure
Ask one group to present their results to the class. Then generalize the results found by the groups in Step 4.

Explorations and Projects Book, Copyright © McDougal Littell Inc.

Algebra 2 Exploration 10 Note

Purpose

The purpose of this Exploration is to have students discover how the graph of $y = ax^2$ is affected by introducing other constants.

Materials/Preparation

A graphing calculator or graphing software is needed.

Procedure

Have students copy the table and then take turns using the calculator to graph both equations in each row simultaneously. They should compare the graphs and complete the third column. For question 1, students should make their predictions independently, compare them with each other, and then check their predictions with the graphing calculator. Students can use the table as well as question 1 to answer question 2.

Closure

Have students discuss question 2 to help them see how to graph equations in the form $y = a(x - h)^2 + k$.

Algebra 2 Exploration 11 Note

Purpose

The purpose of this Exploration is to have students predict the x-intercepts and the x-coordinate of the vertex of a quadratic function written in intercept form.

Materials/Preparation

Each pair of students needs a graphing calculator or graphing software.

Procedure

Students should complete the table by graphing each equation and finding the x-intercepts and vertex. Students using a TI-82 can complete the table using the CALCULATE menu. They should choose 2:root to find the x-intercepts and either 3:minimum or 4:maximum to find the vertex. After completing the table, they should look for patterns.

Closure

Review question 2 as a class activity. Ask students to give the equation of a parabola with particular x-intercepts. Is more than one answer possible? (Yes.)

Algebra 2 Exploration 12 Note

Purpose

The purpose of this Exploration is to have students discover how to factor a quadratic expression by using algebra tiles.

Materials/Preparation

Each pair of students needs 1 x^2-tile, 7 x-tiles, and 12 1-tiles.

Procedure

Students work with a partner and follow Steps 1–3 to factor the expression $x^2 + 7x + 12$. They then repeat this process for three other expressions.

Closure

Write the four quadratic expressions and their factored forms on the board. Ask students if they can see any relationships among the coefficients of the original expression and the constant terms of the factored expression.

Algebra 2 Exploration 13 Note

Purpose
The purpose of this Exploration is to have students discover how the value of the discriminant of a quadratic equation can be used to predict the number of solutions to the equation.

Materials/Preparation
Graphing calculators are needed by each group.

Procedure
Students graph various quadratic equations to find the number of solutions (*x*-intercepts) of each equation. They then find the value of the discriminant for each equation. Students record their results in a table and use them to make a generalization about how the value of the discriminant is related to the number of solutions to the equation.

Closure
Students should conclude that if the discriminant is positive, there are 2 solutions; if the discriminant is 0, there is one solution; and if it is negative, there are no solutions.

Algebra 2 Exploration 14 Note

Purpose
The purpose of this Exploration is to have students discover that the degree of a polynomial function indicates the maximum number of real zeros the function can have.

Materials/Preparation
Each pair of students will need a graphing calculator or graphing software.

Procedure
Students graph four functions and observe how the number of real zeros is related to the function's degree. They then check their observations using four other functions. After graphing several more functions, they state the relationship they think is true.

Closure
Call on several partners to describe their results and share their conjectures. Students should understand that the degree of a polynomial function sets an upper limit on the possible number of real zeros. It is not necessary to say what the values of the zeros actually are, only *how many* there are.

Algebra 2 Exploration 15 Note

Purpose
The purpose of this Exploration is to have students discover relationships between a polynomial's degree, its end behavior, and the number of turning points it has.

Materials/Preparation
Each pair of students needs a graphing calculator or graphing software.

Procedure
Suggest that partners sketch each graph they obtain when using technology. The sketches do not need to be exact but should indicate where turning points occur and how the graphs behave for large positive and negative values of *x*. Students should write down their answers to Questions 1–3.

Closure
Call upon different groups to present their answers to Questions 1–3. Students should understand the effects that the degree of a polynomial function has on its graph.

Explorations and Projects Book, Copyright © McDougal Littell Inc.

Algebra 2 Exploration 16 Note

Purpose
The purpose of this Exploration is to have students discover that they need to restrict the domain of the function $y = x^2$ so that its inverse will be a function.

Materials/Preparation
Each pair of students needs graph paper and a MIRA®, tracing paper, or a ruler.

Procedure
Students graph $y = x^2$ and $y = x$ in the same coordinate plane. They then draw the reflection of $y = x^2$ over the line $y = x$. Questions 1 and 2 have students consider whether the reflection is a function and suggest restricting the domain of $y = x^2$ to see if its reflection is a function.

Closure
In answering Questions 1 and 2, students should see that the inverse of the function $y = x^2$ is not a function, but that they can restrict its domain so that the inverse is a function. Ask students if they can think of another way to restrict the domain of $y = x^2$ so that its inverse will be a function.

Algebra 2 Exploration 17 Note

Purpose
The purpose of this Exploration is to have students discover those values of n for which the domain of the function $y = x^n$ must be restricted so that its inverse will be a function.

Materials/Preparation
Each group needs a graphing calculator or graphing software.

Procedure
For $n = 3$, 4, 5, and 6, students graph $y = x^n$ and $y = x$ in the same coordinate plane and use the draw-inverse feature to reflect $y = x^n$ over the line $y = x$. Questions 1 and 2 ask students to describe how the functions and their reflections differ when n is odd or even, and when the domain of $y = x^n$ should be restricted.

Closure
Students should understand that even power functions must have their domains restricted so that their reflections over the line $y = x$ are functions. Odd power functions need no such restriction.

Algebra 2 Exploration 18 Note

Purpose
The purpose of this Exploration is to have students organize data in a box plot and to see that the data can be divided at the 25%, 50%, and 75% points.

Materials/Preparation
Each pair of students needs scissors and graph paper.

Procedure
Students record the data on a strip of graph paper. The data should be written in numerical order and each number should be written in one square. Students then cut the paper so that there are no extra squares.

They fold the strip of graph paper in half and then in half again. Students unfold the strip and draw a line on each fold.

Closure
Students should see that the strip shows the 25%, 50%, and 75% points of their data. The numbers at both ends are the shortest and longest string of letters. The middle fold is the point at which 50% of the data are above or below this point. The first and last folds are the points below which 25% of the data fall and above which 25% of the data fall.

Algebra 2 Exploration 19 Note

Purpose
The purpose of this Exploration is to investigate the distribution of sample proportions.

Materials/Preparation
Each group needs a calculator.

Procedure
Students record their answers, collect the answers, and write the responses on the board. Provide the correct answer. Each group uses the random number generator to choose 6 random samples of 5 responses. For each sample, the group writes the sample proportion as a percent. The class then makes a histogram and examines it for any clustering. The class calculates the population proportion and compares it with the results of Step 4.

Closure
Students should understand they are simulating a random survey of 6 groups of 5 people and that they are using the results to estimate a population proportion.

Algebra 2 Exploration 20 Note

Purpose
The purpose of this Exploration is to have students explore a real-world situation that exhibits a pattern of exponential decay.

Materials/Preparation
Each group will need 100 pennies, a cup, and a graphing calculator. You may wish to review the procedure for drawing a scatter plot.

Procedure
Students should record the number of times the cup is emptied as well as the number of pennies remaining. Then they will have the data needed to make their scatter plots.

Closure
Groups can share their equations and graphs with each other. All students should arrive at an understanding that a quantity that decreases regularly by a fixed percent (in this case, about 50%) will approach 0 rapidly.

Algebra 2 Exploration 21 Note

Purpose
The purpose of this Exploration is to have students discover how the values of a and b affect the graph of $y = ab^x$.

Materials/Preparation
Each group needs a graphing calculator.

Procedure
Urge students to experiment with different windows to obtain satisfactory graphs. Students should sketch how the graphs appear on the calculator screen and should indicate the scales used on the axes. Instruct students to record the values of b and a that they use in Steps 3 and 5, respectively.

Closure
Discuss the graphs obtained by different groups. Ask students to use their results to predict the general appearance of graphs of functions such as $y = 5^x$, $y = \left(\frac{1}{5}\right)^x$, $y = 2\left(\frac{4}{3}\right)^x$, and $y = -2\left(\frac{4}{3}\right)^x$. Check the predictions on a graphing calculator. Use Step 6 to summarize how the values of a and b affect the graph of $y = ab^x$.

Explorations and Projects Book, Copyright © McDougal Littell Inc.

Algebra 2 Exploration 22 Note

Purpose
The purpose of this Exploration is to have students discover that as the interest rate approaches 100% and the frequency of compounding increases that the value of an account with one dollar in it approaches a constant value.

Materials/Preparation
Each group should have a scientific or graphing calculator.

Procedure
Students can work together to complete the second and third columns of the table.

Then each student should complete one of the four remaining columns.

Closure
Discuss the result of increasing the frequency of compounding as the interest rate approaches 100%. Students should see that the value of the dollar invested for a one-year period eventually levels off to about $2.72.

Algebra 2 Exploration 23 Note

Purpose
The purpose of this Exploration is to have students investigate the inverse of the function $f(x) = 2^x$.

Materials/Preparation
Each group needs a MIRA® transparent mirror and graph paper.

Procedure
Students use a table of values to graph $f(x) = 2^x$ and label the points. They then graph the line $y = x$ on the same coordinate plane and reflect each point of $f(x) = 2^x$ with the MIRA®. They label the reflected points and use them to explain how the input values of a function are related to the output values of the inverse function.

Closure
Students should understand that input and output values for a function are reversed for a function and its inverse. In other words, the domain and range values are reversed.

Algebra 2 Exploration 24 Note

Purpose
The purpose of this Exploration is to have students discover the product, quotient, and power properties of logarithms.

Materials/Preparation
A scientific calculator is needed.

Procedure
Students use a calculator to find the common logarithm of the numbers 1 to 9 and also the common logarithm of some multiples of 10. Using the table, they complete logarithm equations which demonstrate the product property, the quotient property, and the power property.

Closure
Students should conclude that the logarithm of the product of two numbers is the sum of the logarithms of each number, the logarithm of the quotient of two numbers is the difference of the logarithms of each number, and that the logarithm of the power of a number is the exponent of the number times the logarithm of its base.

Algebra 2 Exploration 25 Note

Purpose
The purpose of this Exploration is to have students discover how the graph of an equation of the form $y = \frac{a}{x-h} + k$ is related geometrically to the graph of $y = \frac{a}{x}$.

Materials/Preparation
Each pair of students needs a graphing calculator or graphing software.

Procedure
As students complete Steps 1–3, they may find it helpful to sketch each graph includ-ing asymptotes. They should write the equation alongside the sketch. This procedure can facilitate a class discussion and provide students with a record of their work.

Closure
Discuss the graphs and asymptotes for all equations. Students should be able to predict accurately how the graph of any equation of the form $y = \frac{a}{x-h} + k$ is related to the graph of $y = \frac{a}{x}$.

Algebra 2 Exploration 26 Note

Purpose
The purpose of this Exploration is to have students discover relationships between the equation for a rational function and the vertical asymptotes of the function.

Materials/Preparation
Each pair of students needs a graphing calculator or graphing software.

Procedure
As students graph their functions using technology, suggest that they sketch each of the graphs they obtain. The sketches can be used to facilitate a class discussion of students' results and provide them with a record of their work.

Closure
Discuss each graph with the class. Students should understand that each vertical asymptote corresponds to a zero of the denominator of the given function.

Algebra 2 Exploration 27 Note

Purpose
The purpose of this Exploration is to have students discover the distance and midpoint formulas.

Materials/Preparation
Each pair of students needs centimeter graph paper and a metric ruler.

Procedure
Students find the distance between two points and then verify their measurements by applying the Pythagorean theorem. Next, students use a ruler to estimate the midpoint of a segment. They find the arithmetic means of the x- and y-coordinates of the endpoints of the segments, and check to see how they are related to the midpoint.

Closure
Students should be able to explain how to find the distance between any two points in a coordinate plane. They should understand that the coordinates of the midpoint are found by using the coordinates of the endpoints of the segment and taking the means of the x- and y-coordinates.

    Explorations and Projects Book, Copyright © McDougal Littell Inc.

Algebra 2 Exploration 28 Note

Purpose
The purpose of this Exploration is to have students discover that each point on a parabola is an equal distance from the focus and the directrix.

Materials/Preparation
Each group needs focus-directrix paper.

Procedure
Students label a directrix line below the center of a circle. The center of the circle is the focus of the parabola, and the vertex is the midpoint of the perpendicular line segment joining the directrix to the focus. They then use the concentric circles to label two points whose distance from the center of the circle is equal to their distance from the directrix line. They continue to mark points on concentric circles with larger radii until they have sketched the points of a parabola defined by the given directrix line and focus.

Closure
Students should understand that each point of a parabola is an equal distance from the focus and the directrix.

 Algebra 2 Exploration 29 Note

Purpose
The purpose of this Exploration is to have students discover that an ellipse is all points in a plane such that the sum of the distances from two fixed points is constant.

Materials/Preparation
Each pair of students needs graph paper, a 10-inch piece of string, two push pins, and a piece of cardboard.

Procedure
Students draw a coordinate axes on graph paper, plot two points, and pin the graph paper to the cardboard at those points. They attach a string to each of the points and use a pencil to pull it taut. By moving the pencil above and below the axis, they trace out an ellipse. Students then repeat the activity with the fixed points in different positions.

Closure
Students should be able to define an ellipse as the set of points in a plane whose distance from two fixed points is constant.

 Algebra 2 Exploration 30 Note

Purpose
The purpose of this Exploration is to have students explore arithmetic and geometric sequences.

Materials/Preparation
Each group needs paper and scissors.

Procedure
One student of a pair cuts strips of paper in half repeatedly and stacks the pieces. The other student in the pair cuts strips from one end of a piece of paper and stacks the strips. The first student should notice that cutting strips in half repeatedly generates a tall stack of papers. The second student should notice that his or her stack increases slowly because only one piece is added at a time. Students are asked to describe how their stacks increase and write a formula for the sequence generated.

Closure
Students should understand that they have generated two different types of sequences: one which has a common ratio and another which has a common difference.

Algebra 2 Exploration 31 Note

Purpose
The purpose of this Exploration is to have students generate a sequence by using repeated addition or multiplication.

Materials/Preparation
A graphing calculator is needed.

Procedure
Students enter a starting value and then add a constant to the last value by using the last-answer key. They then keep pressing ENTER to see the same constant added repeatedly. This generates an arithmetic sequence. They repeat the procedure by multiplying by a constant. This generates a geometric sequence. Encourage students to experiment with various starting values and various constants.

Closure
Students should conclude that an arithmetic sequence can be generated by repeatedly adding the common difference to the previous term. They also should conclude that a geometric sequence can be generated by repeatedly multiplying the previous term by the common ratio.

 Algebra 2 Exploration 32 Note

Purpose
The purpose of this Exploration is to have students discover the multiplication counting principle.

Materials/Preparation
Each group needs paper of four different colors and scissors.

Procedure
Students use colored strips of paper to determine the number of flags that can be made with two horizontal bars when three colors are used with no repetition, three colors are used with repetition, and four colors are used without repetition. Students count the number of flags and try to find patterns between that number and the number of colors used. They then use these patterns to predict the number of flags possible when ten colors are used without repetition and when four colors are used with repetition.

Closure
Students should intuitively understand the multiplication counting principle.

 Algebra 2 Exploration 33 Note

Purpose
The purpose of this Exploration is to have students discover the relationship between the number of edges in a complete graph and the number of vertices in the graph.

Materials/Preparation
Students should know how to graph a scatter plot on their graphing calculators. They should set their viewing window so that $0 < x \le 10$ and $0 < y \le 40$.

Procedure
Students should record the number of edges for each complete graph. Check to see that each group of students graphs the number of edges as a function of the number of vertices.

Closure
Groups can share their answers and results with each other. All students should recognize that the number of edges in a complete graph can be found by using the expression $\frac{n(n-1)}{2}$, where n represents the number of vertices in the graph.

Explorations and Projects Book, Copyright © McDougal Littell Inc.

Algebra 2 Exploration 34 Note

Purpose
The purpose of this Exploration is to have students explore the concept of combinations.

Procedure
Students work in groups of 4 or 5. Each member assumes he or she is the first-prize winner in the Grand Sweepstakes and lists the ways the others in the group can win the second- and third-place prizes. The group then combines these lists, counts the total number of ways to award the 3 prizes, and writes their answer in the form $_nP_r$. Next, each group uses the lists to count the number of ways the three winners can be chosen for the Lucky 3 Drawing. They express this total in the form $\frac{_nP_r}{r!}$.

Closure
Students should understand that when groups of n elements of a set are taken r at a time and position is not important, the $r!$ groups are not unique. Therefore, dividing the total number of permutations of the set, $_nP_r$, by $r!$ will give the combinations of the set, $_nC_r$.

Algebra 2 Exploration 35 Note

Purpose
The purpose of this Exploration is to have students learn what a simulation is and how one can be used to model a real-world situation.

Materials/Preparation
Each pair of students should have a die or a number cube with sides numbered from 1 to 6.

Procedure
For Step 1, one student can roll the die and the other can record the numbers that come up. For Step 4, students can switch their roles of rolling the die and recording the results.

Closure
Have several pairs of students describe their results for Step 2. Combine the results of all pairs to get one result for the whole class. When discussing Step 3, students should understand that the fractions chosen by the manager ($\frac{1}{2}$, $\frac{1}{3}$, and $\frac{1}{6}$) have a sum of 1.

Algebra 2 Exploration 36 Note

Purpose
The purpose of this Exploration is to have students examine a situation in which events are not independent.

Materials/Preparation
Each student needs a small slip of paper.

Procedure
The class chooses a movie that most students have seen. Each student writes whether they are male or female and whether they liked or disliked the movie. If the student did not see the movie, they write "no opinion." The slips are collected and a table is made.

Closure
Students should understand that the events *male* or *female* and *liked movie* or *disliked movie* are not independent, and that the probability that a person liked or disliked the movie is different when considering males or females than it is when you consider the whole class.

Algebra 2 Exploration 37 Note

Purpose
The purpose of this Exploration is to conduct a binomial experiment and to introduce students to a binomial distribution.

Materials/Preparation
Each student in the class needs a coin.

Procedure
Each student simulates random guessing by flipping a coin and answering *True* if heads comes up and *False* if tails comes up. Students find the number of questions they answered correctly. (The translation and answers are in the answers to the Exploration.) A relative frequency histogram is made. Students use this histogram to find experimental probabilities. They also calculate theoretical probabilities and compare them with the experimental ones.

Closure
Ask students to copy the histogram into their journals. Have each student turn to a classmate and ask a question that can be answered using the histogram.

 Algebra 2 Exploration 38 Note

Purpose
The purpose of this Exploration is to have students discover that the corresponding ratios of side lengths in similar triangles do not depend on the lengths of the sides.

Materials/Preparation
Each pair of students needs graph paper and a protractor.

Procedure
Students draw right triangles on graph paper, each with a 60° angle and discuss why the triangles they have drawn are similar. They then find the ratio of the length of the leg opposite the 60° angle to the length of the hypotenuse. They should determine that the ratio is the same for each triangle even though the lengths of the sides are different.

Closure
Students should understand that the corresponding ratios of side lengths in similar triangles do not depend on the lengths of the sides, but they do depend on the measures of the acute angles.

 Algebra 2 Exploration 39 Note

Purpose
The purpose of this Exploration is to have students use the tangent ratio and similar triangles to find the distance across a room.

Materials/Preparation
Each pair of students needs a ruler, a yardstick, or a meterstick.

Procedure
One student stands across the room while the other lines up a ruler vertically 12 in. in front of his or her eyes. This student then uses the ruler to line up the partner within his or her line of sight. The students then set up similar triangles by using the actual height and ruler height of the partner. The tangent ratio is then calculated for each triangle and is used to find the estimated distance across the room.

Closure
Students should understand that the tangent ratio can be used to find distances that are difficult to measure.

Explorations and Projects Book, Copyright © McDougal Littell Inc.

Algebra 2 Exploration 40 Note

Purpose
The purpose of this Exploration is to introduce students to the concept of radian measure.

Materials/Preparation
Each group needs a cylinder, string, tape, a ruler, a marker, and a protractor.

Procedure
Students determine the radius of their cylinder by measuring its diameter. They then mark the midpoint of the string and repeatedly mark lengths equal to one radius in each direction from the midpoint. The string is then taped to the cylinder at the midpoint

(representing the origin) and wrapped around it, with the counterclockwise direction representing positive and the clockwise direction representing negative. Students then answer questions about their model.

Closure
Discuss questions 1–3 in class. Students should understand that a radian is the *measure* of a central angle that intercepts an arc whose length is equal to the radius.

Algebra 2 Exploration 41 Note

Purpose
The purpose of this Exploration is to have students investigate whether two side lengths of a triangle and the measure of a non-included angle are enough information to determine a unique triangle.

Materials/Preparation
Each pair of students needs a ruler, a protractor, and a compass.

Procedure
Students construct a 30° angle along a ray and then mark off an 8 cm segment along the side of the angle. From the endpoint of the side, they draw arcs with different radii.

They then determine which radii complete a triangle with the given angle and given side. This is the side-side-angle condition studied in geometry.

Closure
Students should conclude that two sides and a non-included angle do not always determine a unique triangle.

Algebra 2 Exploration 42 Note

Purpose
The purpose of this Exploration is to introduce students to the concept of parametric equations and to have them understand that such equations can be used to model and analyze motion in two dimensions.

Materials/Preparation
graphing calculator with parametric mode

Procedure
Students initially determine the parametric equations for the descent of a small airplane. They then graph the equations in parametric mode on a calculator after determining the appropriate values of Tmin and Tmax for the

viewing window. Encourage students to estimate Tmax by solving the first parametric equation for *t* and using 150,000 for a possible value of *x*. After seeing a complete graph, students then trace the graph to determine how long it takes the plane to land.

Closure
Students should understand that parametric equations can be used to model situations that involve motion in two dimensions.

Algebra 2 Exploration 43 Note

Purpose

The purpose of this Exploration is to have students plot the sine and cosine functions and analyze them.

Materials/Preparation

Each pair of students needs a scientific calculator and graph paper.

Procedure

Students use a calculator to complete a table of values for $y = \sin \theta$ and $y = \cos \theta$ for θ between 0° and 360°. They plot points from the table to graph both functions. Students compare the two graphs and find the number of angles on the graph that produce a given sine or cosine value.

Closure

Discuss questions 1 and 2 in class. For question 1, students should point out the shape of the curves, the maximum and minimum values, and the θ-intercepts. For question 2, students can see how many values satisfy each equation by examining the graphs.

Explorations and Projects Book, Copyright © McDougal Littell Inc.

Algebra 2 Projects
Teacher Notes

Project Notes

Mathematical Goals

- Conduct an experiment and record data in a table.
- Draw a scatter plot of the data.
- Write a linear equation based upon the data and use it to predict values beyond the data.

Planning

Materials

- strong rubber band
- 2 large paper clips
- a paper cup
- 20 marbles
- a ruler (preferably transparent)
- graph paper
- pencil

Project Teams

Students can choose a partner and decide how to conduct the experiment together. After collecting their data, they can share the work of analyzing the data and writing the report.

Guiding Students' Work

Before students conduct the experiment, it may be helpful to work with the whole class on a list of goals for the experiment, and then have each pair of students discuss the reasoning for the goals in their report. Students should share responsibilities for the project and contribute to each part of it.

Second-Language Learners

Students learning English are likely to benefit from working cooperatively with English-fluent students when writing their reports.

Rubric for Chapter 2 Project

4 Students conduct the experiment and accurately record the data. They draw the scatter plot correctly and all labels are made on the graph. They write an accurate equation to model the data and correctly calculate an estimate for the length of the rubber band with 20 marbles in the cup. The report is well written and contains a clear analysis of the four points listed in the text. The

 Explorations and Projects Book, Copyright © McDougal Littell Inc.

report also indicates an understanding of the mathematical ideas of the project. Students complete the extension ideas and investigate the three possibilities listed.

3 Students complete the experiment and record the data accurately. Their graphs are drawn correctly, and the calculations and equations made are correct for the data collected. The written report touches on the four points listed in the text and reflects an understanding of the mathematical ideas, but students did not extend the project to check their work or look at other factors.

2 Students complete the experiment and record the data in the table. A mistake is made in the calculation of the equation for the line or in the estimate for 20 marbles. The report is written and is complete but does not convey a thorough understanding of the mathematical ideas of the project. Students did not extend the project using the ideas listed in the text.

1 Students did not complete the experiment or complete only part of it and then guess the results for the remaining parts. Students draw the graphs incorrectly or not at all, and miscalculate the equation of the line. A report is written but is incomplete and does not convey any understanding of the concepts of the project. Students should be encouraged to speak with the teacher as soon as possible to review their work and to make a new start on the project.

For the Student

Rubric for Chapter 2 Project

4 You conduct the experiment and accurately record the data. You draw the scatter plot correctly and all labels are made on the graph. You write an accurate equation to model the data and correctly calculate an estimate for the length of the rubber band with 20 marbles in the cup. The report is well written and contains a clear analysis of the four points listed in the text. The report also indicates an understanding of the mathematical ideas of the project. You complete the extension ideas and investigate the three possibilities listed.

3 You complete the experiment and record the data accurately. Your graphs are drawn correctly, and the calculations and equations made are correct for the data collected. The written report touches on the four points listed in the text and reflects an understanding of the mathematical ideas, but you did not extend the project to check your work or look at other factors.

2 You complete the experiment and record the data in the table. A mistake is made in the calculation of the equation for the line or in the estimate for 20 marbles. The report is written and is complete but does not convey a thorough understanding of the mathematical ideas of the project. You did not extend the project using the ideas listed in the text.

1 You did not complete the experiment or complete only part of it and then guess the results for the remaining parts. You draw the graphs incorrectly or not at all, and miscalculate the equation of the line. A report is written but is incomplete and does not convey any understanding of the concepts of the project. You should speak with your teacher as soon as possible to review your work and to make a new start on the project.

Mathematical Goals

- Analyze patterns in the Sierpinski Triangle and in other transformations.
- Find values in a transformation used to create the Sierpinski Triangle.
- Enter and execute a program on a TI-82 graphing calculator to display the Sierpinski Triangle.
- Find values in a transformation used to create other fractals and display the fractal using a TI-82 graphing calculator.

Planning

Materials

- TI-82 graphing calculator, paper and pencil

Project Teams

Students work with a partner to complete the project. The partners should work closely together to discuss and perform each aspect of the project.

Guiding Students' Work

This project is an excellent example of using transformation matrices to create a fractal. If students understand what happens to points in certain types of transformations, they can use matrices to help draw the images. When students are finding the values in the matrices, encourage them to work step by step. Also, students may want to reread the project a few times to develop an understanding of the process used to solve for the variables.

Second-Language Learners

You might want to encourage students to determine the meaning of the term *self-similar* by looking at the word parts and at the picture of the Sierpinski Triangle. Elicit from them that *self-similar* describes a figure made up of smaller figures that look exactly like the original figure.

Using Technology

The program for the TI-83 is identical to the program for the TI-82, with one minor difference. The dim function on the TI-82 does not take parentheses; the dim function on the TI-83 does. So the line that reads $\{3,1\} \rightarrow \dim[D]$ on the TI-82 becomes $\{3,1\} \rightarrow \dim([D])$ on the TI-83.

Rubric for Chapter 4 Project

4 Students enter the program in their graphing calculators and display the Sierpinski Triangle on their calculator screen. Students also find correct values for the six variables for one of the given transformations. Students write a complete report that contains all the information asked for; it is evident from the report that students understand the concepts discussed in the project. Students extend the project and complete a self-assessment.

3 Students enter the program in their graphing calculators and display the Sierpinski Triangle on their calculator screen. Students also make an effort to find values for the six variables for one of the given transformations in the project, but one or two miscalculations prevent them from displaying the fractal. Students write a report describing their work, but it is incomplete. Students attempt to extend the project and provide a self-assessment.

2 Students enter the program in their calculators but cannot display the Sierpinski Triangle because of errors in entering the program. Students do not complete the calculations to find the values of the six variables listed. As a result, no other fractals are generated. If a report is written, it is incomplete and does not contain most of the work requested for the project. Students do not extend the project or provide a self-assessment.

1 Students try to enter the program but do not succeed in doing so. Students do not attempt to complete any other part of the project. Students should be encouraged to speak with the teacher as soon as possible to review their work and to make a new start on the project.

For the Student

Rubric for Chapter 4 Project

4 You enter the program in your graphing calculator and display the Sierpinski Triangle on your calculator screen. You also find correct values for the six variables for one of the given transformations. You write a complete report that contains all the information asked for; it is evident from the report that you understand the concepts discussed in the project. You extend the project and complete a self-assessment.

3 You enter the program in your graphing calculator and display the Sierpinski Triangle on your calculator screen. You also make an effort to find values for the six variables for one of the given transformations in the project, but one or two miscalculations prevent you from displaying the fractal. You write a report describing your work, but it is incomplete. You attempt to extend the project and provide a self-assessment.

2 You enter the program in your calculator but cannot display the Sierpinski Triangle because of errors in entering the program. You do not complete the calculations to find the values of the six variables listed. As a result, no other fractals are generated. If a report is written, it is incomplete and does not contain most of the work requested for the project. You do not extend the project or provide a self-assessment.

1 You try to enter the program but do not succeed in doing so. You do not attempt to complete any other part of the project. You should speak with your teacher as soon as possible to review your work and to make a new start on the project.

Project Notes

Mathematical Goals

- Perform an experiment and record data.
- Formulate a quadratic model for the data.
- Display the model and data points on a graph.
- Compare the model with the actual values.

Planning

Materials

- large (metal) can, nail, hammer, metric ruler, watch
- graphing calculator or graphing software

Project Teams

Students can select a partner and perform the experiment together. Then they can decide how to proceed to complete the project.

Guiding Students' Work

Punching the hole in the bottom of the can should be done under teacher supervision. Also, caution students to be careful when using the hammer and nail to create the hole.

This is a good project to illustrate to students the importance of keeping their work organized. An organized table of data values will make it easier to draw a scatter plot and calculate values for the quadratic model. Also, and perhaps more importantly, writing equations in an organized way presents the values so that they are more easily calculated and compared. Students should first simplify the equation so that it contains only the variables t and $h(t)$, then use this simplified equation to substitute t values and find an estimated water height.

Second-Language Learners

Students learning English can benefit from working on the research and writing a report of the project with the help of a peer tutor or aide.

Rubric for Chapter 5 Project

4 Students conduct the experiment and record the results in a data table. Students accurately substitute values into the equation and compare the measures and calculated values for experimental and predicted water height. Students graph both a scatter plot and the quadratic model and relate the two. A well-written report is developed that includes a goal statement, a complete data table, an evaluation, the graph, and an explanation, as well as some ideas on the extension of the project. The report shows an understanding of the mathematical content of the project.

3 Students perform the experiment and record the results in a data table. Students measure, substitute, and calculate values for the equation but make at least one mathematical error. Students graph the scatter plot and the quadratic model and compare the two. A report is written that contains all of the required parts and shows an understanding of the mathematics, but an extension of the project is not done.

2 Students complete the experiment and record the data values but have difficulty with the quadratic model. As a result, predicted values are incorrect and the graph of the quadratic model as well as the equation itself are incorrect. Students write a report that relates the mathematical ideas of the project with the experimental values, but some errors in understanding the concepts involved in the project are evident in the report.

1 Students complete the experiment but do not attempt to calculate predicted values. A quadratic model is not found and no attempt is made to relate the experimental data with a model. An incomplete report is written that does not indicate an whole-hearted attempt at doing the project or an understanding of the ideas being explored. Students should be encouraged to speak with the teacher as soon as possible to review their work and to make a new start on the project.

For the Student

Rubric for Chapter 5 Project

4 You conduct the experiment and record the results in a data table. You accurately substitute values into the equation and compare the measures and calculated values for experimental and predicted water height. You graph both a scatter plot and the quadratic model and relate the two. A well-written report is developed that includes a goal statement, a complete data table, an evaluation, the graph, and an explanation, as well as some ideas on the extension of the project.

3 You perform the experiment and record the results in a data table. You measure, substitute, and calculate values for the equation but make at least one mathematical error. You graph the scatter plot and the quadratic model and compare the two. A report is written that contains all of the required parts and shows an understanding of the mathematics, but an extension of the project is not done.

2 You complete the experiment and record the data values but have difficulty with the quadratic model. As a result, predicted values are incorrect and the graph of the quadratic model as well as the equation itself are incorrect. You write a report that relates the mathematical ideas of the project with the experimental values, but some errors in understanding are evident.

1 You complete the experiment but do not attempt to calculate predicted values. A quadratic model is not found and no attempt is made to relate the experimental data with a model. An incomplete report is written. You should speak with your teacher as soon as possible to review your work and to make a new start on the project.

Mathematical Goals

- Time and record a person as he or she walks a 60 ft course.
- Calculate each person's actual speed and predicted maximum speed.
- Graph and compare the actual and predicted maximum speeds.

Planning

Materials

- tape measure
- stopwatch

Project Teams

Students can select their partner and come up with a list of possible subjects to participate in the experiment together. Then the partners can decide how they want to divide up the remaining project tasks.

Guiding Students' Work

Make sure that students' measurements are accurate. For example, students are to measure only the leg length that begins at the bottom of the hip where the leg starts and ends at the bottom of the heel where the leg ends. Also, if students are using a track as a course, they should walk along a part of the track that has been measured to be 60 feet. When students are plotting actual and predicted speeds, make sure they select the correct variables. Leg length is the independent variable for both graphs, so it is plotted on the horizontal axis. Speed is the dependent variable for both graphs (actual speed for the first graph and predicted speed for the second graph), so it is plotted on the vertical axis.

Second-Language Learners

Students learning English may benefit from conducting their experiments and working on their reports with the help of a peer tutor or aide.

Rubric for Chapter 7 Project

4 Students select ten subjects and make accurate measurements. Each subject is timed and a chart showing all times and speeds is completed. Actual and predicted speeds are calculated correctly, and students plot these values on a graph. A well-written report is done that includes all of the requested information. The comparison of the graphs in the report indicates an understanding of the mathematics of the project. Students also extend the project by exploring walking speeds on other planets or by discussing the centripetal force formula.

3 Students select ten subjects and accurately take measurements. The subjects are timed and a chart is completed showing all times and speeds. Some calculations are incorrect, or minor errors are made in plotting the points. Students submit a report that includes all the charts, graphs, and explanations, and that shows an understanding of the concepts of the project. Students also extend the project by looking into walking speeds on other planets or by exploring the centripetal force formula.

2 Students select ten subjects, accurately take measurements and complete the experiment, but they do not display their results correctly. Values are miscalculated and the graphs of the data are incorrect. Students do make an attempt to understand the project. Their report contains all the project data and information requested, but it is clear that some of the main ideas are not completely understood. Students attempt to extend the project, but it is not completed.

1 Students select only a few subjects for the experiment and complete some of the measurements. However, they do not record all of the lengths and speeds and do not calculate correctly the actual or predicted speeds. Students plot only one graph or do not complete a graph at all. If a report is written, it is incomplete and does not show an understanding of the project. Students should be encouraged to speak with the teacher as soon as possible to review their work and to make a new start on the project.

For the Student

Rubric for Chapter 7 Project

4 You select ten subjects and make accurate measurements. Each subject is timed and a chart showing all times and speeds is completed. Actual and predicted speeds are calculated correctly, and you plot these values on a graph. A well-written report is done that includes all of the requested information. The comparison of the graphs in the report indicates an understanding of the mathematics of the project.

3 You select ten subjects and accurately take measurements. The subjects are timed and a chart is completed showing all times and speeds. Some calculations are incorrect, or minor errors are made in plotting the points. You submit a report that includes all the charts, graphs, and explanations, and that shows an understanding of the concepts of the project.

2 You select ten subjects, accurately take measurements and complete the experiment, but you do not display your results correctly. Values are miscalculated and the graphs of the data are incorrect. You do make an attempt to understand the project. Your report contains all the project data and information requested, but it is clear that some of the main ideas are not completely understood.

1 You select only a few subjects for the experiment and complete some of the measurements. However, you do not record all of the lengths and speeds and do not calculate correctly the actual or predicted speeds. You plot only one graph or do not complete a graph at all. You should speak with your teacher as soon as possible to review your work and to make a new start on the project.

Project Notes

Mathematical Goals

- Collect and organize data using a scatter plot and table.
- Model data with a linear function and an exponential function.
- Graph linear and exponential functions.
- Select the best model for the data collected.

Planning

Materials

- piece of paper, wastebasket, yardstick
- graph paper, graphing calculator or graphing software

Project Teams

Students may work with a partner and assist each other in completing the experiment. Then they can decide which model best fits each of their own data.

Guiding Students' Work

To get a more accurate set of data, suggest that students repeat the experiment two or three times and use the results of the combined trials in their table and graph. If students are working in pairs, they may want to have each person complete the experiment and then combine the data into one table and graph. Also, if students are using a graphing calculator, encourage them to use the value of r, the correlation coefficient, that the calculator displays for both the linear model and the exponential model in their report. Once students have graphed their two equations and the scatter plot, discuss the indications of the graphs verbally before having them write their reports.

Second-Language Learners

A peer tutor or aide might help students learning English discuss and organize their ideas for the written report.

Rubric for Chapter 8 Project 1

4 Students complete the experiment and record the results correctly. They make an accurate scatter plot of the data with axes and scale shown. Their descriptions are clear and correctly relate the data collected with the mathematical ideas. Both their linear and exponential models are calculated and written correctly, then graphed accurately. They repeat the experiment a number of times, and also repeat the experiment with a real basketball and hoop. Their final report is well thought out and clearly presented.

 Explorations and Projects Book, Copyright © McDougal Littell Inc.

3 Students complete the experiment and table and calculate both a linear and an exponential model, but they may not make all of the calculations correctly or do not relate all of the mathematical ideas to the data. Students include all of the information required for the report and show they extended the project by completing the experiment more times and using a real basketball and hoop. The report is clear and shows a considerable effort.

2 Students complete the experiment but may not accurately record, calculate, or describe the data. Only some of the models are drawn on the graph, and the table may be incomplete. They repeat only the wastebasket experiment but do not do the experiment with a real basketball and hoop. A report is written but may not include all of the ideas necessary to convey the meaning of the activity.

1 Students do not show that they understand the mathematical ideas of the chapter and their work is incomplete. The descriptions of the graph are inaccurate and the calculations in the table are not complete. The linear and exponential functions models are not correctly related to the data and the report does not convey an understanding of the material or a significant effort to complete the activity. Students should be encouraged to speak with the teacher as soon as possible to review their work and to make a new start on the project.

For the Student

Rubric for Chapter 8 Project 1

4 You complete the experiment and record the results correctly. You make an accurate scatter plot of the data with axes and scale shown. Your descriptions are clear and correctly relate the data collected with the mathematical ideas. Both your linear and exponential models are calculated and written correctly, then graphed accurately. You repeat the experiment a number of times, and also repeat the experiment with a real basketball and hoop. Your final report is well thought out and clearly presented.

3 You complete the experiment and table and calculate both a linear and an exponential model, but you may not make all of the calculations correctly or do not relate all of the mathematical ideas to the data. You include all of the information required for the report and show you extended the project by completing the experiment more times and using a real basketball and hoop. The report is clear and shows a considerable effort.

2 You complete the experiment but may not accurately record, calculate, or describe the data. Only some of the models are drawn on the graph, and the table may be incomplete. You repeat only the wastebasket experiment but do not do the experiment with a real basketball and hoop. Your report does not include all of the ideas necessary to convey the meaning of the activity.

1 You do not show that you understand the mathematical ideas of the chapter and your work is incomplete. The descriptions of the graph are inaccurate and the calculations in the table are not complete. The linear and exponential functions models are not correctly related to the data. You should speak with your teacher as soon as possible to review your work and to make a new start on the project.

Project Notes

Mathematical Goals

- Collect and organize experimental data in a table.
- Calculate a bounce factor from the data.
- Write an exponential equation that describes rebound height as a function of the number of bounces.

Planning

Materials

- a ball
- two metersticks or a tape measure

Project Teams

Students can choose their partners and decide on how to divide up their project responsibilities. They should choose a convenient place to do the experiment and record their results.

Guiding Students' Work

To ensure enough trials in the experiment, students should use a specific number of drop heights, such as 10 or 15. This will also ensure a better mean bounce factor. Also, discuss with students that the mean bounce factor is always a number greater than 0 and less than 1 because all of the recorded bounce factors are greater than 0 and less than 1.

Second-Language Learners

Students learning English are likely to benefit from working cooperatively with English-fluent students when writing their reports.

Rubric for Chapter 8 Project 2

4 Students complete the experiment and record the results in a table. The data from the table are analyzed correctly and the bounce factors and mean bounce factor are calculated correctly. Students write a clear and thorough report relating the project goals with the mathematical concepts of the chapter. They include prediction tables as well as a correctly written exponential model for the experiment. Students extend the project using other balls and do research on a ball in a sport.

3 Students complete the experiment and record the results in a table. Students also calculate all of the bounce factors correctly, and make predictions about the number of bounces in their report. The report is written clearly and indicates an understanding of the mathematics, but it also shows a minimum amount of work in the prediction tables and in the analysis of the ideas. Students do not extend the project beyond the specific tasks in the text.

2 Students perform the experiment and make a table for the data but do not calculate some of the bounce factors or the mean bounce factor correctly. Students make predictions from the data, but they do not indicate an understanding of the mathematical ideas about exponential equations and their meanings, and the values of *a* or *b* in the equation are not correct. Students turn in a report and make an attempt at understanding the project, but the report is unclear and does not extend the project beyond the bounce experiment or the analysis of the data.

1 Students record only a few bounce heights in a table and do not show a record of the data. Students do not make a prediction table but guess what the equation will be and what the number of bounces will be without experimentation. A report is turned in, but it is incomplete and does not state project goals, describe procedures, or present data. Students should be encouraged to speak with the teacher as soon as possible to review their work and to make a new start on the project.

For the Student

Rubric for Chapter 8 Project 2

4 You complete the experiment and record the results in a table. The data from the table are analyzed correctly and the bounce factors and mean bounce factor are calculated correctly. You write a clear and thorough report relating the project goals with the mathematical concepts of the chapter. You include prediction tables as well as a correctly written exponential model for the experiment. You extend the project using other balls and do research on a ball in a sport.

3 You complete the experiment and record the results in a table. You also calculate all of the bounce factors correctly, and make predictions about the number of bounces in your report. The report is written clearly and indicates an understanding of the mathematics, but it also shows a minimum amount of work in the prediction tables and in the analysis of the ideas. You do not extend the project beyond the specific tasks in the text.

2 You perform the experiment and make a table for the data but do not calculate some of the bounce factors or the mean bounce factor correctly. You make predictions from the data, but you do not indicate an understanding of the mathematical ideas about exponential equations and their meanings, and the values of *a* or *b* in the equation are not correct. You turn in a report and make an attempt at understanding the project, but the report is unclear and does not extend the project beyond the bounce experiment or the analysis of the data.

1 You record only a few bounce heights in a table and do not show a record of the data. You do not make a prediction table but guess what the equation will be and what the number of bounces will be without experimentation. A report is turned in, but it is incomplete and does not state project goals, describe procedures, or present data. You should speak with your teacher as soon as possible to review your work and to make a new start on the project.

Project Notes

Mathematical Goals

- Collect and organize athletic data for both men and women.
- Display the data in a scatter plot.
- Calculate both linear and exponential regression models of the data.
- Predict future performances based upon the models.

Planning

Materials

- graphing calculator or statistical software
- Olympic data source

Project Teams

Students can decide on the members of their group and then work together to select, draw, and interpret the data. The team members work together to understand the equations and calculations of the project and how to complete the graphs.

Guiding Students' Work

Working together and discussing all aspects of the project can help students to understand the goals of the project and how to complete the necessary calculations. Encourage students to discuss their ideas within the groups. Also, it may help to review the meaning of linear and exponential equations as well as the shapes of their graphs. Discussing both exponential growth and exponential decay may help some students create their exponential model.

Second-Language Learners

The idiomatic expression *compete against the clock* may not be familiar to students learning English. If necessary, explain that it means "to try to accomplish a certain goal speedily, or before there is no time left."

Rubric for Chapter 8 Project 3

4 Students collect and organize data from an Olympic sport and accurately draw scatter plots. The linear and exponential models that are drawn are done accurately. A report is written that includes graphs of the scatter plots and their regression equations, equations for the linear and exponential models and how they were found, and an evaluation of the models. The report is written clearly and an understanding of the mathematics of the project is conveyed. Students also extend the project by comparing results with other groups or discussing human limits.

 Explorations and Projects Book, Copyright © McDougal Littell Inc.

3 Students collect and organize data and accurately draw scatter plots, but either the linear or the exponential model has at least one error in it. A report is written and an attempt is made to explain the equations and ideas of the project, but some errors are made in the analysis of the models. The report includes the table, scatter plots, graphs, models, and an evaluation of the models. Students also extend the project by comparing their result with other groups or by discussing human limits.

2 Students collect and organize data and draw the scatter plots but do not draw the linear and exponential models correctly or draw only one of the two models. Students write a report, but it does not include all of the graphs, all of the equations, and it only analyzes part of the data. An attempt is made to understand the meaning of the project and to predict future performances, but it is clear from the report that students do not have a good understanding of the key concepts involved. Students also do not extend the project.

1 Students collect data but do not organize it correctly. Both the linear model and the exponential model, if completed at all, are incorrect. If a report is written, it is incomplete because it does not contain graphs that explain the data. No evaluation of limits is done, and the project is not extended in any way. Students should be encouraged to speak with the teacher as soon as possible to review their work and to make a new start on the project.

For the Student

Rubric for Chapter 8 Project 3

4 You collect and organize data from an Olympic sport and accurately draw scatter plots. The linear and exponential models that are drawn are done accurately. A report is written that includes graphs of the scatter plots and their regression equations, equations for the linear and exponential models and how they were found, and an evaluation of the models. The report is written and an understanding of the mathematics of the project is conveyed.

3 You collect and organize data and accurately draw scatter plots, but either the linear or the exponential model has at least one error in it. A report is written and an attempt is made to explain the equations and ideas of the project, but some errors are made in the analysis of the models. The report includes the table, scatter plots, graphs, models, and an evaluation of the models.

2 You collect and organize data and draw the scatter plots but do not draw the linear and exponential models correctly or draw only one of the two models. You write a report, but it does not include all of the graphs, all of the equations, and it only analyzes part of the data. An attempt is made to understand the meaning of the project and to predict future performances, but it is clear from the report that you do not have a good understanding of the key concepts involved.

1 You collect data but do not organize it correctly. Both the linear model and the exponential model, if completed at all, are incorrect. If a report is written, it is incomplete because it does not contain graphs that explain the data. You should speak with your teacher as soon as possible to review your work and to make a new start on the project.

Project Notes

Mathematical Goals

- Express the surface area of a cylinder as a function of its base radius only.
- Find the dimensions of the cylinder that minimize surface area.
- Investigate other shapes and minimize their surface area for a given volume.
- Select the best shape with minimum surface area for a given volume.

Planning

Materials

- graphing calculator or graphing software
- spreadsheet software

Project Teams

Students can select their groups and all members can work together on the ideas and calculations for the project. Groups may find it helpful to discuss the ideas of the project and to decide how to solve the problems.

Guiding Students' Work

Some students may need a review of the formulas for surface area and volume. If this is the case, review the formulas for the basic shapes, such as cylinders, cubes, and prisms. Also, the project involves writing the formula for surface area in terms of base radius only. If students are having difficulty with this, guide them in their solution by explaining the hint given in Step 1. If students cannot understand one type of solution method, have them try a different method. For example, if students are using a graph to try to minimize surface area but do not know how to read the graph, have them use a spreadsheet. Then have them relate the spreadsheet to the graph.

Second-Language Learners

Students learning English can benefit from working in small groups to design their containers and write their reports.

Rubric for Chapter 9 Project

4 Students correctly express the surface area of a cylinder as a function of base radius only and accurately find the dimensions that minimize surface area. Students then investigate other shapes and minimize their surface areas. Students make a well-organized presentation of their report, describing their procedures and using data to support their conclusions. The report includes all of the information requested. Students also extend the project by completing at least one of the suggestions given.

---

3 Students write the surface area as a function of base radius only and accurately find the dimensions that minimize the surface area of the cylinder. Students' investigate other shapes and minimize their surface areas as well, but make errors in some of the calculations. The presentation is made and conclusions are drawn, but there are some errors in logic or conclusions are not supported by data. Students extend the project using one of the suggestions given.

2 Students make an attempt to write the surface area as a function of base radius but make an error in their calculations and do not minimize the surface area correctly. Students make the same mistake when investigating other shapes. Students try to make a presentation, but it is not done well because of the lack of understanding of the ideas of the project. Students draw incorrect conclusions and try to support them with data. The written report is not clear. Students do not extend the project.

1 Students do not correctly minimize the surface area of a cylinder because they do not write the surface area as a function of base radius only. Students do not investigate other shapes for possible containers and therefore no comparison is made to find the best shape. If a presentation is made, it demonstrates a poor attempt at completing the project. Students should be encouraged to speak with the teacher as soon as possible to review their work and to make a new start on the project.

For the Student

Rubric for Chapter 9 Project

4 You correctly express the surface area of a cylinder as a function of base radius only and accurately find the dimensions that minimize surface area. You then investigate other shapes and minimize their surface areas. You make a well-organized presentation of your report, describing your procedures and using data to support your conclusions.

3 You write the surface area as a function of base radius only and accurately find the dimensions that minimize the surface area of the cylinder. You investigate other shapes and minimize their surface areas as well, but make errors in some of the calculations. The presentation is made and conclusions are drawn, but there are some errors in logic or conclusions are not supported by data.

2 You make an attempt to write the surface area as a function of base radius but make an error in your calculations and do not minimize the surface area correctly. You make the same mistake when investigating other shapes. You try to make a presentation, but it is not done well because of the lack of understanding of the ideas of the project. You draw incorrect conclusions and try to support them with data. The written report is not clear.

1 You do not correctly minimize the surface area of a cylinder because you do not write the surface area as a function of base radius only. You do not investigate other shapes for possible containers and therefore no comparison is made to find the best shape. You should speak with your teacher as soon as possible to review your work and to make a new start on the project.

Project Notes

Mathematical Goal

- Design a logo composed of conic sections for an organization.

Planning

Materials

- graphing calculator or graphing software
- posterboard
- markers or other coloring tools

Project Teams

Students can work alone or with a partner to complete the project. If students work with a partner, they should work together on all phases of the project, including selecting the organization, choosing the conic sections for the logo, and designing the logo.

Guiding Students' Work

Students may have difficulty writing the equations for their conic sections. If so, work through the logic with them so they can translate their ideas into the mathematical equations. Also, if students have difficulty selecting an organization, you may want to develop a list of possible companies with names that lend themselves to logos containing conic sections.

Second-Language Learners

Students learning English should be able to design and present their logos to the class independently, but they might benefit from discussing with English-proficient students what each of the signs, represented by the logos or icons, means.

Rubric for Chapter 10 Project

4 Students select an organization and design an interesting logo using conic sections. The logo is appropriate for the organization and contains all of the features listed in the text. The poster of the logo is well drawn and neatly done. Students make an interesting presentation of their design to the class and include all of the aspects of designing the logo in the presentation. Students extend the project in one of the three ways listed.

3 Students select an organization and design a logo using conic sections. The logo is appropriate for the organization and the poster is neatly done. Students make a presentation of their logo to the class, but the presentation is incomplete because students do not explain all aspects of the project, such

Explorations and Projects Book, Copyright © McDougal Littell Inc.

as the equations and their restrictions or how the logo relates to the organization. Students extend the project in one of the three ways listed.

2 Students select an organization and design a logo using conic sections, but the design selected does not relate to the organization or is not easily understood. A neatly drawn poster is made of the logo. Students make a presentation but do not explain all of the parts of the project. No attempt is made to extend the project.

1 Students select an organization and come up with an idea for a logo but do not draw the logo with a graphing calculator or graphing software. No poster is made of a logo, and if a presentation is made, it is incomplete because it does not include an explanation of the equations used in the project or how the logo was designed. Students should be encouraged to speak with the teacher as soon as possible to review their work and to make a new start on the project.

For the Student

Rubric for Chapter 10 Project

4 You select an organization and design an interesting logo using conic sections. The logo is appropriate for the organization and contains all of the features listed in the text. The poster of the logo is well drawn and neatly done. You make an interesting presentation of your design to the class and include all of the aspects of designing the logo in the presentation. You extend the project in one of the three ways listed.

3 You select an organization and design a logo using conic sections. The logo is appropriate for the organization and the poster is neatly done. You make a presentation of your logo to the class, but the presentation is incomplete because you do not explain all aspects of the project, such as the equations and their restrictions or how the logo relates to the organization. You extend the project in one of the three ways listed.

2 You select an organization and design a logo using conic sections, but the design selected does not relate to the organization or is not easily understood. A neatly drawn poster is made of the logo. You make a presentation but do not explain all of the parts of the project. No attempt is made to extend the project.

1 You select an organization and come up with an idea for a logo but do not draw the logo with a graphing calculator or graphing software. No poster is made of a logo, and if a presentation is made, it is incomplete because it does not include an explanation of the equations used in the project or how the logo was designed. You should speak with your teacher as soon as possible to review your work and to make a new start on the project.

Mathematical Goals

- Gather data on college costs.
- Organize the data in a spreadsheet.
- Analyze the data using different scenarios of saving for college.
- Compare the scenarios and discuss their feasibility.

Planning

Materials

- sources to find data on college costs
- spreadsheet software

Project Teams

Students can select the members of their group and can work together on all aspects of the project, including gathering the data, deciding how to analyze the data, completing the calculations, and writing the report.

Guiding Students' Work

If students decide to select data from different types of colleges, make sure that they do not mix the data selections and compare the colleges or universities incorrectly. If students do not have access to sources for data, you can provide the information at the right for them.

Second-Language Learners

Students learning English will benefit from working with a peer tutor or in small groups to create the spreadsheets and write their reports for this project.

Rubric for Chapter 11 Project

4 Students collect data on college costs for various colleges and universities and use a spreadsheet correctly to project future costs and savings. Students investigate several scenarios for saving and extend the project by comparing both private and public institutions. Students complete a report and convey their data and findings clearly and concisely.

Average College Costs		
Year	Public Institutions	Private Institutions
1979–80	$2,165	$4,912
1980–81	$2,373	$5,470
1981–82	$2,663	$6,166
1982–83	$2,945	$6,920
1983–84	$3,156	$7,508
1984–85	$3,408	$8,202
1985–86	$3,571	$8,885
1986–87	$3,805	$9,676
1987–88	$4,050	$10,512
1988–89	$4,274	$11,189
1989–90	$4,504	$12,018
1990–91	$4,757	$12,910
1991–92	$5,135	$13,907
1992–93	$5,379	$14,634
1993–94	$5,695	$15,532

Explorations and Projects Book, Copyright © McDougal Littell Inc.

3 Students collect data about various colleges and universities and use a spreadsheet to project future costs and savings. Some of the calculations are incorrect, however, and, therefore, the analysis is somewhat inaccurate. Students write a report that contains all of the data and information used in the project. The report is well written and complete.

2 Students collect college cost data and attempt to analyze the data in a spreadsheet but make mistakes both in their calculations and in the analysis of the results. Students only look at a few ways to save for college and do not explore other possibilities for comparison. Students write a report, but it is poorly organized and does not contain a good discussion of the feasibility of the scenarios.

1 Students gather some cost data on colleges and universities but do not correctly analyze it in a spreadsheet. An analysis of the data is not completed and only one, if any, scenario is investigated. If a report is written, it is incomplete and does not indicate that any effort was made to complete the project. Students should be encouraged to speak with the teacher as soon as possible to review their work and to make a new start on the project.

For the Student

Rubric for Chapter 11 Project

4 You collect data on college costs for various colleges and universities and use a spreadsheet correctly to project future costs and savings. You investigate several scenarios for saving and extend the project by comparing both private and public institutions. You complete a report and convey your data and findings clearly and concisely.

3 You collect data about various colleges and universities and use a spreadsheet to project future costs and savings. Some of the calculations are incorrect, however, and, therefore, the analysis is somewhat inaccurate. You write a report that contains all of the data and information used in the project. The report is well written and complete.

2 You collect college cost data and attempt to analyze the data in a spreadsheet but make mistakes both in your calculations and in the analysis of the results. You only look at a few ways to save for college and do not explore other possibilities for comparison. You write a report, but it is poorly organized and does not contain a good discussion of the feasibility of the scenarios.

1 You gather some cost data on colleges and universities but do not correctly analyze it in a spreadsheet. An analysis of the data is not completed and only one, if any, scenario is investigated. If a report is written, it is incomplete and does not indicate that any effort was made to complete the project. You should speak with your teacher as soon as possible to review your work and to make a new start on the project.

Mathematical Goal

- Develop a strategy for winning a game.

Planning

Materials

- Cups
- Counters
- Egg carton

Project Teams

Students can choose a partner to play the game and then collect the materials needed. They can follow Steps 1–3 to begin playing.

Guiding Students' Work

As students set up their boards and start to play, you can circulate around the room to make sure each group is playing the game according to the rules. Encourage students to play several games and to discuss their strategies for winning.

Second-Language Learners

Students learning English should have no difficulties understanding any of the vocabulary used in this project.

Rubric for Chapter 12 Project 1

4 Students play the game and develop strategies for winning. They give a clear and interesting oral report to the class and demonstrate successful strategies for winning. They explain how the strategies work and how they were developed.

3 Students play the game and develop strategies for winning. Their oral report includes a demonstration of the strategies, but the explanation of how they were developed is not entirely clear.

2 Students play the game but cannot seem to develop any strategies for winning. They give an oral report and attempt to explain their strategies, but the class is not convinced they work.

1 Students start to play the game but are not sure about how to proceed. They have difficulty understanding the rules and do not develop any strategies for winning. Students should be encouraged to speak with the teacher as soon as possible to review their work and to make a new start on the project.

Explorations and Projects Book, Copyright © McDougal Littell Inc.

For the Student

Rubric for Chapter 12 Project 1

4 You play the game and develop strategies for winning. You give a clear and interesting oral report to the class and demonstrate successful strategies for winning. You explain how the strategies work and how they were developed.

3 You play the game and develop strategies for winning. Your oral report includes a demonstration of the strategies, but the explanation of how they were developed is not entirely clear.

2 You play the game but cannot seem to develop any strategies for winning. You give an oral report and attempt to explain your strategies, but the class is not convinced they work.

1 You start to play the game but are not sure about how to proceed. You have difficulty understanding the rules and do not develop any strategies for winning. You should speak with your teacher as soon as possible to review your work and to make a new start on the project.

Mathematical Goals

- Select a real-world situation to model with a flip book.
- Design and create a flip book modeling the situation.
- Calculate the number of combinations the flip book shows.

Planning

Materials

- pad of paper, posterboard, scissors
- photos from magazines or coloring utensils

Project Teams

Students can work individually to make their flip books, but if they decide to work in pairs, every part of the project should be completed as a team.

Guiding Students' Work

The description of the flip book and how it works will be better understood by students if they can see an example before trying to make their own. If possible, put together a real flip book for students to see, such as the planning a dinner flip book described in the project. Also, if students are having difficulty coming up with an idea for a flip book, it may help to have a list of areas where they may find ideas, such as selecting classes for the coming school year, clothing combinations, color combinations for parts of a design or map, or paths they can take home from school.

Second-Language Learners

The professions *police sketch artist*, *landscaper*, and *fashion designer* may not be familiar to some students learning English. If necessary, explain that a police sketch artist is "an artist who helps police track down criminals by using witness accounts to draw composite pictures of the criminals." A landscaper is "someone who designs and builds gardens, or decorates grounds." A fashion designer is "someone who designs fashions that are made into clothes." Students learning English may also wish to work on creating their flip books with the help of a peer tutor or aide.

Rubric for Chapter 12 Project 2

4 Students produce a flip book that is original and innovative. It is neatly drawn and well organized. A report is made that contains all of the information relating to the production of the book including the number of combinations in the book. The report is easy to read and discusses how other people in different professions can use a flip book for their job. Students extend the project by completing one or more of the suggestions given in the project.

3 Students produce a flip book that displays an interesting idea and is neatly drawn and put together. A report is made, but the report is either missing information relating to producing the book or it is not clear nor well written. The report does contain a discussion of how flip books can be used in careers, and students extend the project using one of the suggestions given in the project.

2 Students produce a flip book that displays an idea, but it is poorly put together. A report is made and contains some of the information relating to the book, but it is incomplete and is not well written. Students discuss some of the ideas about the flip book in their report. Students do not make any attempt to extend the project.

1 Students produce a flip book, but it is very poorly done and is incomplete. The flip book shows a lack of effort for the project. If a report is done, it is incomplete and contains only one or two of the pieces of information relating to the book. The report also shows a lack of effort to complete the project. Students make no attempt to extend the project. Students should be encouraged to speak with the teacher as soon as possible to review their work and to make a new start on the project.

For the Student

Rubric for Chapter 12 Project 2

4 You produce a flip book that is original and innovative. It is neatly drawn and well organized. A report is made that contains all of the information relating to the production of the book including the number of combinations in the book. The report is easy to read and discusses how other people in different professions can use a flip book for their job. You extend the project by completing one or more of the suggestions given in the project.

3 You produce a flip book that displays an interesting idea and is neatly drawn and put together. A report is made, but the report is either missing information relating to producing the book or it is not clear nor well written. The report does contain a discussion of how flip books can be used in careers, and you extend the project using one of the suggestions given in the project.

2 You produce a flip book that displays an idea, but it is poorly put together. A report is made and contains some of the information relating to the book, but it is incomplete and is not well written. You discuss some of the ideas about the flip book in your report. You do not make any attempt to extend the project.

1 You produce a flip book, but it is very poorly done and is incomplete. The flip book shows a lack of effort for the project. If a report is done, it is incomplete and contains only one or two of the pieces of information relating to the book. You should speak with your teacher as soon as possible to review your work and to make a new start on the project.

Mathematical Goals

- Survey at least twenty students on the taste of generic and name brand beverages.
- Evaluate the results of the survey.
- Analyze the evaluations to see if people can distinguish between generic beverages.

Planning

Materials

- generic version of a drink and one or more brand name versions of the same drink
- small paper cups for beverage sampling

Project Teams

Students can perform the survey and complete the project individually or in pairs. If students work in pairs, they should complete all phases of the project together, including calculating the various probabilities.

Guiding Students' Work

Students may need help understanding the meaning of the two formulas used in the project. If necessary, take the time to go over the variables and ideas involved in the equations and how they were developed.

Second-Language Learners

Students learning English should benefit from working cooperatively with a partner on their experiments. They might also wish to work with their partners to conduct the research and write the report.

Rubric for Chapter 12 Project 3

4 Students conduct the survey of twenty people and include their results in a report. The report is well written, neat, and contains the correct answers to the questions. The report also shows a solid understanding of the mathematical ideas being discussed in the project. Students extend the project by conducting another survey with another product and calculate the probabilities for that product.

3 Students conduct the survey of twenty people and include their results in a report. The report is neat and clear, but one or two of the calculations are not done correctly or the answers to some of the questions are not complete. The report indicates a good understanding of the mathematical ideas of the project. Students extend the project by conducting another survey with another product and calculate the probabilities for that product.

2 Students conduct the survey of twenty people and include their results in a report. While the report shows an effort to complete the project and understand the ideas, it does not contain all of the answers to the questions and does not indicate a good grasp of the meaning of the probabilities involved in the project. Students do not attempt to extend the project.

1 Students conduct a survey but survey only a few people. Students may or may not complete a report, but if one is done, it does not contain all of the answers to the questions and is poorly written. It is clear that students do not have an understanding of the probabilities involved in the project. Students should be encouraged to speak with the teacher as soon as possible to review their work and to make a new start on the project.

For the Student

Rubric for Chapter 12 Project 3

4 You conduct the survey of twenty people and include your results in a report. The report is well written, neat, and contains the correct answers to the questions. The report also shows a solid understanding of the mathematical ideas being discussed in the project. You extend the project by conducting another survey with another product and calculate the probabilities for that product.

3 You conduct the survey of twenty people and include your results in a report. The report is neat and clear, but one or two of the calculations are not done correctly or the answers to some of the questions are not complete. The report indicates a good understanding of the mathematical ideas of the project. You extend the project by conducting another survey with another product and calculate the probabilities for that product.

2 You conduct the survey of twenty people and include your results in a report. While the report shows an effort to complete the project and understand the ideas, it does not contain all of the answers to the questions and does not indicate a good grasp of the meaning of the probabilities involved in the project. You do not attempt to extend the project.

1 You conduct a survey but survey only a few people. You may or may not complete a report, but if one is done, it does not contain all of the answers to the questions and is poorly written. It is clear that you do not have an understanding of the probabilities involved in the project. You should speak with your teacher as soon as possible to review your work and to make a new start on the project.

Mathematical Goals

- Measure and record an angle of elevation using a transit.
- Measure and record distances from a tall object.
- Apply trigonometric ratios to calculate the height of a tall object using the angle of elevation and distance measurements.

Planning

Materials

- protractor
- drinking straw
- a piece of string
- small weight (such as a key or a washer)
- masking tape
- tape measure

Project Teams

Students can select their own partners and can work together to make the transit. Then they can use the transit with both methods to find the height of a tall object. Students should also work together to compile a report of their project.

Guiding Students' Work

It may be difficult for students to understand how to use a transit. If this is the case, make your own transit before explaining the project and demonstrate how it is used. Also, the steps listed in calculating the height of a tall object using the indirect approach involve the use of geometry. Students may find it helpful to redraw the figure given in the project pages on a piece of paper and label the parts of the triangles (the angles and lengths) being calculated at each step. This may help in understanding the logic behind the approach.

Second-Language Learners

Students learning English may benefit from working with a peer tutor or aide to write their summary reports.

Rubric for Chapter 13 Project

4 Students make their transit and measure the angle of elevation and distances accurately. Students then calculate the height of the tall object correctly using both methods and assemble their measurements and results in a report. The report contains all of the project information and conveys this information so that it is clear and easily understood. The project is extended by completing one of the suggestions given in the text.

3 Students make their transit correctly. They measure the angle of elevation accurately as well as the distances needed to complete the calculations. Students try to calculate the height of a tall object but make an error in applying and using the trigonometric ratios. A report is written and contains all of the data and calculations completed. The report also presents the ideas clearly. Students accomplish or attempt to extend the project by completing one of the suggestions given in the text.

2 Students make their transit correctly but do not use it properly to measure the angle of elevation. Their calculations of the height of the tall object using trigonometric ratios are not accurate, but students make an attempt at completing the project. Students write a report and it contains most of the information from the project. Students do not attempt to extend the project.

1 Students do not make their transit correctly and, as a result, do not have an accurate measurement for an angle of elevation. Students do not attempt to calculate the height of the tall object using either method and, if a report is written, it is incomplete and shows little effort to complete the project. Students should be encouraged to speak with the teacher as soon as possible to review their work and to make a new start on the project.

For the Student

Rubric for Chapter 13 Project

4 You make your transit and measure the angle of elevation and distances accurately. You then calculate the height of the tall object correctly using both methods and assemble your measurements and results in a report. The report contains all of the project information and conveys this information so that it is clear and easily understood. The project is extended by completing one of the suggestions given in the text.

3 You make your transit correctly. You measure the angle of elevation accurately as well as the distances needed to complete the calculations. You try to calculate the height of a tall object but make an error in applying and using the trigonometric ratios. A report is written and contains all of the data and calculations completed. The report also presents the ideas clearly. You accomplish or attempt to extend the project by completing one of the suggestions given in the text.

2 You make your transit correctly but do not use it properly to measure the angle of elevation. Your calculations of the height of the tall object using trigonometric ratios are not accurate, but you make an attempt at completing the project. You write a report and it contains most of the information from the project. You do not attempt to extend the project.

1 You do not make your transit correctly and, as a result, do not have an accurate measurement for an angle of elevation. You do not attempt to calculate the height of the tall object using either method and, if a report is written, it is incomplete and shows little effort to complete the project. You should speak with your teacher as soon as possible to review your work and to make a new start on the project.

Project Notes

Mathematical Goals

- Perform an experiment to model simple harmonic motion.
- Relate experimental measurements to values in a trigonometric equation involving cosine.
- Graph the cosine equation.
- Compare and evaluate the results.

Planning

Materials

- a spring, paper clip, masking tape, 1 lb weight, string, meterstick
- stopwatch

Project Teams

Students can select their project teams and can work together to gather all of the materials and perform the experiment. Team members should also work together to write and graph the equations and to develop a written report for the group.

Guiding Students' Work

It may be easier for students to find the materials for the project at school and perform the experiment there. Also, before the groups perform the experiment, discuss the ideas of equilibrium position, oscillation, and amplitude, as they apply to the experiment. This will help students when they need to model their oscillation. Also, discuss why simple harmonic motion would be modeled with the cosine function and not the sine function by relating the graph for simple harmonic motion with that of the cosine function.

Second-Language Learners

Students learning English may benefit from writing their reports with the help of a peer tutor or aide.

Rubric for Chapter 14 Project

4 Students perform the experiment and make accurate measurements for the values of d and T. They then correctly relate these values to the cosine equation. An accurate graph is made and included in a well-written report, along with the other items listed in the text. Also included in the report is an in-depth comparison and evaluation of the experiment's model. Students also extend the project by addressing the idea of the damping function.

3 Students perform the experiment and make accurate measurements for the values of d and T. They then relate these values to the cosine function but make an error in the calculation of the equation or in the graph of the function. A report is written and contains all of the information relating to the project but does not make a thorough comparison or evaluation of the model. Students extend the project by investigating the damping function.

2 Students perform the experiment and make estimates for d and T but incorrectly relate them to the cosine function. Their graph is also incorrect and the written report shows that students do not understand the main ideas of the project. The report does contain an attempt at an evaluation of the model, but it is not complete or well done. Students do not make an attempt to extend the project.

1 Students make an attempt at performing the experiment but do not calculate the values of d and T correctly and do not make an effort to complete the project. As a result, an equation is not found and a graph is not drawn. If a report is written, it is poorly done and does not indicate an attempt to complete the project or an understanding of the mathematical ideas of the project. Students should be encouraged to speak with the teacher as soon as possible to review their work and to make a new start on the project.

For the Student

Rubric for Chapter 14 Project

4 You perform the experiment and make accurate measurements for the values of d and T. You then correctly relate these values to the cosine equation. An accurate graph is made and included in a well-written report, along with the other items listed in the text. Also included in the report is an in-depth comparison and evaluation of the experiment's model. You also extend the project by addressing the idea of the damping function.

3 You perform the experiment and make accurate measurements for the values of d and T. You then relate these values to the cosine function but make an error in the calculation of the equation or in the graph of the function. A report is written and contains all of the information relating to the project but does not make a thorough comparison or evaluation of the model. You extend the project by investigating the damping function.

2 You perform the experiment and make estimates for d and T but incorrectly relate them to the cosine function. Your graph is also incorrect and the written report shows that you do not understand the main ideas of the project. The report does contain an attempt at an evaluation of the model, but it is not complete or well done. You do not make an attempt to extend the project.

1 You make an attempt at performing the experiment but do not calculate the values of d and T correctly and do not make an effort to complete the project. As a result, an equation is not found and a graph is not drawn. If a report is written, it is poorly done and does not indicate an attempt to complete the project or an understanding of the mathematical ideas of the project. You should speak with your teacher as soon as possible to review your work and to make a new start on the project.

Answers to
Explorations

Answers to Algebra 1 Explorations

Exploration 1

1.

Square number	Grains of rice needed for square
1	1
2	2
3	$2 \cdot 2 = 4$
4	$2 \cdot 2 \cdot 2 = 8$
5	$2 \cdot 2 \cdot 2 \cdot 2 = 16$
6	$2 \cdot 2 \cdot 2 \cdot 2 \cdot 2 = 32$
7	$2 \cdot 2 \cdot 2 \cdot 2 \cdot 2 \cdot 2 = 64$
8	$2 \cdot 2 \cdot 2 \cdot 2 \cdot 2 \cdot 2 \cdot 2 = 128$
9	$2 \cdot 2 \cdot 2 \cdot 2 \cdot 2 \cdot 2 \cdot 2 \cdot 2 = 256$
10	$2 \cdot 2 \cdot 2 \cdot 2 \cdot 2 \cdot 2 \cdot 2 \cdot 2 \cdot 2 = 512$

2. 29; 63; $n - 1$; On each square, the number of factors of 2 is one less than the number of the square.

3. about 215 bags of wheat; Answers may vary. An example is given. The total value of the wheat would be greater than the value of 64 gold pieces.

Exploration 2

1. Robin's answer; They gave the driver $14.50 in all, so $7.25 is a reasonable estimate of half and $13.50 is not.

2. Answers may vary. If your answer is 13.50, your calculator divided first. If your answer is 7.25, your calculator added first.

3. addition; $14.50 \div 2 = 7.25$; division; $12.50 + 1 = 13.50$

4. 0.428571428; division; 6; subtraction

5. If Jeff enters a left parenthesis before he enters 12.50 and a right parenthesis after he enters the first 2, the calculator will add 12.5 and 2 before dividing.

Exploration 3

Number of triangles	Number of toothpicks
4	9
5	11
6	13
7	15
8	17
...	...
14	29

Questions

1. Answers may vary. An example is given. Each time the number of triangles increases by 1, the number of toothpicks increases by 2. In each row, the number of toothpicks is one more than twice the number of triangles.

2. 21; 201; 2,000,001; Answers may vary. An example is given. I used the pattern I described in Question 1.

3. $2n + 1$ toothpicks

Exploration 4

1. Answers may vary. An example is given. Step 1: Stand in front of the chair with your back to it. Step 2: Step back until your legs are near or actually touching the chair. Step 3: Bend your knees, leaning slightly forward above the waist until you are seated on the chair.

2–4. Answers may vary.

Exploration 5

1. If the die is fair, each outcome is equally likely to happen, so each number should occur about 4 times.

2–6. Answers may vary. Since the number of rolls is small, results may vary greatly.

2. Predictions should be reasonably close.

3. Most graphs should be similar.

4. Each fraction should be close to $\frac{1}{4}$.

5. An example is given. I think the more rolls there are, the closer the ratios will be to $\frac{1}{4}$.

6. They should be reasonably close.

Exploration 6

1. Subtract two 1-tiles from both sides of the equation. Then divide both sides into five equal parts to find that each x-tile is equal to one 1-tile; $x = 1$.

2. Subtract five 1-tiles from both sides of the equation. Then divide both sides into two equal parts to find that each x-tile is equal to five 1-tiles; $x = 5$.

3. Subtract five 1-tiles from both sides of the equation. Then divide both sides into three equal parts to find that each x-tile is equal to two 1-tiles; $x = 2$.

4. Subtract four 1-tiles from both sides of the equation. Then divide both sides into three equal parts to find that each x-tile is equal to three 1-tiles; $x = 3$.

Exploration 7

1. Answers may vary.

2. Students with coordinates such as $(-2, -3)$, $(-1, -2)$, $(0, -1)$, $(1, 0)$, $(2, 1)$, $(3, 2)$, and so on, should be standing. All the people standing up are located on a straight line.

3. For each equation, all the people will be located on a line.

Exploration 8

1, 2. Results may vary. Ratios should be close to 0.75.

3. Graphs may vary. Check students' work.

4. $y = 0.75x$; Check students' work.

5. The points plotted in Step 3 should lie close to the line graphed in Step 4. This result would support Leonardo da Vinci's observation.

Explorations and Projects Book, Copyright © McDougal Littell Inc.

Exploration 9

1. a. 2; (0, 0)

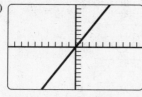

b. 2; (0, 3)

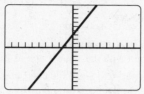

c. 2; (0, −3)

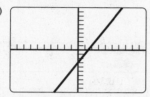

2.

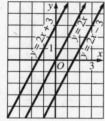

The three lines are parallel. Each line has slope 2, which is the coefficient of x in each equation. The y-coordinate of the point where each graph crosses the y-axis is equal to the number that is added to or subtracted from $2x$ in the equation.

3. The graph will be a line that is parallel to the lines in Step 1. The slope will be 2, since the coefficient of x is 2, and the graph will cross the y-axis at (0, 6), since 6 is added to $2x$ in the equation.

Exploration 10

Answers will vary. Examples are given.

1.

Number of pieces of spaghetti	Number of marbles needed to break spaghetti
1	3
2	7
3	11
4	16
5	20

2. Let n = the number of marbles and m = the number of pieces of spaghetti;

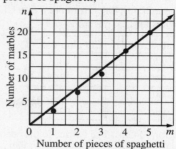 $n = 4m$.

3. If $m = 6$, $n = 24$; about 24 marbles.

4. Moving the chairs does affect the results. If the chairs are moved farther apart, fewer marbles are needed to break the spaghetti; if the chairs are moved closer together, more marbles are needed.

Exploration 11

1–3.

3. Answers may vary. An example is given. All the circled points lie below and to the right of the points labeled with zeros

4. Yes; Yes.

5.

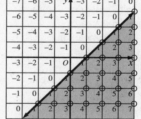

The border is the graph of the equation $x − y = 1$. Points on the line make the sides $x − y$ and 1 of the inequality $x − y \geq 1$ equal.

Exploration 12

1–4. Answers may vary. Students should recognize that comparing total numbers of points does not tell you who has the best aim. It is better to compare average numbers of points per drop.

Exploration 13

1.

No. of CDs	Cost at store ($)	CD club cost ($)
14	154	90
15	165	105
16	176	120

2. the CD club; No, since the cost for each CD is less at the store than through the club, at some point the savings per CD will overtake the initial savings from the 8 free CDs and the total cost will be less at the store.

3.

No. of CDs	Cost at store ($)	CD club cost ($)
20	220	180
30	330	330
40	440	480
50	550	630

4. The costs are equal for 30 CDs. The entries in the second and third columns of the table are the same for 30 CDs. If you are choosing based only on costs, choose the club if the number of CDs you plan to buy is greater than or equal to 14 and less than 30; choose the discount store otherwise. If you plan to buy 30 CDs, choose either.

5. $y = 11x$

6. $y = 15(x - 8)$

7.

8. The costs are equal for 30 CDs. The graphs intersect at $x = 30$. If you are choosing based only on costs, choose the club if the number of CDs you plan to buy is greater than or equal to 14 and less than 30; choose the discount store otherwise. If you plan to buy 30 CDs, choose either.

9. Both methods give the same answer. Answers may vary. Examples: The table method gives specific values. This can be helpful when the value you need appears in the table. However, if the value you need does not appear in the table, it may be difficult to find an exact solution. A graph gives a good visual picture of the situation, but may take more time than a table to create.

Exploration 14

1. a–c. The graph is the graph of all three equations.

2. All three graphs are identical.

3. Given any two of the equations, one can be obtained by multiplying both sides of the other by some number.

4. a–c. The graph is the graph of all three systems.

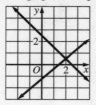

5. Each system has the solution $\left(2, \frac{1}{2}\right)$. This makes sense because each system consists of the equation $5x - 6y = 7$ and an equation with the same graph as $2x + 2y = 5$.

6. the system in part (c); Since the coefficients of y are opposites, this system can be solved by adding.

Exploration 15

Product of powers	Expanded product	Product as a single power
$10^2 \cdot 10^1$	$(10 \cdot 10)(10)$	10^3
$10^4 \cdot 10^2$	$(10 \cdot 10 \cdot 10 \cdot 10)(10 \cdot 10)$	10^6
$10^7 \cdot 10^1$	$(10 \cdot 10 \cdot 10 \cdot 10 \cdot 10 \cdot 10 \cdot 10)(10)$	10^8
$10^5 \cdot 10^6$	$(10 \cdot 10 \cdot 10 \cdot 10 \cdot 10)(10 \cdot 10 \cdot 10 \cdot 10 \cdot 10 \cdot 10)$	10^{11}
$10^0 \cdot 10^3$	$(1) \cdot (10 \cdot 10 \cdot 10)$	10^3

Quotient of powers	Expanded quotient	Quotient as a single power
$\dfrac{10^3}{10^2}$	$\dfrac{10 \cdot 10 \cdot 10}{10 \cdot 10}$	10
$\dfrac{10^6}{10^4}$	$\dfrac{10 \cdot 10 \cdot 10 \cdot 10 \cdot 10 \cdot 10}{10 \cdot 10 \cdot 10 \cdot 10}$	10^2
$\dfrac{10^{12}}{10^3}$	$\dfrac{10 \cdot 10 \cdot 10 \cdot 10 \cdot 10 \cdot 10 \cdot 10 \cdot 10 \cdot 10 \cdot 10 \cdot 10 \cdot 10}{10 \cdot 10 \cdot 10}$	10^9
$\dfrac{10^1}{10^3}$	$\dfrac{10}{10 \cdot 10 \cdot 10}$	10^{-2}
$\dfrac{10^0}{10^2}$	$\dfrac{1}{10 \cdot 10}$	10^{-2}

Exploration 16

1–3. Check students' work.

1. Let h = the length of the hypotenuse; $h^2 = 1^2 + 1^2 = 2$, so $h = \sqrt{2}$.

2. Let h = the length of the hypotenuse; $h^2 = 2^2 + 2^2 = 4 + 4 = 8$, so $h = \sqrt{8}$ Drawing segments from the midpoint of the hypotenuse to the midpoints of the legs forms two smaller right triangles. The legs of each smaller triangle are 1 unit long and each hypotenuse is $\sqrt{2}$ units long. Then the hypotenuse of the original triangle is $\sqrt{2} + \sqrt{2} = 2\sqrt{2}$.

3. 3 units: $\sqrt{18}$ units and $3\sqrt{2}$ units; 4 units: $\sqrt{32}$ units and $4\sqrt{2}$ units; 5 units: $\sqrt{50}$ units and $5\sqrt{2}$ units; The pattern seems to be that for any number $\sqrt{x^2 + x^2} = x\sqrt{2}$

4. Since $\sqrt{8} = \sqrt{4 \cdot 2}$ it makes sense that $\sqrt{8} = \sqrt{4} \cdot \sqrt{2} = 2\sqrt{2}$. Since $\sqrt{18} = \sqrt{9 \cdot 2}$, it makes sense that $\sqrt{18} = \sqrt{9} \cdot \sqrt{2} = 3\sqrt{2}$. Similarly, it makes sense that $\sqrt{32} = \sqrt{16} \cdot \sqrt{2} = 4\sqrt{2}$ and $\sqrt{50} = \sqrt{25 \cdot 2} = 5\sqrt{2}$.

Explorations and Projects Book, Copyright © McDougal Littell Inc.

Exploration 17

1.

Length of Side 1 (ft)	Length of Side 2 (ft)	Perimeter (ft)	Area (ft²)
1	14	30	14
14	1	30	14
2	13	30	26
13	2	30	26
3	12	30	36
12	3	30	36
4	11	30	44
11	4	30	44
5	10	30	50
10	5	30	50
6	9	30	54
9	6	30	54
7	8	30	56
8	7	30	56

2. 7 ft by 8 ft or 8 ft by 7 ft; 1 ft by 14 ft or 14 ft by 1 ft; Answers may vary. An example is given. I would recommend the 7 ft by 8 ft or 8 ft by 7 ft pen because its area is 4 times as large as the area of the 1 ft by 14 ft pen.

3. The graph is shaped like an upside-down U.

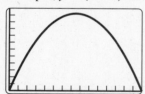

4. length of Side 2 $= \frac{1}{2}(30 - 2x) = 15 - x$; Let y be the area of the pen; $y = x(15 - x) = 15x - x^2$.

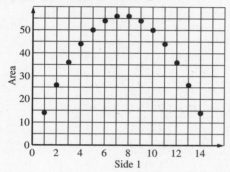

5. Answers may vary. An example is given. The graphs have the same shape; the graph in Step 3 consists of those points on the graph in Step 4 for which x and y are both integers.

Exploration 18

1. The greater the value of the coefficient of x^2, the narrower and steeper the parabola.

2. Check students' work. The graph of $y = 4x^2$ will be even narrower and steeper than the graph of $y = 3x^2$.

3. The smaller the coefficient of x^2, the wider and flatter the parabola.

4. Check students' work. The graph of $y = \frac{1}{4}x^2$ will be even wider and flatter than the graph of $y = \frac{1}{3}x^2$.

5. As the value of a increases from 0 to 1 and beyond, the graph of $y = ax^2$ gets narrower and steeper.

6. As the value of a decreases from 0 to −1 and beyond, the graph of $y = ax^2$ gets narrower and steeper, and the "U" opens downward.

Exploration 19

1.

$3x(x + 2) = 3x^2 + 6x$

2.
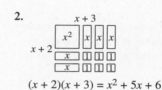

$(x + 2)(x + 3) = x^2 + 5x + 6$

3.
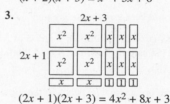

$(2x + 1)(2x + 3) = 4x^2 + 8x + 3$

4. Answers may vary. Check students' work.

Exploration 20

1–6. Check students' work.

7. x represents the height of the box. The rectangle outlined in red is the base of the box.

8. Answers may vary. An example is given. For an $8\frac{1}{2}$ in. by 11 in. rectangle, the length is $11 - 2x - 2\left(\frac{5}{8}\right) = 9.75 - 2x$; the width is $8\frac{1}{2} - 2x = 8.5 - 2x$, and the height is x.

9. Answers may vary.

Exploration 21

1. 1 and B, 2 and D, 3 and A, 4 and C

Equation 1   Equation 2

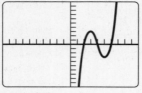

Equation 3   Equation 4

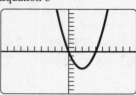
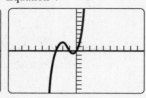

2. 1: –3 and 1; 2: 2, 4, and 6; 3: 0 and 4; 4: –3, –1, and 0;
Each x-intercept makes one of the factors in factored form equal to 0.

3. The x-intercepts of the graph are the solutions to the polynomial equation; the solutions are where either of the factors x and x – 6 is zero, or at 0 and 6.

Exploration 22

1–3. Answers may vary. Let m = the total number of marked beans, s = the number of beans in the sample, and n = the number marked in the sample.

1. $\frac{m}{B}$

2. $\frac{n}{s}$; The two fractions should be approximately equal.

3. If, for example, 22 beans are marked in Step 2 and 3 of 15 beans are marked in the sample drawn in Step 4, then $\frac{22}{B} = \frac{3}{15}$. Solving for B gives: $(15B)\left(\frac{22}{B}\right) = (15B)\left(\frac{3}{15}\right)$; $330 = 3B$; $B = 110$. There are about 110 beans in the coffee can.

Exploration 23

1. Answers may vary. An example is given. 12 and 3

2.

l	w
12	3
3	12
2	18
18	2
1	36
36	1
4	9
9	4
6	6

3.

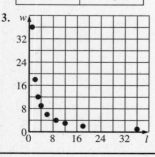

4. a. Yes; 8 units.

Exploration 24

1. By lining up the end of a bar that represents $\frac{1}{2}$ with the end of a bar that represents $\frac{1}{3}$, you can see that the difference is the length of a bar that represents $\frac{1}{6}$.

2.

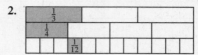

Questions

1. All three numerators in each equation are 1. Also, the first two denominators are consecutive integers, and the denominator of the difference is the product of the integers.

a. $\frac{1}{20}$ b. $\frac{1}{30}$ c. $\frac{1}{42}$

2. $\frac{1}{x(x+1)}$

Exploration 25

1–4. Answers may vary. An example is given for a sheet of typing paper, about 280 mm by 216 mm, oriented vertically, with the fold in Step 2 made 51 mm up from the bottom. Angle measures are rounded to the nearest degree and lengths to the nearest millimeter.

1.

$\triangle ABC$	
Measure of $\angle A$	90°
Measure of $\angle B$	38°
Measure of $\angle C$	52°
Length of $\overline{AB}$	280 mm
Length of $\overline{BC}$	353 mm
Length of $\overline{AC}$	216 mm

$\triangle DEF$	
Measure of $\angle D$	90°
Measure of $\angle E$	38°
Measure of $\angle F$	52°
Length of $\overline{DE}$	229 mm
Length of $\overline{EF}$	290 mm
Length of $\overline{DF}$	179 mm

2. $\angle A$ and $\angle D$ have the same measure, $\angle B$ and $\angle E$ have the same measure, and $\angle C$ and $\angle F$ have the same measure.

3. a. about 1.2
   b. about 1.2
   c. about 1.2

The three ratios are the same.

4. I think it means the triangles have angles with equal measure and three pairs of sides whose lengths have the same ratio.

Explorations and Projects Book, Copyright © McDougal Littell Inc.

Answers to Geometry Explorations

Exploration 1

1–3. Check students' work.

4, 5. The table values for the first seven steps are given.

Step	Number of new segments	Total number of segments
1	1	1
2	2	3
3	4	7
4	8	15
5	16	31
6	32	63
7	64	127

6. The figure shown is Step 2 is repeated over and over again, on a smaller and smaller scale.

7. The number of new segments doubles at each step; the total number of segments increases by a power of two at each step. At Step n, the number of new segments is 2^{n-1}; the total number of segments is $2^n - 1$.

8. 1023 segments; $2^{10} - 1 = 1023$

Exploration 2

1. No.

2, 3. Check students' work.

4. Yes (where the two trays meet).

5. Yes (see art); No; Yes (see art).

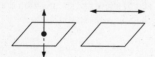

Exploration 3

1. Check students' work.

2. Yes; No (unless planes B and C are the same plane); Yes; they are parallel.

3. Yes; Yes.

4. Yes; Yes; Yes; the sketches demonstrate the three situations.

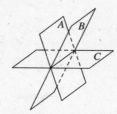
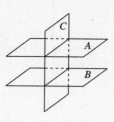
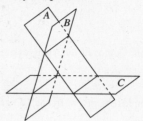

5. Check students' work.

6. They are parallel.

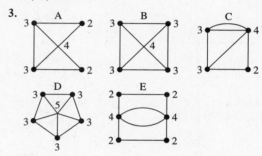

Exploration 4

1. Check students' work.

2. A, C, and E

3.

Exploration 5

1–3. Check students' work.

4. corresponding angles

5. They appear to be parallel; they also appear to be parallel. If two lines are intersected by a transversal and corresponding angles are congruent, then the lines are parallel.

Exploration 6

1. slope of j = slope of $k = -\frac{2}{5}$

2. Answers may vary. Check students' work. The lines have equal slopes or are both vertical.

3. The slopes of nonvertical parallel lines are equal.

4. slope of $l = -\frac{4}{3}$; slope of $m = \frac{3}{4}$

5. Answers may vary. Check students' work. The product of the slopes of the lines is -1, or one of the lines is vertical and the other horizontal.

6. The product of the slopes of two nonvertical perpendicular lines is -1.

Exploration 7

1–4. Sample rules include "triangles with a right angle," "triangles with only acute angles," or "triangles with no congruent sides."

Exploration 8

1–3. Check students' work.

4. Students should find that for every triangle, $m\angle 4 = m\angle 1 + m\angle 2$.

Exploration 9

1. a right triangle

2. The corresponding sides and angles of the triangles are congruent.

3. $\triangle BCA \cong \triangle XZY$

4. Diagrams may vary. Examples are given. In each diagram below, $\triangle ABC \cong \triangle YXZ$.

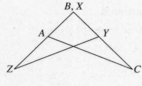

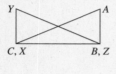

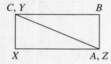

5. Answers may vary. Examples are given. In each diagram below, $\triangle ABC \cong \triangle YXZ$.

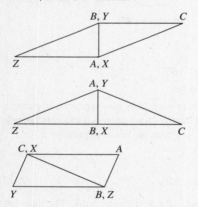

Exploration 10

1–3. Check students' work.

4. All three vertices are on circle C. C is on the perpendicular bisector of each of the three segments whose endpoints are vertices of the triangle. If a point lies on the perpendicular bisector of a segment, then the point is equidistant from the endpoints of the segment. Then C is equidistant from the three vertices.

5. All groups should have the same results. The intersection of the perpendicular bisectors of the sides of a triangle is equidistant from the vertices of the triangle.

6. The conjecture given in the answer to Step 5 is true for all triangles.

Exploration 11

Steps 1–4. Answers may vary. Check students' work.

5. Students should find that $AC < AB + BC$ and that $AC > AB - BC$ for every choice of points A and C.

6. No; A, B, and C are collinear. No; C is between A and B.

7. $AC < AB + BC$ and $AC > AB - BC$

Exploration 12

3. The opposite sides are congruent.

4. The opposite angles are congruent.

5. The diagonals intersect at their midpoints.

6. The results are the same.

7. Opposite sides of a parallelogram are congruent. Opposite angles of a parallelogram are congruent. The diagonals of a parallelogram bisect each other.

Exploration 13

1–3. Check students' work. One common placement of the parallelogram is $E(0, 0)$, $F(10, 0)$, $G(13, 4)$, and $H(3, 4)$.

4, 5. Answers may vary. Examples are given using the placement described above.

4. Slope of $\overline{EF}$ = slope of $\overline{GH}$ = 0 and slope of $\overline{FG}$ = slope of $\overline{EH} = \frac{4}{3}$. Since both pairs of opposite sides of $EFGH$ are parallel, $EFGH$ is a parallelogram by definition.

5. The midpoint of $\overline{EG}$ = midpoint of $\overline{FH}$ = (6.5, 2). The diagonals of a parallelogram bisect each other.

6. Answers may vary. An example is given. Since the placements of the parallelogram are different, the co-ordinates of the vertices and of the midpoint are different. Also, the different orientations mean that the slopes are not all the same. Since all the parallelograms are congruent, the opposite sides of the parallelogram are parallel for every placement and the diagonals bisect each other for every placement.

7. No. The different placements of the quadrilaterals in Step 2, and the results of Steps 4 and 5, show that the position does not affect the fact that the diagonals bisect each other.

Exploration 14

1–2. Check students' work.

3. They are right angles.

4. They are equal.

5. Check students' work.

6. The diagonals of a rhombus are perpendicular. Each diagonal bisects two angles of the rhombus.

Exploration 15

1, 2. Check students' work.

3. The base and height of the triangle are the base and height of the rectangle. The area of one triangle is half the area of the rectangle. The area of the triangle is half the product of its base and its height.

Explorations and Projects Book, Copyright © McDougal Littell Inc.

4. Check students' work.

5.

$x + z$; Yes; the area of the parallelogram is the product of its base and its height.

6.

x and $x + 2z$; $2x + 2z$; Yes; the area of the trapezoid is half the product of its height and the sum of the lengths of its bases.

Exploration 16

1–2. Check students' work.

3. counterclockwise

4. Each distance is twice the distance between lines m and n.

5. Each distance is still twice the distance between lines m and n.

Exploration 17

1–3. Check students' work.

4. Results do not depend on the right triangle that is chosen.

5. The area of the central square is c^2, the area of the large square is $(a + b)^2$ and the area of each right triangle is $\frac{1}{2}ab$. According to the results of Step 3, Area of the central square = Area of the large square − Area of the 4 right triangles, or $c^2 = (a + b)^2 - 4\left(\frac{1}{2}ab\right) = a^2 + 2ab + b^2 - 2ab = a^2 + b^2$. Then the square of the length of the hypotenuse is equal to the sum of the squares of the lengths of the legs.

Exploration 18

1, 2. Check students' work.

3. See answers in back of book.

4. Let the lengths of the sides of a triangle be a, b, and c, with c the length of the longest side. Then if $a^2 + b^2 = c^2$, the triangle is a right triangle; if $a^2 + b^2 > c^2$, the triangle is an acute triangle; if $a^2 + b^2 < c^2$, the triangle is an obtuse triangle.

5. a. acute

  b. obtuse

  c. acute

Exploration 19

1. Answers may vary slightly due to rounding.

$m \angle A$	opposite / hypotenuse	adjacent / hypotenuse
20°	0.34	0.94
40°	0.64	0.77
60°	0.87	0.50
80°	0.98	0.17

2. The ratio $\frac{\text{opposite}}{\text{hypotenuse}}$ increases; the ratio $\frac{\text{adjacent}}{\text{hypotenuse}}$ decreases.

3. As $m \angle A$ approaches 0°, the length of the leg opposite $\angle A$ approaches 0, so $\frac{\text{opposite}}{\text{hypotenuse}}$ approaches 0. The length of the adjacent leg approaches the length of the hypotenuse, so $\frac{\text{adjacent}}{\text{hypotenuse}}$ approaches 1. As $m \angle A$ approaches 90°, the length of the leg opposite $\angle A$ approaches the length of the hypotenuse, so $\frac{\text{opposite}}{\text{hypotenuse}}$ approaches 1. The length of the adjacent leg approaches 0, so $\frac{\text{adjacent}}{\text{hypotenuse}}$ approaches 0.

4. 45°

Exploration 20

1–4. Check students' work.

5. about $\frac{\text{Shaded area}}{\text{Area of target}}$

Exploration 21

1–3. Check students' work.

4. the wide tube; The amount of popcorn that filled the thin tube does not fill the wide tube.

5. Yes.

6. Answers may vary. An example is given. I think the radius has more effect. The tube with the greater radius had greater volume even though it was much shorter than the tube with the smaller radius.

Exploration 22

1–3. Check students' work.

4. Answers may vary. The sum of the measures of the interior angles is greater than 180°.

5. The sum of the measures of the interior angles is greater than 180°.

Answers to Algebra 2 Explorations

Exploration 1

1.

This action models subtracting x from both sides.

2.

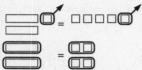

$x = 2$; check: $3x + 1 = x + 5$; $3(2) + 1 \stackrel{?}{=} 2 + 5$; $7 = 7$ ✓

3. **a.** $x = 1$ **b.** $x = 2$
   c. $x = 3$ **d.** $x = 1$

4. Answers may vary. An example is given. If there are variables on both sides, add the same variable expression to both sides or subtract the same variable expression from both sides to get all the variable terms on the same side of the equation.

Exploration 2

1–4. Check students' work. Tables may vary. An example is given.

Slope of line	Slope of perpendicular line
1	-1
2	$-\dfrac{1}{2}$
$-\dfrac{1}{3}$	3
$\dfrac{2}{3}$	$-\dfrac{3}{2}$

5. Answers may vary. Examples are given. The product of the slopes of two perpendicular lines is -1. If the slope of a line is m, then the slope of a line perpendicular to the line is $-\dfrac{1}{m}$.

Exploration 3

1–5. Answers may vary.

Exploration 4

1. Answers may vary. The slope represents the change in thickness per page of the book. Since there is one piece of paper for every two pages, the thickness of a piece of paper is twice the slope.

2. **a.** Answers may vary. The T-intercept represents the thickness of the book without any pages, that is the total thickness of the covers.

   b. Answers may vary.

Exploration 5

The ages of people in the photographs are as follows. Philip: 27; Clarice: 38; Alan: 40; Eva: 32; Luke: 41

1. all the guesses for a given actual age

2. Answers may vary. If they do, it means that a guess was correct.

3. **a.** The guess was less than the actual age; $e < a$.

   b. The guess was greater than the actual age; $e > a$.

4. Answers may vary.

5. Answers may vary. For example, many young people may wish to appear older and so would want most points to fall above the line, while many older people may wish to appear younger and would want most points to fall below the line.

Exploration 6

1.

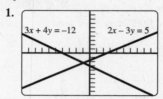

2. Yes; $(-0.941, -2.294)$

3.

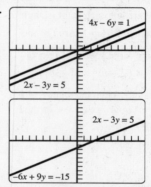

The graphs of the equations $2x - 3y = 5$ and $4x - 6y = 1$ do not intersect; they are parallel. The graphs of the equations $2x - 3y = 5$ and $-6x + 9y = -15$ coincide.

Questions

1. They can intersect in a single point, they can be parallel and not intersect at all, or they can coincide. If they intersect in a single point, the system has one solution. If they are parallel, the system has no solution. If they coincide, the system has infinitely many solutions.

2. The slopes must be different or else the slope of exactly one of the lines must be undefined.

Exploration 7

1–3. Answers may vary.

4. Multiply every number in the matrix by $\dfrac{\text{number of students in the school}}{\text{number of students in your class}}$.

Explorations and Projects Book, Copyright © McDougal Littell Inc.

Exploration 8

1, 2. Check students' work.

3. $\begin{bmatrix} 1 & 0 \\ 0 & -1 \end{bmatrix}$ reflection over the x-axis;

$\begin{bmatrix} -1 & 0 \\ 0 & 1 \end{bmatrix}$ reflection over the y-axis;

$\begin{bmatrix} 0 & 1 \\ 1 & 0 \end{bmatrix}$ reflection over the line $y = x$;

$\begin{bmatrix} 0 & -1 \\ -1 & 0 \end{bmatrix}$ reflection over the line $y = -x$

Exploration 9

1. $\begin{bmatrix} 1 & 0 \\ 0 & 1 \end{bmatrix}$; $\begin{bmatrix} 1 & 0 \\ 0 & -1 \end{bmatrix}$; $\begin{bmatrix} -1 & 0 \\ 0 & 1 \end{bmatrix}$; $\begin{bmatrix} -1 & 0 \\ 0 & -1 \end{bmatrix}$; $\begin{bmatrix} 0 & 1 \\ 1 & 0 \end{bmatrix}$; $\begin{bmatrix} 0 & 1 \\ -1 & 0 \end{bmatrix}$;

$\begin{bmatrix} 0 & -1 \\ 1 & 0 \end{bmatrix}$; $\begin{bmatrix} 0 & -1 \\ -1 & 0 \end{bmatrix}$

2. $\begin{bmatrix} 1 & 0 \\ 0 & 1 \end{bmatrix}\begin{bmatrix} 3 & 4 & 7 \\ 1 & 3 & 1 \end{bmatrix} = \begin{bmatrix} 3 & 4 & 7 \\ 1 & 3 & 1 \end{bmatrix}$; $\begin{bmatrix} 1 & 0 \\ 0 & -1 \end{bmatrix}\begin{bmatrix} 3 & 4 & 7 \\ 1 & 3 & 1 \end{bmatrix} =$

$\begin{bmatrix} 3 & 4 & 7 \\ -1 & -3 & -1 \end{bmatrix}$; $\begin{bmatrix} -1 & 0 \\ 0 & 1 \end{bmatrix}\begin{bmatrix} 3 & 4 & 7 \\ 1 & 3 & 1 \end{bmatrix} = \begin{bmatrix} -3 & -4 & -7 \\ 1 & 3 & 1 \end{bmatrix}$; $\begin{bmatrix} -1 & 0 \\ 0 & -1 \end{bmatrix}$

$\begin{bmatrix} 3 & 4 & 7 \\ 1 & 3 & 1 \end{bmatrix} = \begin{bmatrix} -3 & -4 & -7 \\ -1 & -3 & -1 \end{bmatrix}$; $\begin{bmatrix} 0 & 1 \\ 1 & 0 \end{bmatrix}\begin{bmatrix} 3 & 4 & 7 \\ 1 & 3 & 1 \end{bmatrix} = \begin{bmatrix} 1 & 3 & 1 \\ 3 & 4 & 7 \end{bmatrix}$;

$\begin{bmatrix} 0 & 1 \\ -1 & 0 \end{bmatrix}\begin{bmatrix} 3 & 4 & 7 \\ 1 & 3 & 1 \end{bmatrix} = \begin{bmatrix} 1 & 3 & 1 \\ -3 & -4 & -7 \end{bmatrix}$; $\begin{bmatrix} 0 & -1 \\ 1 & 0 \end{bmatrix}\begin{bmatrix} 3 & 4 & 7 \\ 1 & 3 & 1 \end{bmatrix} =$

$\begin{bmatrix} -1 & -3 & -1 \\ 3 & 4 & 7 \end{bmatrix}$; $\begin{bmatrix} 0 & -1 \\ -1 & 0 \end{bmatrix}\begin{bmatrix} 3 & 4 & 7 \\ 1 & 3 & 1 \end{bmatrix} = \begin{bmatrix} -1 & -3 & -1 \\ -3 & -4 & -7 \end{bmatrix}$

3. $\begin{bmatrix} 1 & 0 \\ 0 & 1 \end{bmatrix}$; identity

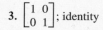

$\begin{bmatrix} 1 & 0 \\ 0 & -1 \end{bmatrix}$; reflection over x-axis

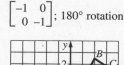

$\begin{bmatrix} -1 & 0 \\ 0 & 1 \end{bmatrix}$; reflection over y-axis

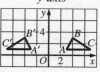

$\begin{bmatrix} -1 & 0 \\ 0 & -1 \end{bmatrix}$; 180° rotation

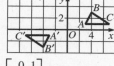

$\begin{bmatrix} 0 & 1 \\ 1 & 0 \end{bmatrix}$; reflection over $y = x$

$\begin{bmatrix} 0 & 1 \\ -1 & 0 \end{bmatrix}$; 270° rotation

$\begin{bmatrix} 0 & -1 \\ 1 & 0 \end{bmatrix}$; 90° rotation

$\begin{bmatrix} 0 & -1 \\ -1 & 0 \end{bmatrix}$; reflection over $y = -x$

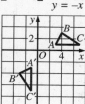

4.

Matrix	Transformation
$\begin{bmatrix} 1 & 0 \\ 0 & 1 \end{bmatrix}$	identity/360° rotation
$\begin{bmatrix} 0 & -1 \\ 1 & 0 \end{bmatrix}$	90° rotation
$\begin{bmatrix} -1 & 0 \\ 0 & -1 \end{bmatrix}$	180° rotation
$\begin{bmatrix} 0 & 1 \\ -1 & 0 \end{bmatrix}$	270° rotation
$\begin{bmatrix} 1 & 0 \\ 0 & -1 \end{bmatrix}$	reflection over x-axis
$\begin{bmatrix} -1 & 0 \\ 0 & 1 \end{bmatrix}$	reflection over y-axis
$\begin{bmatrix} 0 & 1 \\ 1 & 0 \end{bmatrix}$	reflection over $y = x$
$\begin{bmatrix} 0 & -1 \\ -1 & 0 \end{bmatrix}$	reflection over $y = -x$

Exploration 10

Equation 1	Equation 2	How is the graph of equation 2 geometrically related to the graph of equation 1?
$y = x^2$	$y = (x - 1)^2$	translated 1 unit to the right
$y = x^2$	$y = x^2 + 1$	translated up 1 unit
$y = 2x^2$	$y = 2(x + 3)^2$	translated 3 units to the left
$y = 2x^2$	$y = 2x^2 - 4$	translated down 4 units
$y = -\frac{1}{2}x^2$	$y = -\frac{1}{2}(x + 1)^2 + 3$	translated 1 unit to the left, up 3 units
$y = -\frac{1}{2}x^2$	$y = -\frac{1}{2}(x - 2)^2 + 1$	translated 2 units to the right, up 1 unit

Questions

1. a. The graph is the graph of $y = x^2$ shrunk vertically by a factor of 3 and translated 5 units up.

b. The graph is the graph of $y = x^2$ translated 1 unit to the right, stretched vertically by a factor of 4, and reflected over the x-axis.

c. The graph is the graph of $y = x^2$ translated 4 units to the left and down 3 units.

2. a. The graph of $y = ax^2 + k$ is the graph of $y = ax^2$ translated $|k|$ units up if k is positive and down if k is negative.

b. The graph of $y = a(x - h)^2$ is the graph of $y = ax^2$ translated $|h|$ units left if h is positive and right if h is negative.

Exploration 11

Equation	What are the x-intercepts of the graph?	What are the coordinates of the vertex?
$y = x(x - 1)$	0 and 1	$(0.5, -0.25)$
$y = 2x(x - 2)$	0 and 2	$(1, -2)$
$y = -x(x + 3)$	0 and -3	$(-1.5, 2.25)$
$y = -\frac{1}{2}x(x + 4)$	0 and -4	$(-2, 2)$
$y = (x + 2)(x - 4)$	-2 and 4	$(1, -9)$
$y = 3(x - 1)(x + 3)$	1 and -3	$(-1, -12)$

1. a.

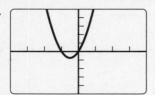

b.

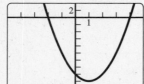

c.

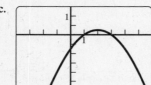

d.

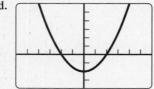

2. $p, q; \dfrac{p + q}{2}$

Exploration 12

1. $(x + 1)(x + 4)$

2. $(x + 4)(x + 2)$

3. $(x + 2)(x + 2)$

Exploration 13

1, 2.

Equation	Number of solutions	$b^2 - 4ac$
$0 = -3x^2 + 5x + 5$	2	85
$0 = 5x^2 + 3x + 2$	0	-31
$0 = 6x^2 + 12x + 6$	1	0
$0 = x^2 + 8x - 3$	2	76
$0 = x^2 - 2x + 4$	0	-12
$0 = x^2 + 4x + 4$	1	0

3. If the discriminant is positive, the equation has two solutions. If the discriminant is zero, the equation has one solution. If the discriminant is negative, the equation has no solutions.

Exploration 14

1.

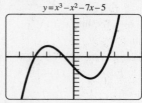
$y = x^3 - x^2 - 7x - 5$

3 real zeros

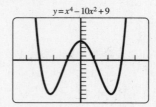
$y = x^4 - 10x^2 + 9$

4 real zeros

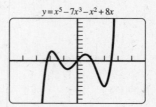
$y = x^5 - 7x^3 - x^2 + 8x$

5 real zeros

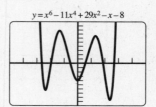
$y = x^6 - 11x^4 + 29x^2 - x - 8$

6 real zeros

2. The number of real zeros is the same as the degree.

3.

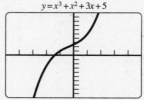
$y = x^3 + x^2 + 3x + 5$

1 real zero

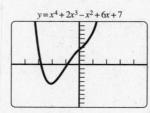
$y = x^4 + 2x^3 - x^2 + 6x + 7$

2 real zeros

Explorations and Projects Book, Copyright © McDougal Littell Inc.

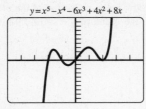

$y = x^5 - x^4 - 6x^3 + 4x^2 + 8x$

4 real zeros

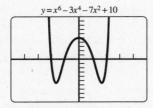

$y = x^6 - 3x^4 - 7x^2 + 10$

4 real zeros

No; the number of real zeros is less than or equal to the degree.

4. The number of real zeros is less than or equal to the degree.

Exploration 15

Steps 1 and 2: Coodinates that involve approximations may vary due to rounding. Examples are given. $y = 4x^2 - 8x - 3$: As x takes on large negative or positive values, the graph rises; one turning point, $(1, -7)$. $y = x^3 - x^2 - 3x + 1$: As x takes on large negative values, the graph falls; as x takes on large positive values, the graph rises; two turning points, $(-0.72, 2.27)$, $(1.39, -2.42)$. $y = x^4 + 2x^3 - 5x^2 - 7x + 3$: As x takes on large negative or positive values, the graph rises; three turning points, $(-2.26, -3.72)$, $(-0.58, 5.10)$, $(1.34, -7.32)$. $y = 2x^5 + 6x^4 - 2x^3 - 14x^2 + 5$: As x takes on large negative values, the graph falls; as x takes on large positive values, the graph rises; four turning points, $(-2, -3)$, $(-1.40, -4.66)$, $(0, 5)$, $(1, -3)$. $y = 3x^6 - 13x^4 + 15x^2 + x - 17$: As x takes on large negative or positive values, the graph rises; five turning points, $(-1.46, 16.3)$, $(-0.865, -12.66)$, $(-0.0334, -17.02)$, $(0.919, -10.88)$, $(1.44, -13.60)$. $y = x^7 - 8x^5 + 18x^3 - 6x$: As x takes on large negative values, the graph falls; as x takes on large positive values, the graph rises. six turning points, $(-1.92, -3.33)$, $(-1.38, -8.52)$, $(-0.349, 1.37)$, $(0.349, -1.37)$, $(1.38, 8.52)$, $(1.92, 3.33)$.

Questions:

1. They rise; they rise.

2. They rise; they fall.

3. Let n be the degree of the polynomial function and t the number of turning points.

a. $t = n - 1$

b. $t \leq n - 1$

Exploration 16

1, 2.

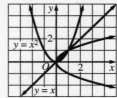

Questions

1. No; for $y = \pm \sqrt{x}$, there are two outputs for every input except 0.

2. a half-parabola; Yes.

Exploration 17

1.

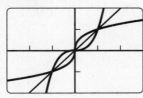

Yes.

2. $y = x^4$

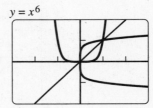

No.

$y = x^5$

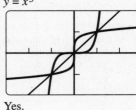

Yes.

$y = x^6$

No.

Questions

1. Answers may vary. The graphs of $y = x^n$ for n odd have the shape of a sideways and backwards "S." No horizontal line intersects the graph in more than one point. The reflections of these graphs are graphs of functions. The graphs of $y = x^n$ for n even are shaped like parabolas. (For $n = 2$, the graph is a parabola.) Every horizontal line that intersects such a graph (except for the one intersecting the vertex) intersects the graph in two points. The reflections of these graphs are not the graphs of functions.

2. n even; The domains may be restricted to $x \geq 0$ or $x \leq 0$.

Exploration 18

1. The middle fold tells you that half of the data points lie to the left of the fold and half to the right. The left-most fold tells you that one-quarter of the data points lie to the left of the fold and three-quarters lie to the right. The right-most fold tells you that one-quarter of the data points lie to the right of the fold and three-quarters lie to the left.

2. Answers may vary.

Exploration 19

Correct answer to test question: B

1–5. Answers may vary.

Exploration 20

1. Results may vary. Check students' work.

2. a.

x = number of times cup is emptied	y = expected number of pennies remaining
0	100
1	$100\left(\frac{1}{2}\right)$
2	$100\left(\frac{1}{2}\right) \cdot \left(\frac{1}{2}\right) = 100\left(\frac{1}{2}\right)^2$
3	$100\left(\frac{1}{2}\right)^2 \cdot \left(\frac{1}{2}\right) = 100\left(\frac{1}{2}\right)^3$
4	$100\left(\frac{1}{2}\right)^3 \cdot \left(\frac{1}{2}\right) = 100\left(\frac{1}{2}\right)^4$
5	$100\left(\frac{1}{2}\right)^4 \cdot \left(\frac{1}{2}\right) = 100\left(\frac{1}{2}\right)^5$
6	$100\left(\frac{1}{2}\right)^5 \cdot \left(\frac{1}{2}\right) = 100\left(\frac{1}{2}\right)^6$

3. $y = 100\left(\frac{1}{2}\right)^x$, where y = the number of pennies remaining and x = the number of times the cup is emptied; the graph of the equation should be close to the points on the scatter plot

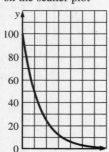

Exploration 21

1.

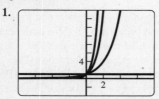

The graphs have the same y-intercept, 1.

2.

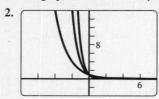

The graph of $y = b^x$ is the image of the graph of $y = \left(\frac{1}{b}\right)^x$ reflected over the y-axis.

3. Graphs may vary. Each graph is the reflection of the other over the y-axis. For $b > 1$, the graph of $y = b^x$ represents exponential growth. Since $0 < \frac{1}{b} < 1$, the graph of $y = \left(\frac{1}{b}\right)^x$ represents exponential decay.

4.

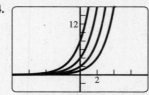

For each graph, the numerical coefficient is the y-intercept.

5. Graphs may vary. Each graph is the reflection of the other over the x-axis.

6. Summaries may vary. The value of a determines the y-intercept of the graph. The table further describes the graphs.

	Above or below x-axis?	Represents exponential:
$a > 0, b > 1$	above	growth
$a > 0, 0 < b < 1$	above	decay
$a < 0, b > 1$	below	decay
$a < 0, 0 < b < 1$	below	growth

Exploration 22

Compounding	n	Formula	r = 0.05	r = 0.10	r = 0.50	r = 1.00
annually	1	$\left(1 + \frac{r}{1}\right)^1$	1.05	1.10	1.50	2.00
semiannually	2	$\left(1 + \frac{r}{2}\right)^2$	1.0506	1.1025	1.5625	2.25
quarterly	4	$\left(1 + \frac{r}{4}\right)^4$	1.0509	1.1038	1.6018	2.4414
monthly	12	$\left(1 + \frac{r}{12}\right)^{12}$	1.0512	1.1047	1.6321	2.6130
daily	365	$\left(1 + \frac{r}{365}\right)^{365}$	1.0513	1.1052	1.6482	2.7146
hourly	8760	$\left(1 + \frac{r}{8760}\right)^{8760}$	1.0513	1.1052	1.6487	2.7181
every minute	525,600	$\left(1 + \frac{r}{525,600}\right)^{525,600}$	1.0513	1.1052	1.6487	2.7183
every second	31,536,000	$\left(1 + \frac{r}{31,536,000}\right)^{31,536,000}$	1.0513	1.1052	1.6487	2.7183

2. Increasing the frequency of compounding initially increases the earnings, but the effect levels off eventually. For r = 0.05, for example, the yield is no greater for compounding every second than for compounding daily.

3. No; the effect of more frequent compounding eventually becomes negligible. This happens very quickly for values of r that correspond to real-world interest rates.

Explorations and Projects Book, Copyright © McDougal Littell Inc.

Exploration 23

1.

x	f(x)
−2	$\frac{1}{4}$
−1	$\frac{1}{2}$
0	1
1	2
2	4
3	8

2–4.

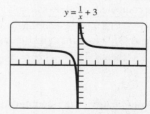

Questions

1. a. 3
   b. −2
   c. 0
2. a. exponents; powers of 2
   b. powers of 2; exponents

Exploration 24

N	1	2	3	4	5	6	7	8	9	10
log N	0	0.3010	0.4771	0.6021	0.6990	0.7782	0.8451	0.9031	0.9542	1.0000
N	20	30	40	50	60	70	80	90	100	1000
log N	1.3010	1.4771	1.6021	1.6990	1.7782	1.8451	1.9031	1.9542	2.0000	3.0000

Questions

1. a. 0.9031   b. 8; 8
2. a. 40   b. 80   c. 70   d. 90
3. MN
4. a. 4
   b. 10
   c. 6
   d. 3
5. $\frac{M}{N}$
6. a. 9
   b. 100
   c. 1000
7. M^k

Exploration 25

1.

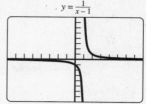

$x = 1$; $y = 0$; translated 1 unit right

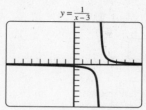

$x = 3$; $y = 0$; translated 3 units right

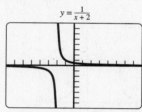

$x = -2$; $y = 0$; translated 2 units left

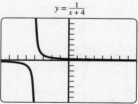

$x = -4$; $y = 0$; translated 4 units left

2.

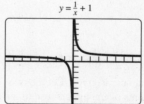

$x = 0$; $y = 1$; translated 1 unit up

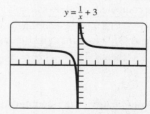

$x = 0$; $y = 3$; translated 3 units up

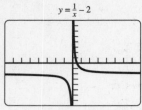

$y = \frac{1}{x} - 2$

$x = 0$; $y = -2$; translated 2 units down

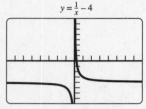

$y = \frac{1}{x} - 4$

$x = 0$; $y = -4$; translated 4 units down

3. translated 4 units right; translated 1 unit left; translated 3 units up; translated 5 units down

Exploration 26

1.

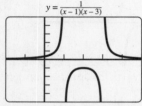

$y = \frac{1}{(x-1)(x-3)}$

$x = 1$; $x = 3$

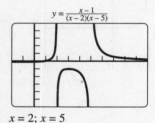

$y = \frac{x-1}{(x-2)(x-5)}$

$x = 2$; $x = 5$

Exploration 27

1. Check students' work. 5 cm; $d = \sqrt{3^2 + 4^2} = 5$ cm

2. Answers may vary. An example is given. Let the two given points be the endpoints of the hypotenuse of a right triangle. Draw a horizontal line segment and a vertical line segment to form a right triangle. Then the distance, d, between the points can be computed as follows: $d = \sqrt{(\text{change in } x\text{-coordinates})^2 + (\text{change in } y\text{-coordinates})^2}$. Given the points $(-2, 1)$ and $(3, 1)$ to form a right triangle with legs of length 5 and 12. Then $d = \sqrt{5^2 + 12^2} = 5$

3. about $\left(2\frac{1}{2}, 4\right)$

4. $2\frac{1}{2}$; 4; The mean of the x-coordinates = the x-coordinate of the midpoint, and the mean of the y-coordinates = the y-coordinate of the midpoint.

5. Answers may vary. An example is given. The x-coordinate

of the midpoint is the mean of the x-coordinates of the given points. The y-coordinate of the midpoint is the mean of the y-coordinates of the given points. Given the points $(3, 8)$ and $(-1, 6)$, the coordinates of the midpoint of the line segment joining the points are

$$\left(\frac{3 + (-1)}{2}, \frac{8 + 6}{2}\right) = (1, 7).$$

Exploration 28

1–4. Check students' work.

Questions

1. It is the vertex of the parabola.

2. The distance between any point on a parabola and its focus is equal to the perpendicular distance from the point to the directrix of the parabola.

3. The parabola opens down.

Exploration 29

1, 2. Check students' work.

Questions

1. $F_1P + F_2P = F_1Q + F_2Q$

2. The figure I drew is the set of all points in a plane such that, for all points, the sum of the distances to the two points F_1 and F_2 is the same.

3. The ellipse became more and more round. The ellipse looks more and more like a circle.

Exploration 30

No. of Cuts	No. of Pieces	
	A	B
1	2	2
2	4	3
3	8	4
4	16	5
5	32	6

1. Method A: the number doubles; Method B: the number increases by 1.

2. See table.

3. Method A: $t_n = 2 \cdot 2^{n-1}$; Method B: $t_n = 2 + (n-1)$

Exploration 31

1, 2. Answers may vary. Examples are given.

1. For a starting value of 5 with 3 added, the calculator produces the sequence 5, 8, 11, 14, 17, 20, ...

2. For a starting value of 5 multiplied by 3, the calculator produces the sequence 5, 15, 45, 135, 405, 1215, ...

Questions

1. If a sequence is produced by adding a constant, consecutive terms have a common difference, the constant. If a sequence is produced by multiplying by a constant, consecutive terms have a common ratio, the constant.

Explorations and Projects Book, Copyright © McDougal Littell Inc.

2. arithmetic

3. geometric

Exploration 32

1–4. Choice of colors may vary. Examples, using red, blue, white, and green are given.

1. Red/Blue, Red/White, Blue/Red, Blue/White, White/Red, White/Blue; 6; 2×3

2. Red/Blue, Red/White, Red/Green, Blue/Red, Blue/White, Blue/Green, White/Red, White/Blue, White/Green, Green/Red, Green/Blue, Green/White; 12; 3×4

3. The pattern is number of flags = (number of colors) × (number of colors − 1); $10 \times 9 = 90$.

4. 9; Answers may vary. An example is given. There are 3 choices of color for the top bar and 3 choices of color for the bottom bar, or $3 \times 3 = 9$ flags in all; $9 = 3^2$.

5. 16; There are 4 choices of color for the top bar and 4 choices of color for the bottom bar, so $4 \times 4 = 16$ flags can be made.

Exploration 33

1.

number of vertices	number of edges
2	1
3	3
4	6
5	10
6	15
7	21

2.

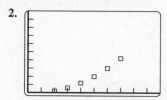

3. 28 edges; For each added vertex, you add a number of edges equal to the original number of vertices. Adding an eighth vertex adds seven edges to the previous number, for a total of 28 edges.

4. Let n = the number of vertices and $f(n)$ = the number of edges; $f(n) = \dfrac{n(n-1)}{2}$. Each vertex can be connected to all the other vertices, so there are $n(n-1)$ edges. Only half of them are unique since each edge is counted twice in that number.

5. Yes.

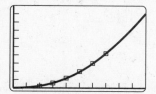

Exploration 34

1–4. Results may vary, depending on the number of students in each group.

1. For a four-member group, there are $3 \times 2 = 6$ ways; for a five-member group, there are $4 \times 3 = 12$ ways.

2. For a four-member group, there are $4 \times 3 \times 2 = {}_4P_3$ ways; for a five-member group, there are $5 \times 4 \times 3 = {}_5P_3$ ways. If there are n people in the group, there are $n(n-1)(n-2)$ ways to award the three prizes, that is, ${}_nP_3$ ways.

3. 6 times; You can write 6 as 3! because there are 3! ways to order the names in each group of three.

4. For a four-member group, there are 4 ways, or $\dfrac{{}_4P_3}{6}$ ways, to award the prizes; for a five-member group, there are 10 ways, or $\dfrac{{}_5P_3}{6}$ ways, to award the prizes. The list in Step 2 gives the number of ways to award the prizes when the order of the names is important. If the order of the names is not important, as in Step 4, then the number of ways to award the prizes is equal to the answer in Step 2 divided by 3!.

Exploration 35

1, 2. Answers may vary. Sample trial results are given.

1. 1, 2, 2, 1, 9, 3, 1, 2, 5, 3

2. for the sample above, 9 coupons; 1 coupon; about 3 coupons

3. Answers may vary. An example is given. I would let 1, 2, or 3 represent a 10% discount because the chance of rolling a 1, 2, or 3 is $\frac{1}{2}$. I would let a 4 or 5 represent a 15% discount because the chance of rolling a 4 or 5 is $\frac{1}{3}$. I would let a 6 represent a 30% discount because the chance of rolling a 6 is $\frac{1}{6}$.

4. Answers may vary. Sample trial results are given. 12, 9, 2, 13, 7, 3, 4, 5, 14, 2; You need about 7 coupons.

Exploration 36

Answers may vary. Examples are given.

1. a. $P(A \text{ and } B) = \dfrac{9}{35}$,
$P(A) \cdot P(B) = \dfrac{19}{35} \cdot \dfrac{4}{7} = \dfrac{76}{245}$

b. No; since $P(A \text{ and } B) \neq P(A) \cdot P(B)$, events A and B are not independent.

2. $\dfrac{11}{16}, \dfrac{3}{16}, \dfrac{1}{8}$

Exploration 37

1. Answers may vary. **2.** $\dfrac{1}{2}; \dfrac{1}{64}$

3. The translation of the test and answers are as follows.
1. More people live in California than in all of Australia. True.
2. The main crop of the Ukraine is wheat. True.
3. Kenya gained its independence in 1963. True.
4. Calcutta is the capital of India. False; the capital is New Delhi.
5. Shanghai is a country in Asia. False; Shanghai is a city in Asia.
6. Malawi lies on the western shore of a large lake. True.

4. Histograms may vary, but they should generally be bell-shaped.

5. Answers may vary, though students may note that it appears to be close to 0. Students should realize that an experimental probability may vary from a theoretical probability, especially if relatively few trials are performed.

6. Probabilities based on the histograms will vary, though the theoretical probabilities are $\frac{11}{32}$ and $\frac{21}{32}$. Theoretically, it is more likely to answer three or fewer questions correctly. Since the probabilities of being correct or incorrect are equal, you are as likely to get 0 right (miss all 6) as to get 6 right, to get 1 right (miss 5) as to get 5 right, and to get 2 right as to get 4 right. So, getting 3 or fewer right is as likely as getting 3 or more right. Because getting 4 or more right is a proper subset of getting 3 or more right, it is thus more likely to get 3 or fewer right than to get 4 or more correct.

Exploration 38

1–3. Check students' work.

Questions

1. The corresponding angles of the three triangles are congruent.

2. The ratio is about 0.87 for both triangles.

3. The ratio will be the same for any similar triangle. The ratio for $\triangle AFG$ is the same.

Exploration 39

1–4. Check students' work.

Questions

1. Answers may vary. Students' ratios should be $\frac{\text{ruler height}}{12 \text{ in.}}$.

2. Answers may vary. Students' ratios should be $\frac{\text{actual height}}{d}$.

3. Answers may vary. Students' equations should be $d = \frac{12 \cdot \text{actual height}}{\text{ruler height}}$.

Exploration 40

1. about 6.3

2. No; because the ratio of the circumference to the radius is the same for all circles, the size of the cylinder does not matter.

3. They are the same distance from the origin but in different directions. Yes.

Exploration 41

Radius r (cm)	Number of Triangles
2	0
4	1
6	2
8	1
10	1

Questions

1. 4 cm; Yes; the height is always the length of the perpendicular dropped from the vertex at C to the line containing the opposite side. Since AC and $\angle A$ are the same for all triangles, h is the same for all triangles.

2. 1; 4 cm

3. a. 6 cm   b. $h < r < b$

4. 1; 4 cm, 8 cm, 10 cm

5. $r > b$; $r \le b$

Exploration 42

1. 200; 12,000; –15

2.

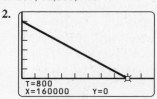

T=800
X=160000   Y=0

3. 800 s; 160,000; about 30.3 mi

Exploration 43

1.

Angle θ	$\sin \theta$	$\cos \theta$
0°	0	1
30°	0.5	0.8660
60°	0.8660	0.5
90°	1	0
120°	0.8660	–0.5
150°	0.5	–0.8660
180°	0	–1
210°	–0.5	–0.8660
240°	–0.8660	–0.5
270°	–1	0
300°	–0.8660	0.5
330°	–0.5	0.8660
360°	0	1

2.

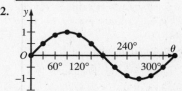

3.

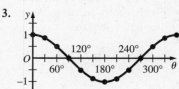

Questions

1. The graphs have the same shape, domain, and range. They have different θ-intercepts, maximum points, and minimum points. The graph of $\cos \theta$ is the graph of $\sin \theta$ shifted 90° to the left.

2. a. 2   b. 2   c. 1   d. 2

Explorations and Projects Book, Copyright © McDougal Littell Inc.